# The Caribbean

D0303259

9112000039 0369

# The Caribbean

## A Brief History

### THIRD EDITION

## GAD HEUMAN

BLOOMSBURY ACADEMIC
LONDON · NEW YORK · OXFORD · NEW DELHI · SYDNEY

BLOOMSBURY ACADEMIC
Bloomsbury Publishing Plc
50 Bedford Square, London, WC1B 3DP, UK
1385 Broadway, New York, NY 10018, USA

BLOOMSBURY, BLOOMSBURY ACADEMIC and the Diana logo
are trademarks of Bloomsbury Publishing Plc

This third edition first published in Great Britain 2019

Copyright © Gad Heuman, 2006, 2013, 2019

Gad Heuman has asserted his right under the Copyright, Designs and
Patents Act, 1988, to be identified as Author of this work.

For legal purposes the Acknowledgements on p. xi constitute
an extension of this copyright page.

Cover image from the author's private collection.

All rights reserved. No part of this publication may be reproduced or
transmitted in any form or by any means, electronic or mechanical,
including photocopying, recording, or any information storage or retrieval
system, without prior permission in writing from the publishers.

Bloomsbury Publishing Plc does not have any control over, or responsibility for,
any third-party websites referred to or in this book. All internet addresses given
in this book were correct at the time of going to press. The author and publisher
regret any inconvenience caused if addresses have changed or sites have
ceased to exist, but can accept no responsibility for any such changes.

A catalogue record for this book is available from the British Library.

A catalog record for this book is available from the Library of Congress.

ISBN: HB: 978-1-3500-3692-5
PB: 978-1-3500-3691-8
ePDF: 978-1-3500-3694-9
eBook: 978-1-3500-3693-2

Typeset by Deanta Global Publishing Services, Channel, India
Printed and bound in Great Britain

To find out more about our authors and books visit www.bloomsbury.com
and sign up for our newsletters.

| BRENT LIBRARIES | |
| --- | --- |
| 91120000390369 | |
| Askews & Holts | 19-Dec-2018 |
| 972.9 | £21.99 |
| | |

*Another to Ruth*

# CONTENTS

# LIST OF ILLUSTRATIONS

# ACKNOWLEDGEMENTS

I have been very fortunate in working on an area which has attracted such a distinguished group of scholars, many of whom I now count as friends. This has been helped by my involvement in two professional bodies, the Association of Caribbean Historians (ACH) and the Society for Caribbean Studies. I am not the first to note that being part of the ACH is like being a member of a large family; its meetings each year in a different area of the Caribbean are invariably interesting, pan-Caribbean and also quite intimate. In England, the Society for Caribbean Studies serves a similar role and, although it cannot match the ACH for exotic conference sites, it none the less has also brought together scholars from all over the world working on the region. I have profited immensely from being a part of both organizations.

The University of Warwick has provided a very different kind of home. Its History Department has under its umbrella the School of Comparative American Studies and the Centre for Caribbean Studies. These different entities have provided intellectual and social sustenance, and I am very grateful to my colleagues and my students for their support.

Several friends have read a draft of this book and made very valuable suggestions. They are Jerome Handler, Michael Krasner and James Walvin. My family have also been incredibly supportive about this project. My two children, Daniel and Adam, have considerable experience of the Caribbean; they lived there as very young children and have returned frequently with me. Daniel has worked independently in the region, done anthropological fieldwork there and has also read and commented on the manuscript. Daniel and Adam have both pushed me to complete this book. However, my greatest debt is to Ruth Heuman; she has not only commented on the book as it went along but also patiently dealt with my preoccupation with it. This book is dedicated to her, with thanks and love.

# PREFACE TO THE THIRD EDITION

Since the publication of the second edition, there have been important developments in the Caribbean and numerous new publications. For example, China has taken a greater interest in the region and the Caribbean has had to consider the effects of Brexit, the British decision to leave the European Union. There has been a significant rapprochement between the United States and Cuba, marked by President Barack Obama's visit to the island in 2016. In addition, natural disasters have badly affected parts of the Caribbean, including two category-five hurricanes in September 2017. That other force of nature, Usain Bolt, retired in 2017 but was the only sprinter to have won the 100-metre and 200-metre titles in three successive Olympics. CARICOM, the Caribbean Community, has accepted the argument for reparations for the damage caused by slavery and native genocide. This new edition takes into account these developments and many others as well. It also includes many significant new publications in the Suggestions for Further Reading.

I am grateful to the anonymous readers who made suggestions for this new edition. As a result, several chapters have been updated and expanded and there is considerably more material on the contemporary Caribbean. The accompanying website has also been improved and I hope this will prove useful for teachers and students.

# ORIGINAL PREFACE

This book sets out to examine the history of the Caribbean, from its earliest inhabitants to cultural and political developments in the recent past. In a format which is designed to be brief, however, it is not possible to provide a comprehensive coverage of the region's history. As a result, I have chosen to concentrate on the social history of the Caribbean.

My own research has centred on slave and post-emancipation societies in the Caribbean. More specifically, I have worked on the social structure of slave societies, the free people of colour and the nature of resistance during slavery and after emancipation. These topics are explored in this book as well as more recent developments, such as the impact of Marcus Garvey, the growth of the Rastafarian movement and the role of the United States in the region, especially in the twentieth century. *The Caribbean* also explores the Cuban Revolution and the wider revolutionary movements, and deals with current issues, such as emigration, the environment, race relations and the cultures of the Caribbean.

In light of the debate on the region itself, it is important to highlight what is meant by the Caribbean. In this book, the Caribbean refers to the islands of the region, from Cuba to Trinidad, as well as the mainland territories of the Guianas (Guyana, Suriname and French Guiana) and Belize in Central America. The islands vary enormously in size: some are tiny such as Bequia in the Grenadines, with its 7 square miles and a population of around 5,000 people. At the other end of the spectrum, Cuba's population is well over 11 million, and the island has more than 44,000 square miles. Geographically, the larger islands – Cuba, Jamaica, Haiti and the Dominican Republic (sharing the island of Hispaniola) and Puerto Rico – comprise the Greater Antilles, while the islands to the east of Puerto Rico down to Grenada form the Lesser Antilles. Most of the islands are volcanic in origin and often mountainous, although several islands, such as

Barbados, Anguilla and Antigua, are formed from coral limestone and have far less rugged terrain. All these territories have experienced similar histories of slavery, colonialism and exploitation and share a common history, despite their linguistic, cultural and geographic differences. Finally, although the Caribbean has been one of the most colonized places in the world, this book is more interested in exploring how the people of the Caribbean have reacted to the colonial presence than with the structures of imperial authority.

# CHAPTER ONE

# The Amerindians and European patterns of settlement

When Christopher Columbus landed in the Caribbean in 1492, he encountered a world entirely different from his own. The population and its way of life resembled nothing he had experienced in late-fifteenth-century Europe. Although Columbus believed he had discovered the Orient, he had instead stumbled on a world of Amerindians whose ancestors had migrated from South America to the Caribbean region, beginning around 2500 BC.

Yet the first Amerindians had arrived in the Caribbean several thousand years earlier. Travelling from South America, they settled in Trinidad roughly 7,000 years ago. Their trek was made easier because Trinidad was then still part of the mainland of South America. Gradually, over several thousand years, the descendants of these early migrants inhabited the eastern Caribbean as far north as Puerto Rico and including the eastern-most island of Barbados.

About one thousand years later, beginning around 4000 BC, there was a separate migration from Central America to the Caribbean. These people travelled from the Yucatan in present-day eastern Mexico to the western part of Cuba. Subsequently, their descendants occupied the rest of Cuba and moved eastwards to Hispaniola (now the Dominican Republic and Haiti) and to Puerto Rico. Like the Amerindians who emanated from South America, these were hunter-fisher-gatherer people who had no

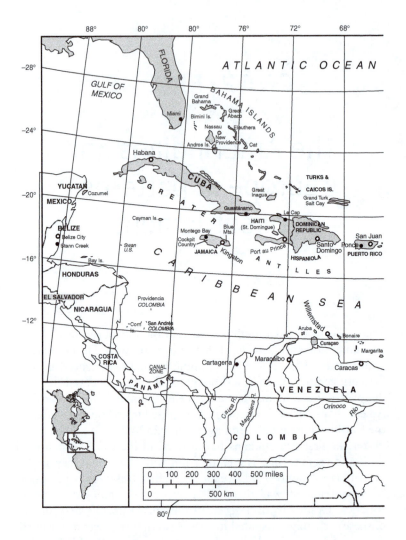

**FIGURE 1.1** *Map of the Caribbean.*

settled agriculture. Included in this group were the Guanahatabeys
(also known as the Ciboneys)in western Cuba, who had all but
disappeared by the time Columbus sailed into the region. These
early migrants from South and Central America have left very little
archaeological evidence, although we do have some artefacts, such
as stone tools, food remains and burial sites.

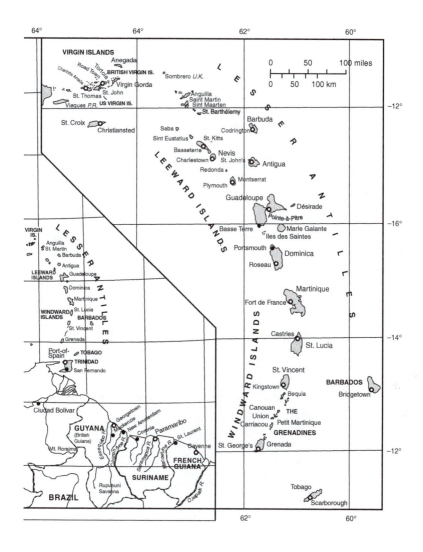

The second major wave of migration, which began around 2500 BC, has produced far more archaeological material. Originating in the Orinoco basin of South America, these Amerindians settled in most areas of the eastern and western Caribbean. They were agriculturalists and, unlike the early peoples of the Caribbean, settled in permanent villages and had a distinctive form of pottery.

Moreover, they spoke languages based on a single language family known as Arawakan. The now-dated description of these people as Arawak comes from the confusion of using their language to name the people.

The most developed of these societies emerged after about AD 600 in Hispaniola and Puerto Rico. They called themselves Tainos and used that name to describe themselves to Columbus and those that followed him. We therefore use the term Taino to describe the people who predominated in the Greater Antilles. For the Amerindians themselves, Taino meant good or noble. From about AD 1100 onwards, the Tainos in the more densely populated islands moved away from societies organized along tribal lines to societies characterized by chiefdoms or *cacicazgos*. The leaders of these societies were known as chiefs or *caciques*. One of the leading specialists on the Amerindians, Jalil Sued-Badillo, suggests that there was a direct relationship between population size and social complexity. This meant that in densely populated islands such as

FIGURE 1.2 *Taino religious object, 1200–1492 AD.*

*Source:* National Museum of the American Indian, Smithsonian Institution (5/3753). Photo by David Heald.

Hispaniola, it was possible to develop more sophisticated forms of political organization centring around powerful chiefs. In the more sparsely populated islands of Jamaica and Cuba, this was not the case: they had not moved beyond the less complex stage of tribal organization.[1]

In the case of Hispaniola, there were four or possibly five chiefdoms, each covering a very large area of the island. Puerto Rico appears to have had only one chiefdom, but this was also extensive: it included a large part of the south-western coast and reached halfway across the island. In these chiefdoms, the *caciques* had great authority, much of which was based on their religious aura. They were seen as lesser gods and made use of religion and magic to help them maintain control of their societies. In addition, *caciques* were the only people allowed to practise polygamy: this meant that these chiefs could form alliances linking members of various groups. For example, Behechío, the *cacique* of the territory of Jaragua (today part of Haiti), reportedly had thirty wives while his neighbouring chief and rival had twenty.

Unlike the Europeans, Amerindian societies were characterized by matrilineal descent. This meant that sons and wives did not inherit the *cacique*'s position; instead, power was passed through the chief's mother's nieces or nephews and brothers or sisters. Women could therefore become *cacicas* or chiefs in their own right. At the death of the *cacique* Behechío, for example, his sister Anacaona succeeded him. Although she was married to a *cacique* from another province, Anacaona returned to her own territory to assume Behechío's position. Matrilineal descent was also important for the Spanish: some of them married leading females of the indigenous communities and thereby acquired power and possessions.

The *caciques* not only had religious and spiritual power but they could also control significant amounts of labour for clearing and cultivating fields. The chiefs were able to do this through their own subjects as well as those of their wives' kin. This meant that the chiefs often had hundreds of workers at their disposal. For example, Spanish records from Puerto Rico show that two *caciques* there had 600 or more labourers under their control, although most of the chiefs had between 100 and 250.

*Caciques* had even more power to call up their subjects for military service. The Spanish often recorded thousands of warriors assembled against them. In one of the largest battles between the

Amerindians and the Spanish in Hispaniola, there were more than 7,000 indigenous warriors. This was not unusual: in Puerto Rico, there were battles involving between 3,000 and 11,000 Amerindians. In 1495, Columbus described an indigenous offensive:

> The Indians were more than two thousand persons, all bearing their spears, which they hurled with that spear-thrower more rapidly than with a bow; and all were strong, and painted with coloureds, with guaizas [decorative shell mask-pendants, usually inland] and mirrors and masks and mirrors of copper and gold on their heads, giving frightening yells, as they were wont to do at certain times.[2]

But not all the indigenous chiefs opposed the Spanish. Some of the *caciques* allied themselves with the Spanish against their traditional indigenous enemies. One of them, Guadanagarí, formed an alliance with Columbus on his first voyage and continued to encourage the Spanish to attack his enemies. In another example, 3,000 Amerindian warriors backed Columbus' son, Bartolomé, against another leading *cacique*.

The Amerindians in the Caribbean thus had developed a relatively sophisticated society long before Columbus and his successors landed in the Caribbean. Since the Spanish established their main settlement on the island of Hispaniola and since it remained their base of operations in the region for the next thirty years, our knowledge of the Amerindians – and especially the Tainos of the Greater Antilles – derives mostly from Spanish sources. As we have seen, this has been supplemented by significant archaeological evidence.

The Tainos impressed the Spanish with their relative sophistication in agricultural techniques. Their cultivation system was based on the production of various crops, including manioc, a root crop from which the Indians produced cassava bread. Cassava bread was particularly useful since it could be preserved for long periods of time. The Indians also grew sweet potatoes and a wide range of other crops, such as yams, peanuts and beans as well as fruits such as guavas and pineapples. In addition, the Tainos hunted small game and fished; the combination of these activities produced sufficient food for themselves although not for the Europeans whose demands were to destroy this carefully balanced system.[3]

Similarly, for a people without writing and some of the other attributes of the Amerindian civilizations in Mexico, Central America and Peru, the Tainos possessed complex settlements. Their villages contained an average of between 1,000 and 2,000 people, and each village was governed by a chief. Taino houses were made of wood and thatch and were generally arranged around a central plaza. These plazas, which had been associated with the playing of an Amerindian ball game, became sacred sites after about AD 1200 where religious rituals were carried out. The villages were organized into district and regional chiefdoms, and the villagers themselves were divided into classes, which the Spanish observers equated with their own nobility and commoners. In effect, theirs was a stratified society, dominated by hereditary rulers. There was also a gendered division of labour among the Tainos. While men cleared the agricultural sites and also hunted and fished, women did most of the daily agricultural work. Women had a valued place in the social hierarchy of Taino society.

By contrast, the Caribs' focus was more on warfare and raiding, and they had begun to displace the Tainos in the Lesser Antilles. Like the Tainos, the Caribs had migrated from South America to the eastern Caribbean, and by the time of Columbus' landfall in 1492, the Caribs controlled most of the Lesser Antilles. The Caribs have received considerable attention, partly because Europeans believed that the Caribs practised cannibalism. Even now, there is considerable debate about the Caribs and cannibalism. Although the evidence is not conclusive, it is likely that, if it existed, their cannibalism had largely ritualistic functions. Moreover, the Spanish often claimed that the Indians who opposed them were cannibals and used that as a basis for enslaving them.[4]

The Caribs had a less complex social structure than the Tainos. They lacked the inherited chiefs which characterized the Tainos, choosing instead temporary war chiefs, and they also did not have the plazas and other public structures of the Tainos. The emphasis of the Caribs was on warfare and on trade; unlike the Tainos, for example, they raided other groups for their wives rather than making payments or doing service for them. In the end, the Caribs posed greater problems for the Europeans who sought to control them.

Columbus' first voyage had been a voyage of discovery; his second, a year later in the autumn of 1493, was a very different venture. His aim, and that of his patrons, the king and queen of

Spain, was to found a Spanish colony on the island of Hispaniola. Ferdinand and Isabella instructed him to establish gold mines, to trade with the Indians and to convert them to Christianity. They therefore provided him with a fleet of seventeen ships and about 1500 male settlers.

But there were serious problems from the outset. Since most of the Spanish settlers were seeking gold, they were dependent on the Tainos for their food supplies. At the same time, the Spanish soon developed systems of forced labour for the Indians which interfered with their food production. Initially, the Spanish sought tribute in gold from the Indians in the gold areas of Hispaniola: each Indian between the ages of fourteen and seventy was to supply a tribute of gold at three-monthly intervals. Outside of the gold-producing areas, the tribute was to be in cotton or other goods. The disruption of the food supply became progressively worse as the Tainos fled from their villages in the face of the Spanish onslaught.

Subsequently, in 1497, Columbus developed the *repartimiento* system, which meant that whole groups of Indians were to be allocated to individual Spaniards for service and tribute. But even the dragooning of Indian labour did not produce a sufficient yield from the gold mines. At the same time, the Tainos protested against their treatment: they abandoned their agricultural settlements, leading to serious problems of famine. Moreover, the appetite of the Europeans was enormous, especially compared to the consumption of the Indians, and the Indian agricultural economy simply could not produce the surpluses required by the Europeans. In addition, European diseases had devastating consequences for the Indians, and the result for the Tainos was famine, decimation and demoralization.[5]

The Indian population was not only declining because of the impact of the Spanish; it was also failing to grow. Indians committed suicide in significant numbers, faced with the shattering of their economy and ecology and the disruption of their social structure and community life. Their fertility rates also dropped markedly in the face of the trauma associated with the demands of the Europeans. All of this posed serious problems for Columbus, who proved unable to govern the colony successfully.

Because of the low yield from the gold mines and the insufficient amounts of food supplied by the Tainos, the Spanish settlers had to rely on supplies sent from Spain. Columbus himself had to return to Spain to answer questions about his leadership, and after his third voyage to the region in 1498, he spent the next two years seeking desperately to improve the situation. Indeed, many colonists themselves returned to Spain, since they could not make a living in Hispaniola, while others rebelled against Columbus' misrule. In the end, the king and queen of Spain had Columbus removed from office and brought back to Spain in 1500.

After a brief interim administration, Nicholás de Ovando was sent to Hispaniola to rescue the colony. With him were 2,500 settlers, including trained agriculturalists; moreover, Ovando was given extensive powers over the Indians. Within two years, Ovando had removed much of the remaining indigenous Taino leadership; in one act of extreme brutality, he had nearly one hundred of the chiefs massacred at a ceremonial event hosted by a friendly Indian leader. Ovando replaced the Indian *caciques* with his own lieutenants who commandeered Indian labour under an expanded system of *repartimiento*.

Under Ovando, the *repartimiento* system allowed the Spanish to assign entire Indian communities to work in the gold mines or in agriculture. The Indians would spend six months at work and then were allowed six months in their own villages to recover. As the Spanish increased their demands, the time left to the Tainos in their own villages was reduced. The *encomienda* was a similar system of forced labour but theoretically involved a more reciprocal relationship between the Indians and the Spanish. In return for their labour, the Indians were to be protected; moreover, each Indian village was meant to retain ownership of its lands. Whatever the subtle differences between the two systems, the reality was a pattern of forced labour and, indeed, de facto slavery.[6]

There were some attempts to safeguard the rights of the Indian population. The first public statement against the treatment of the Indians was a sermon preached by the Dominican friar, Antonio do Montesinos, at Santo Domingo in 1511. His sermon and the subsequent debate in Spain on the protection of the Indians led to a series of regulations, including a prohibition against their enslavement. Montesinos' message was taken up by another Dominican missionary, Bartolomé de las Casas, who became the principal defender of the Indians in the Spanish Empire. Las Casas was appointed to the office of Protector of the Indians in 1516, but it was too late for the Indians of the Caribbean, whose population continued to decline.

Living in unsanitary conditions, especially in the gold mines, and overworked, undernourished and vulnerable to European diseases, the Indians died in increasing numbers. While it is impossible to precisely assess the size of the Indian population before the arrival of Columbus, it seems likely that there were over 1,000,000 Tainos on Hispaniola in 1492. Whatever the true figure, the arrival of the Spanish and, in particular, the brutality of the Ovando regime reduced the size of this population dramatically. At the same time, the size of the Spanish population on the island was growing, partly because of a short-lived gold rush during Ovando's tenure of office. The reality was that an island densely populated by Indians before 1492 was transformed into one consisting primarily of Spaniards in the early sixteenth century. In 1519, a smallpox epidemic effectively wiped out the remaining Taino population.

But the gold supply on Hispaniola did not last; the output of gold reached its peak in 1510 and thereafter declined significantly. After 1519, gold mining effectively ceased on Hispaniola. Since there was also a continuing labour shortage, the Spanish searched elsewhere for labourers in the region. For example, they raided the Bahamian islands for Indians, enslaving them on Hispaniola and depopulating the Bahamas in the process. In addition, the Spanish looked for other territories in the region to colonize and to exploit.

In 1509, the Spanish occupied Jamaica. There, they again encountered significant numbers of Tainos but found no gold. In Cuba and Puerto Rico, which the Spanish also colonized in this period, there was some gold, and the result was similar to the events in Hispaniola. A brief gold rush in each island was followed by the decimation of the Indian population. Both islands survived as stock rearing centres, supplying food and hides to Spain and to the Spanish fleets travelling on their way to the mother country. Indeed, Havana's location on the route back to Spain from the mainland colonies guaranteed its continuing importance. But many Spanish settlers left the islands to seek their fortune in Mexico in the 1520s and in Peru a decade later, leaving the Spanish Caribbean an imperial backwater.

There was one other source of wealth for the Spanish on Hispaniola, which would have its own highly significant history in the region: sugar. The Spanish introduced the cultivation of sugar cane from the Canary Islands in 1515 and by the late 1530s, thirty-four sugar mills had been constructed on the island. Although the first slaves from Africa had been imported to work in the gold mines, more significant numbers of Africans were brought to work on the sugar plantations from the 1520s. Although Hispaniola was to face stiff competition later in the century from Brazil, a few sugar estates were still producing sugar at the end of the sixteenth century. The impact of the African slave trade and of Africans was to have a profound effect on the development of the Caribbean.

As the geographer, David Watts, concluded, the encounter between the Spanish and the Tainos had significant consequences. For Watts,

> the stable, prosperous, welcoming, agriculturally rich and culturally sophisticated [Taino] domains in the Greater Antilles had been destroyed completely, to make way for an ultimately small and predominately transient Spanish population and many more [African] slaves, living in what after 1519 was a fringe, supporting region for Spanish interests on the American mainland.[7]

This created a vacuum in the remainder of the Caribbean which other European powers would not long ignore.

## European colonies in the Eastern Caribbean

During the sixteenth century, the Spanish sought to maintain control of the Caribbean. They struggled to keep interlopers from smuggling goods to the region and, more significantly, to stop privateers from attacking their treasure fleets and their colonies. In addition, the Spanish were intent on deterring other European powers from establishing colonies of their own in the Caribbean. While it was not possible to accomplish all of these aims, the Spanish did succeed in preventing other European settlements in the Caribbean during the sixteenth century.

However, the French and the English did manage to break the Spanish trading monopoly and to cause them serious problems. In the period up to about 1540, the French were most active in plundering the Spanish treasure fleets as they travelled through the

Caribbean on their way to Spain; in the last half of the sixteenth century, it was the English.

The Englishman, John Hawkins, epitomized one aspect of the attempt to breach the Spanish monopoly of trade in the Caribbean. His idea, although technically illegal, was to trade directly with the Spanish colonists in Hispaniola, thereby undermining and undercutting the Spanish-authorized trade agreements. Hawkins would supply cheaper African slaves to the settlers in exchange for sugar and other commodities which he could sell in Europe. In 1562, Hawkins succeeded, although being careful to avoid the capital of Hispaniola and trading with colonists on the northern side of the island. Several years later, however, Hawkins was not so fortunate; the Spanish destroyed most of his fleet of ten ships, although he managed to escape.

Francis Drake had very different aims than Hawkins. While Hawkins was primarily interested in trade, Drake was after more substantial prizes and had a more coherent strategy against the Spanish. It is also clear that his actions were tacitly approved by the English government. One of his most daring exploits was to attack the mule trains carrying gold and silver from Peru to Central America for their rendezvous with the Spanish fleet. More significantly and accompanied by a fleet of twenty ships, Drake sacked Santo Domingo, the capital of Hispaniola, in 1585 before moving on to Cartagena on the mainland of Latin America. Although Drake did considerable damage to the Spanish, he too suffered defeat: a decade after his successful foray against the Spanish, he and Hawkins were repulsed in an attack on Puerto Rico.

There were other visions of the Caribbean and of settlement in the region. Walter Raleigh was not alone in seeking to find El Dorado, the mythical golden man who lived in a golden village up the Orinoco River in present-day Guyana. El Dorado remained hidden, but the buccaneers and pirates sought their own rewards in attacking ships and settlements. Unlike Drake and other privateers, they generally operated independently of European governments and were made up of a mixture of disaffected sailors, religious refugees, and, in the seventeenth century, of escaped European indentured servants. Living on the margins of Caribbean society, often in remote small-island communities such as Tortuga off the northern coast of Hispaniola, they terrorized settlers and shipping across the region. Indeed, the buccaneers helped to glamorize the

Caribbean, giving it the image, as Richard Dunn has suggested, of 'the Wild West of the sixteenth and seventeenth century'. It was an area associated with 'excitement, quick profit and constant peril' as well as great wealth and great savagery.[8]

Yet the actions against the Spanish, however intrepid in the sixteenth century, did not result in the establishment of other European colonies in the region. But the Spanish grip on settlement in the Caribbean could not last. Weakened by the Anglo-Spanish Wars of the late sixteenth century, the Spanish could no longer prevent rival settlements in the seventeenth century. Nor could they deter the Dutch from taking over much of their trade routes in the region. The seventeenth century, then, witnessed the development of French, British and Dutch colonies in the Caribbean, albeit at first in the eastern Caribbean, at some distance from the main Spanish colonies in the region.

St. Kitts was the first permanent non-Spanish colony in the region. It was settled in 1624 by both French and British settlers who shared the island in a defensive alliance against attacks by the Spanish. Three years later, another group of English colonists established a colony on Barbados. Barbados had significant advantages over St. Kitts: it contained no Amerindians on the island at the time and its position on the eastern fringe of the Caribbean and against the prevailing trade winds made it difficult for colonists on neighbouring islands to attack it. As a result, it was the only British island in the Caribbean to escape invasion by another European power. During the next few years, the English also settled the islands of Nevis, Antigua and Montserrat.

The French also established colonies beyond their foothold on St. Kitts. Although the French put fewer resources into their colonial activities, in 1635 they colonized two of the larger islands of the eastern Caribbean, Guadeloupe and Martinique. However, because of the significant Carib population, the French were slow to settle these islands. The Dutch, who were primarily interested in trade in the region, colonized Curaçao, close to the mainland of South America and therefore to trading opportunities with the Spanish. There were also salt deposits on the nearby island of Bonaire, which the Dutch needed for their fishing industry in the days before refrigeration. The Dutch settled on Bonaire as well as on several smaller islands, sharing St. Martin with the French, and occupying the tiny islands of Saba and St. Eustatius, also useful as trading bases with the neighbouring French and British colonies.

Unlike the Spanish patterns of colonization, the colonies in the eastern Caribbean were largely organized by private enterprise. There was no equivalent in these colonies to the role played by the Spanish Crown in financing Columbus and his successors. Instead, merchants and commercial syndicates took the lead in backing these colonies. In the case of Barbados, for example, the first colonizing expedition was financed by a London merchant, William Courteen. In the struggle for control of the colony, Courteen lost out to James Hay, Earl of Carlisle, who became Lord Proprietor of the Caribbee Islands. Carlisle's land policy had significant implications for the development of Barbados: he initiated a system of sizeable land grants to planters in return for payment of an annual rent, payable in tobacco. This meant that landholding on the island was restricted to those with capital or access to credit. Since it is likely that Carlisle also encouraged the importation of white servants to provide the labour for these plantations, Carlisle's policies helped to ensure the development of Barbados as a plantation colony.

In the early days of Barbados as well as that of the other English and French colonies, white servants provided the main labour force on these islands. This would not have surprised seventeenth-century Englishmen: indentured servitude was a common feature of seventeenth-century life. It was a way of socializing the offspring of the middling classes as well as of making use of the labouring poor. In the Caribbean context, voluntary indentured servants (known as *engagés* in the French colonies) emigrated to the colonies for a period of between three and ten years. Their fare was paid, and in return for their passage and their upkeep, they agreed to work for a master for a specified period of time. At the end of their period of servitude, servants initially could expect to receive ten acres of land. However, as the land in these colonies was soon parcelled out, servants had to migrate elsewhere to get any land or received payment in kind, such as tobacco or sugar, as their 'freedom dues'.

Voluntary servants were not the only European labourers in the colonies. Many whites were sent to the Caribbean as a consequence of political developments in Europe; for example, prisoners of war during the English Civil War in the 1640s were often sent to the islands. Inevitably, because of Cromwell's campaigns in Ireland, this meant that a significant number of Irish prisoners of war found themselves shipped to the Caribbean. In addition, convicts were frequently transported to work on the plantations of the Caribbean instead of serving their prison terms in England.

Whatever their origin, white indentured servants were often treated harshly. Their housing was frequently rudimentary, their food inadequate and their punishments severe. Primarily young males, they generally had no family ties in the colonies; indeed, marriage to an indentured servant, however unlikely given the lack of females on the islands, meant a longer term of servitude. A contemporary observer of Barbados, Richard Ligon, complained about overseers beating their servants mercilessly. In response, many servants sought to escape, either to settle in other colonies or to join the buccaneers and pirates. Whites also joined with black slaves to organize conspiracies and to rebel against their masters. Although these conspiracies were usually discovered before they could develop, they indicated the depths of the servants' resentment about their condition.[9]

Indentured servants were required to do the most demanding tasks on the plantations. They helped to clear the land of the often dense forests and subsequently helped to prepare the land for farming and for the crops which would be grown in the colonies. The first major export crop in the Caribbean, tobacco, was initially successful but could not compete either in quality or quantity with tobacco produced in Virginia. When tobacco prices fell drastically in the 1630s, planters turned to cotton but that proved difficult to grow and required significant amounts of capital and labour. Planters in Barbados also grew indigo, which was used in the manufacture of dyes for the textile industry. But indigo also proved unprofitable in the early 1640s. Neither tobacco, cotton nor indigo, then, would transform the Caribbean colonies from their situation as small-scale export economies. It was sugar which would dramatically change the fortunes of Barbados and then the other English and French colonies in the region. Sugar and slavery would provide the basis of an agricultural and demographic transformation in the seventeenth-century Caribbean.

# CHAPTER TWO

# Sugar and slavery

In the late 1630s, Barbados was facing serious economic difficulties. Tobacco prices had collapsed in the world market, and Barbadian tobacco was in any case unable to compete with the quality of tobacco grown in Virginia. To make things worse, the price of cotton was declining. Needing to produce a new crop, Barbadian planters turned to sugar.

Sugar cane had been first domesticated in southeast Asia and had gradually made its way west. The Arabs had brought it to the southern Mediterranean by the eighth century, and Europeans began to cultivate the crop in Sicily, southern Italy, Portugal and later Spain. The Portuguese also cultivated sugar cane on the Atlantic island of Madeira and on São Tomé off the coast of west Africa, where they made use of African slave labour. When the Portuguese colonized Brazil in the sixteenth century, it was a logical step for them to produce sugar, using the knowledge they had gained in the Atlantic islands.[1]

Although initially significant, the output of sugar in Brazil eventually stagnated and was unable to supply the increasing demand for the crop in Europe. Sugar had been regarded as a medicine and as a luxury commodity to be used sparingly and only for the rich. But its use was transformed in the seventeenth century as a replacement for honey and as a sweetener for the food and drinks of working people. In light of this development, Barbadian planters sought to shift to sugar.

It helped that Barbados and much of the rest of the Caribbean was ideally suited to the cultivation of sugar. The climate and the terrain, especially of a relatively flat and compact island such as Barbados, facilitated sugar production. Sugar requires fourteen to eighteen months to mature and is therefore planted in the Caribbean during the rainy season in the autumn and harvested more than a year later between January and June in the dry season. But planters had to have more than an equitable climate and appropriate soils to transform their production to sugar; they also needed capital to provide the equipment and the labour to grow cane. (Figure 2.1)

For unlike tobacco or cotton farmers, sugar planters were also manufacturers. Once cane is harvested, the sucrose content drops rapidly; therefore, in addition to a large field labour force, planters had to have skilled labour and expensive equipment to process the cane. This meant providing sugar mills to extract the juice from the cane, a boiling house to crystallize the juice and produce sugar, a curing house to dry the sugar and drain the molasses and sometimes a distillery for producing rum. These requirements were far beyond

FIGURE 2.1 *Sugar factory in Trinidad, 1836.*
*Source:* © The British Library Board.

the resources of most small-scale tobacco and cotton farmers; moreover, their plots of land were too small to produce sugar on a profitable scale. It was planters who had access to capital and credit who could make the transition to sugar.

Some of this capital and credit came from the Dutch. The great middlemen of Europe, the Dutch had additional reasons to promote the development of sugar in Barbados. Although the Dutch took control of Pernambuco in 1630, the Portuguese rebelled against the Dutch and succeeded in expelling them from Brazil in 1654. The Dutch therefore saw the possibilities of an expanded market at a time when their hold on their sugar-producing colony was weakening. Moreover, the Dutch envisioned significant profits from all aspects of sugar production: these included providing credit, slaves and plantation supplies to the Barbadians. In addition, the Dutch shipped and refined the sugar in the Netherlands, making profits at every stage of the process.

However, more recent evidence also points to the important role of English investors and merchants in supplying capital and credit to Barbadian planters. Many English business firms bought plantations in Barbados in the crucial decade between 1640 and 1650. Moreover, English merchant investors did not just invest in land; they also played a very significant role in supplying planters in Barbados with African slaves during this period. One report even suggested that the English were ahead of the Dutch in supplying slaves to Barbados. In addition, Barbadian planters themselves were significant in the sugar boom of the seventeenth century. Nearly 40 per cent of the large planters in 1680 came from families that had established farms and estates before sugar became the dominant crop in the island.[2]

Beyond the need for capital, there was an additional problem for the Barbadian planters. To produce sugar on a profitable scale, they had to have a much larger labour force than had been required for tobacco or cotton. Yet at the very time when planters were shifting to sugar, they were facing difficulties in attracting white indentured labourers. Because of the demands of growing sugar, planters were treating their servants more harshly. As a result, white servants ran away, rebelled and conspired to resist the planters. Moreover, as the planters acquired more land for their estates, there was less available for the servants once they had completed their terms of indenture. In the face of these conditions, fewer indentured servants were prepared to come to Barbados and the other Caribbean colonies.

There were also other reasons for the decline in the supply of white indentured servants to the Caribbean. Earlier in the seventeenth century, the English believed that their country was overpopulated and therefore encouraged emigration. By the middle of the century, this view was changing; instead, policymakers began to think of the country as underpopulated and needing to retain its labour. When white servants did emigrate, there were more desirable destinations than the Caribbean, such as South Carolina, Virginia and Maryland. In order to compete with the mainland colonies for white servants, the Caribbean colonies were forced to cut the length of servitude, thereby effectively increasing the price of servant labour. In the face of rising costs for white servants and a diminished supply of labourers, planters turned to Africa and to slavery to solve their labour problem.[3]

In Africa, slavery was a long-standing institution. Unlike the New World, African slavery was not tied to producing agricultural commodities on a grand scale; instead, slavery in Africa was generally organized on a more domestic and small-scale basis. Africans could be enslaved for a variety of reasons: these included being captured in warfare, serving as payment for debts and being punished for crimes. But even with the spread of Islam and the resulting Islamic slave trade, the trade in African slaves remained relatively small. It was only when the Portuguese and subsequently other European powers began trading on the west coast of Africa and purchasing slaves that slavery and the slave trade were transformed. Before the Atlantic slave trade was over nearly four hundred years later, more than 12,000,000 Africans had been shipped across the Atlantic and many others died en route to the African coast and on the Middle Passage.[4]

Enslaved Africans were present from the early days of Spanish settlement in the Caribbean. The governor of Hispaniola, Nicholás de Ovando, brought African slaves with him in 1502, beginning a process which lasted until the end of the nineteenth century. Initially, the Spanish supplied their colonies with enslaved people by granting licences to individual traders to import slaves. At the end of the sixteenth century, the Spanish introduced a monopoly contract or *asiento* system, in which a trader or trading company would be given monopoly rights to supply slaves to the colonies.

Although this was a highly prized contract, trading companies were not always able to fulfil the terms of the contract, leaving room for private interlopers to cash in on the demand for slaves.

In the case of the English Caribbean colonies, it was not until 1660 that the first joint-stock companies were established to participate in the slave trade. Both English companies established during the 1660s collapsed, but one of them, the Company of Royal Adventurers Trading into Africa, established forts on the west African coast and managed to deliver about 3,000 enslaved people to Barbados by 1664. Its successor, the Royal Africa Company, was chartered in 1672 and proved to be more successful: it supplied the majority of the enslaved for the English colonies during this period.

Yet the Royal Africa Company faced some of the same difficulties as its predecessors. It was unable to supply all the slaves the colonists needed, and it also had the problem of keeping up its forts on the African coast as well as dealing with interlopers. As a result, Parliament reorganized the trade in 1698, granting private traders the right to participate legally in the trade on payment of a duty to the Royal Africa Company. Since even this attempt to control the interlopers ended a little over a decade later, the eighteenth century experienced the continued rise of the private traders and the decline of the Royal Africa Company.[5]

Other European powers followed the English example. Dutch involvement in the slave trade was particularly significant after 1630, especially after the Dutch captured Elmina, the principal Portuguese slave trading fort on the Gold Coast in 1637. This enabled the Dutch to supply the Barbadians and other colonists with enslaved people. France was also interested in the slave trade, largely because of its colonies in the Caribbean; it established the French Company of the West Indies in 1664, providing the company with a monopoly of the slave trade to its colonies. But significant French involvement in the Atlantic slave trade did not develop fully until the eighteenth century, when its colonies in the Caribbean, and in particular Saint Domingue, began to expand considerably.

Inevitably, there was an enormous human cost to the Atlantic slave trade. The horrors of the trade and of the Middle Passage resulted in high mortality figures, especially in the early days of the trade. Diseases such as smallpox, dysentery and malaria could have devastating effects on cramped ships. Colin Palmer has examined the records of the Royal Africa Company and, specifically, the number of the enslaved the company carried and those who died during the period from 1680 to 1688. Of nearly two hundred ships which left Africa during these years carrying over 60,000 slaves, over 14,000 or 23.7 per cent died on the Middle Passage alone. This excludes enslaved people who died on the forced marches to the African coast and those who also died soon after their arrival in the New World. The evidence from a much broader sample of voyages suggests that mortality on the Middle Passage in the late sixteenth and early seventeenth centuries was around 20 per cent. It dropped to less than half that level by the early nineteenth century, probably because of a combination of better food, more sanitary conditions and faster ships (see Table 2.1).[6]

There were other important considerations in analysing mortality rates on the Middle Passage. One was the African port of origin of the enslaved Africans: for example, the losses on ships leaving the Bight of Biafra were 120 per cent greater than those leaving Angola, the biggest region of embarkation on the slave trade, and far greater than for the whole of sub-Saharan Africa. While the reasons for such differences are not well understood, one possible explanation lies in the distance the enslaved Africans had to travel from the places they were captured to the particular port. It was also the case that children under fifteen years old had higher rates of mortality while adult women often experienced lower death rates.[7]

These mortality figures sometimes made it difficult for planters to choose the type of slaves they preferred. Yet some planters did

TABLE 2.1 Average slave mortality in the Middle Passage, 1590–1867.

| Period | Mean percentage of deaths (%) | Ships in sample |
|---|---|---|
| 1590–1699 | 20.3 | 401 |
| 1700–1749 | 15.6 | 1,091 |
| 1750–1807 | 12.0 | 2,571 |
| 1808–1829 | 8.8 | 1,350 |
| 1830–1867 | 11.5 | 553 |

*Source*: Herbert S. Klein, *The Atlantic Slave Trade* (Cambridge, 1999), p. 138.

have preferences about what they thought were African ethnic groups. In Jamaica, for example, there was a belief that enslaved Africans from the Gold Coast labelled as 'Coromantees' worked hard, even though they were prone to rebellion. Other slaves, such as the 'Ibo' from the Bight of Biafra, were regarded as prone to depression and suicide. But these views, however stereotyped and ill-informed about African ethnicities, did not carry much weight; other considerations, such as gender and age, were more important than the regional origins of the enslaved people.[8] Moreover, it was African suppliers of slaves who determined the mix of enslaved people sent across the Atlantic rather than planters in the Caribbean and the Americas. As Herbert S. Klein has concluded:

> Whatever the contemporary record might report about planters wanting slaves from the Gold Coast and not from Loango, they in fact took what they could get. This meant accepting not only women and children in ever increasing numbers, but also slaves from whatever region provided them.[9]

Whatever their origin, the arrival of enslaved Africans profoundly affected the demography of the Caribbean colonies. As is apparent from Table 2.2, the change in Barbados from a predominately white labour force to a black one occurred gradually over a period of several decades. But there was no doubting the shift in population and the impact of the African enslaved population. From a situation in the middle of the seventeenth century in which whites slightly outnumbered blacks, by the turn of the eighteenth century blacks outnumbered whites by a ratio of more than 3:1.

The impact was far more than demographic. Sugar and slavery transformed the fortunes of the Barbadian planters, many of whom prospered. Visitors to the island now commented on the rich food, dress and accoutrements of the planters. This was a marked change from the days of tobacco when planters slept in hammocks and used barrels and chests instead of four-poster beds and proper furniture.

One of the richest planters on the island, Thomas Modyford, may have been exceptional, but his career points to the possibilities of accumulating vast wealth from sugar. Arriving in Barbados in 1647 with enough money to purchase a half-share in a 500-acre plantation, he told one visitor to the island that he expected to make £100,000 as a planter. He became governor of the island, sold his property in Barbados and moved to Jamaica, where his plantation was one of the largest in the Caribbean. In all, Modyford and his relatives owned more than 20,000 acres of land on the island.[10]

Yet Barbados, too, had its problems, especially with disease. It was prone to epidemics, especially of yellow fever, and one very serious epidemic in the late 1640s killed thousands of colonists. Barbados was 'a fast-living, fast-dying tropical community', one in which fortunes were made quickly and death could also come suddenly.[11] At the same time, the colony attracted an odd assortment of people. For example, some of the women servants brought to

**TABLE 2.2** The labour force on fifteen Barbados plantations, 1640–1667.

| Year | Planter | Acreage | Servants | Slaves |
| --- | --- | --- | --- | --- |
| 1640 | Lancelot Page | 360 | 17 | 0 |
| 1643 | James Holdip | 200 | 29 | 0 |
| 1646 | Sir Anthony Ashley Cooper | 205 | 21 | 9 |
| 1646 | ? | 500 | 40 | 50 |
| 1647 | Thomas Modyford | 500 | 28 | 102 |
| 1648 | ? | 100 | 11 | 3 |
| 1648 | Humphrey Walrond | 250 | 10 | 29 |
| 1649 | William Powrey | 416 | 7 | 23 |
| 1650 | Gideon Low | 150 | 0 | 10 |
| 1654 | Robert Hooper | 200 | 35 | 66 |
| 1656 | George Martin | 259 | 0 | 60 |
| 1657 | John Read | 75 | 21 | 25 |
| 1658 | Thomas Hothersall | 140 | 0 | 30 |
| 1661 | ? | 143 | 5 | 20 |
| 1667 | ? | 350 | 5 | 125 |

*Source*: Dunn, *Sugar and Slaves*, p. 68.

the colony came from the brothels of Britain's major cities; they hoped to improve their lot by marrying prosperous planters. One contemporary account of the island in 1655 described not only its wealth but also its unusual mixture of people:

> This island is one of the richest spots of ground in the world and fully inhabited. But were the people suitable to the island, it were not to be compared ... . This island is inhabited with all sorts: with English, French, Dutch, Scots, Irish, Spaniards they being Jews, with Indians and miserable Negroes born to perpetual slavery, they and their seed ... . This island is the dunghill whereon England doth cast forth its rubbish. Rogues and whores and such like people are those which are generally brought here. A rogue in England will hardly make a cheater here. A bawd brought over puts on a demure comportment, a whore if handsome makes a wife for some rich planter. But in plain, the island of itself is very delightful and pleasant.[12]

The other islands in the Caribbean – English, French and Spanish – were unable to shift to sugar production as quickly as Barbados. In some cases, politics impeded this process. In the Leeward Islands, for example, which consisted of St. Kitts, Nevis, Antigua and Montserrat, the Anglo-French conflicts of the late seventeenth and early eighteenth centuries served to delay their development. Some of these colonies changed hands repeatedly: in St. Kitts, this happened seven times in this period, before it finally wound up in the hands of the English in 1713.

Planters in the Leeward Islands also generally lacked the capital to buy large numbers of the enslaved and build sugar factories. Instead, tobacco remained a staple in these islands far longer than it did in Barbados. Moreover, in the seventeenth century, the ratio of blacks to whites in the Leewards was largely equal; indeed, in many of these islands, whites outnumbered the enslaved. This would change dramatically by the early eighteenth century, when black–white ratios were closer to that of Barbados. By the middle of the eighteenth century, sugar production in the Leewards was three times greater than that of Barbados.

Jamaica also offered enormous opportunities for the development of sugar after the English seized the island from the Spanish in 1655. It was thirty times the size of Barbados and the Leeward Islands combined and almost totally undeveloped. Yet Jamaica had other advantages, especially for buccaneering expeditions against the Spanish. It was well situated for raids against the Spanish colonies, not only in the Caribbean but also in Central America. One of the most famous buccaneers, Henry Morgan, made his base in Jamaica and from there attacked Spanish settlements in Nicaragua, Cuba, Venezuela and Panama, often returning to Jamaica with vast amounts of loot. The city of Port Royal, located on a promontory of land jutting into the Caribbean Sea on the south side of the island, developed to service the buccaneers and prospered in the process.

But sugar planters had other ideas for Jamaica and eventually were able to oust the buccaneers and pirates from the island. It helped that the buccaneers' capital, Port Royal, was destroyed by a devastating earthquake in 1692, but Henry Morgan was already dead by then and the power of the buccaneers had waned considerably. The future of the island lay in the hands of the sugar planters, who were able to establish large plantations across the island. In addition, the planters imported significant numbers of the enslaved in the late seventeenth and early eighteenth centuries; by 1713, black–white ratios in Jamaica had risen to 8:1, significantly higher than the comparable figures in Barbados and the Leewards.

In the French colonies in the Caribbean, planters were more like their counterparts in the Leewards than in Jamaica. The French colonists preferred to concentrate on tobacco, cotton and indigo rather than making the expensive shift to sugar. Moreover, in the middle of the seventeenth century, the French lost one-third of their white population due to the same epidemic which affected Barbados. Consequently, the populations of Martinique and Guadeloupe remained small, with about 5,000 whites in Guadeloupe and under 3,000 in Martinique and a smaller number of the enslaved in each colony. But with the acquisition of Saint Domingue at the end of the seventeenth century, the French began to increase their slave population and concentrate more on the production of sugar.

For the Spanish settlers in Cuba, Hispaniola and Puerto Rico, the production of hides as well as crops such as ginger and cacao were important exports. Tobacco also became an important crop in Cuba in the seventeenth century. There was some sugar production in these islands, but the Hispanic islands retained a more mixed economy. Unlike the French and English Caribbean, their populations remained predominately white; there was a small number of enslaved people and a larger free black and mulatto population. But the importance of these colonies to the Spanish in this period was mostly strategic: the Spanish were more interested in their far richer colonies on the mainland of Latin America and in the gold and silver which they extracted from them. It was not until the latter part of the eighteenth century that Cuba, in particular, would begin the transformation to a sugar economy.

In general, then, the seventeenth century witnessed the beginnings of the large-scale commercial production of sugar. Although the speed of the shift to sugar differed considerably from island to island, the pattern of sugar production linked to the importation of large numbers of enslaved Africans was clearly established in this period. Barbados set the pace for this transformation and had a significant head start over its neighbours. However, the eighteenth century would see other colonies overtake Barbados and achieve wealth and importance far beyond anything imaginable a century earlier.

# CHAPTER THREE

# Slavery, work and the slaves' economy

Despite developing at different times, slave societies in the Caribbean were broadly similar. Barbados' sugar revolution of the seventeenth century did not vary dramatically from what happened in Jamaica and Saint Domingue in the eighteenth century and Cuba and Puerto Rico in the nineteenth. Of course, there were significant differences as well; the technology which drove Cuba's sugar boom, for example, was far more advanced than its predecessors. But life for the enslaved on the sugar plantations of the Caribbean from the seventeenth to the nineteenth centuries shared many of the same features.

Following the example set by Barbados, it was Jamaica and the Leeward Islands which took off in terms of sugar production in the early eighteenth century. Indeed, by the 1740s, Jamaica was the single largest producer of sugar in the British Caribbean. But Saint Domingue's growth was even more phenomenal; by the late eighteenth century, sugar production in Saint Domingue had not only eclipsed that of Jamaica but also nearly all of the British islands combined.

At the same time, Cuba, which was to become the largest producer of sugar in the nineteenth century, was an underpopulated colony consisting primarily of cattle ranches and tobacco farms. After the British occupied Havana for ten months in 1763, however, the focus of the Cuban economy began to shift. As in the other Caribbean colonies, sugar (and also coffee) took over many of the existing tobacco and cattle holdings. With the liberalization of trade at the end of the eighteenth century and also the destruction of the most important sugar economy of the time, Saint Domingue, Cuba embarked on its own sugar revolution. Puerto Rico also experienced a sugar boom in the nineteenth century, although it never developed a full-fledged plantation economy comparable to that of Jamaica or Cuba.

To produce growth of this magnitude, the Atlantic slave trade concentrated in the eighteenth century on the British and French colonies (see Table 3.1). Saint Domingue and Jamaica each imported around 700,000 enslaved people in this period, although Saint Domingue had reached this level by the time of its slave rebellion of 1791. Jamaica had nearly another two decades of involvement in the slave trade before the British abolished the trade in 1808. Other colonies also imported significant numbers of Africans: Martinique and Guadeloupe each accounted for 250,000 slaves during this period, and Barbados' numbers were similar. However, Barbados ceased bringing in large numbers of Africans during the course of the eighteenth century, as its enslaved population began to show a natural positive increase by late in the century. In the nineteenth century, it was Cuba which dominated the trade: it received around 700,000 slaves in the period between 1800 and 1867. This was

**TABLE 3.1** Estimated net slave imports, 1700–1870 (in 'ooos).

|  | 1700–1760 | 1761–1810 | 1811–1870 | Total |
|---|---|---|---|---|
| Spanish Caribbean | 20 | 230 | 692 | 942 |
| British Caribbean | 626 | 930 | – | 1556 |
| French Caribbean | 365 | 650 | 95 | 1110 |
| Dutch Caribbean | 239 | 138 | – | 377 |
| Danish Caribbean | 25 | 32 | – | 57 |
| TOTAL | 1275 | 1980 | 787 | 4042 |

Source: Stanley L. Engerman and B.W. Higman, 'The Demographic Structure of the Caribbean Slave Societies in the Eighteenth and Nineteenth Centuries', in Franklin Knight, ed., General History of the Caribbean, vol. 3: The Slave Societies of the Caribbean (London, 1997), p. 60.

despite the fact that the slave trade was illegal during much of this time.[1]

Since the Atlantic slave trade lasted for such a long time, it is not surprising that the Caribbean colonies received a mixture of African ethnic groups. At different times, the slave trade centred on specific areas of the West African coast. For example, in the early eighteenth century, traders favoured the area from Senegambia to the Bight of Benin. Yet a century later, the trade had moved south and east: over 80 per cent of the enslaved were then being taken from the Bight of Benin and central Africa. By the nineteenth century, Mozambique had become a critically important source of slaves for Cuba.

Despite this shift in the supply of enslaved people, there were concentrations of slaves from specific areas. Half of the arrivals in Saint Domingue came from west-central Africa; similarly, half of those coming to the Guyanas and Suriname were shipped from the Gold Coast. But the other half in each of these cases came from a number of regions in Africa. It is therefore important to realize that the enslaved generally came from a variety of different locations and African ethnic groups.[2]

In the Caribbean, ethnic rivalry often characterized the enslaved populations. Africans spoke different languages and could not always easily communicate with each other. In eighteenth-century Saint Domingue, there were twenty-six different ethnic groups. Some Africans in Jamaica, such as the Akan-speakers from the Gold Coast, apparently did not mix with the other slaves and were disliked by them. Enslaved people from this area were also heavily involved in some of the rebellions of the seventeenth and eighteenth centuries.

There were other divisions in early slave society. Creole, or Caribbean-born slaves, usually regarded themselves as superior to those directly from Africa. In Saint Domingue, these enslaved people mocked newly arrived Africans and sometimes exploited them. Elsewhere, creole slaves often derogatively labelled the enslaved from Africa as 'salt-water Negroes' or 'Guineybirds'. The specific African origin of the enslaved and then the question of African or Caribbean birth were therefore significant barriers to slave unity.[3]

With the development of Caribbean slave society, occupational differentiation – often linked to differences of colour and to gender – served to divide the enslaved further. The three major groups were domestic, skilled and field slaves, although there were

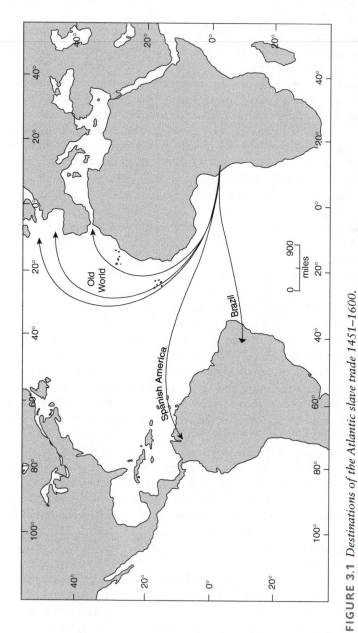

**FIGURE 3.1** *Destinations of the Atlantic slave trade 1451–1600.*

*Source:* © 1969 by the Board of the University of Wisconsin System. Reprinted by permission of the University of Wisconsin Press.

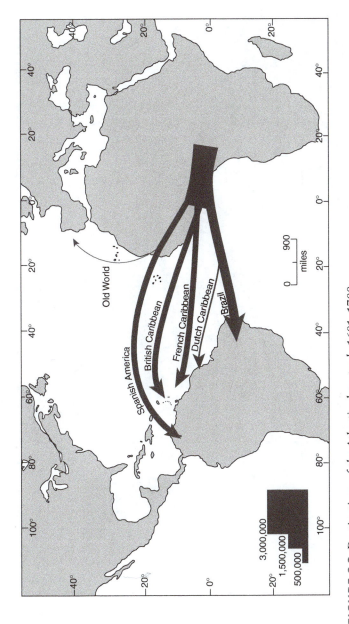

**FIGURE 3.2** *Destinations of the Atlantic slave trade 1601–1700.*

*Source:* © 1969 by the Board of the University of Wisconsin System. Reprinted by permission of the University of Wisconsin Press.

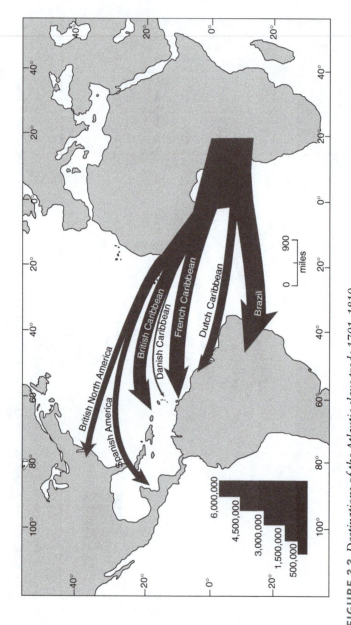

**FIGURE 3.3** *Destinations of the Atlantic slave trade 1701–1810.*

*Source:* © 1969 by the Board of the University of Wisconsin System. Reprinted by permission of the University of Wisconsin Press.

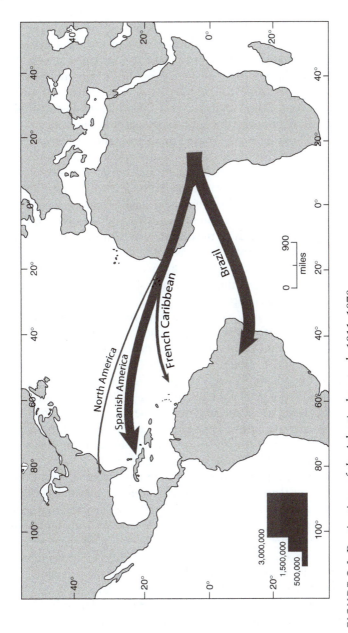

**FIGURE 3.4** *Destinations of the Atlantic slave trade 1811–1870.*

*Source:* © 1969 by the Board of the University of Wisconsin System. Reprinted by permission of the University of Wisconsin Press.

often important subdivisions within each of these categories. There was a hierarchy among the enslaved; those who were in charge of specific areas, were skilled or worked as head domestics were the elite slaves, at least from the point of view of the slave masters. It was the slave owners who determined the rankings among the enslaved and who had the power to promote or demote enslaved people from one group to another. Moreover, status was often related to colour. Slaves of mixed race, also known as coloureds, did not generally work in the lowest status jobs in the field.

A significant proportion of domestic slaves in the Caribbean were coloured women. For enslaved women, work in and around the great house – as washerwomen, cooks and nursemaids – was one of the few areas of advancement out of the fields. Domestic slaves had far less personal freedom than field slaves and may have been isolated from the slave community and from kin; moreover, they had to respond constantly to the demands of their masters. Yet they ate and dressed better than field slaves and had a greater chance of being manumitted. Indeed, domestic slaves could be fiercely loyal to their masters, even at times when the slave owners were under attack by other enslaved people.

Like domestics, many skilled slaves were coloured; but unlike house slaves, all artisans were male. They performed a wide and often very important range of tasks on the plantations and in the wider community. Carpenters, millwrights and coppersmiths were among the most highly valued skilled slaves followed by coopers, sawyers and distillers. For the planters, the boilerman, who was in charge of making the sugar, was one of the most significant of the enslaved on any plantation. On a large estate, there could be several artisans in many of these categories, with a head slave, such as a head boilerman or head cooper, in charge of each.

Skilled slaves enjoyed a degree of mobility denied to most other slaves. Some of them would have been 'hired-out' to other owners, either on plantations or in towns. Though financial arrangements differed in various colonies, many of the enslaved in this group would have earned money, out of which they paid their owners an agreed sum and provided for their own upkeep. Any remaining earnings could be saved towards the purchase of their freedom. 🖉

The lifestyle of these skilled slaves, and especially those living in towns, was very different from that of most of the plantation slaves. This could cause difficulties. In Tortola, one of the Virgin Islands, owners were very concerned about slaves who were allowed to live in towns as housekeepers or artisans. Since these enslaved people lived apart from their masters, the legislature of the Virgin Islands passed a law compelling the enslaved to live on the same premises as their owners. As this example suggests, skilled slaves were sometimes affected more by the demands of their work than by their legal condition as slaves.

In Cuba, the urban enslaved worked in a variety of different jobs from the early sixteenth century onwards. For example, female slaves operated the taverns, the eating houses and the lodges of Havana. In addition, they were the laundresses, the domestic labourers and the prostitutes of the town. Urban male slaves were involved in the building trades, in ship construction and in many other skilled tasks. As elsewhere in the Caribbean, these skilled enslaved people had a significant degree of mobility.

These patterns continued in nineteenth-century Cuba. Since it was easier for the enslaved in the towns to establish more personal relationships with their owners than on the large plantations in the countryside, urban slaves were far more likely to gain their freedom than their counterparts on the estates. Moreover, urban slaves enjoyed a less regimented existence: they could join Afro-Cuban *cabildos* (lodges) and drink in taverns with their *carabelas* (shipmates from Africa).[4]

However, the mass of the plantation slaves, the field slaves, did not have these possibilities. On the contrary, they not only did the hardest manual work, but they were also the most poorly dressed and their homes were the least well furnished. The field slaves were predominately black, they had a significant proportion of African-born among them, and they consisted of men and women. Women were increasingly forced to work in the field gangs, as men had the possibility of doing skilled jobs denied to women. This was especially the case after the abolition of the slave trade when the sex ratio became more evenly balanced. One estimate of the proportion of male and female enslaved people in the field is suggestive: at age 30, more than 80 per cent of female slaves worked in the field while the comparable figure for male slaves was less than 65 per cent.[5]

On many plantations, the enslaved were divided into three work gangs, although there were sometimes four gangs on larger units. In the first gang were the strongest young men and women who did the most laborious tasks. On sugar plantations, this gang was

**FIGURE 3.5** *Sugar cane cultivation in Antigua, 1823.*
*Source:* Courtesy of the John Carter Brown Library at Brown University, USA.

responsible for such jobs as preparing the ground for planting and cutting the cane. The second gang included older and pregnant enslaved people who performed more minor tasks, while the third gang, made up mostly of children, also did less demanding work such as weeding. Each gang had a slave driver, and there was also a head driver responsible for all the gangs.

The organization of slave labour followed this pattern throughout the sugar-producing colonies of the Caribbean. However, not all of the enslaved went to plantation colonies. Belize was a case in point. There, the export crop was not sugar but rather timber. The extraction of mahogany and logwood required a very different form of labour organization than the cultivation of sugar. In Belize, the enslaved worked in groups of ten or twelve rather than in larger gangs in extracting timber. Again, in contrast to the sugar plantations with 300 or 400 slaves, small groups of the enslaved in Belize worked with their owners in cutting the wood. Although the work was often difficult and dangerous, life for the timber-cutting slave was less regimented and generally subject to less arbitrary punishment than for their counterparts on sugar plantations.[6]

There were other Caribbean societies which did not produce sugar. The enslaved in Barbuda grew provisions for the plantations in Antigua. Many in the Bahamas made their living from salvaging shipping wrecks, those in Bonaire mined salt, and the enslaved in Santo Domingo were involved in ranching and growing coffee. Even on sugar plantation colonies, such as Cuba, enslaved people grew coffee and other commodities, which involved a different structure and generally meant less onerous conditions for the enslaved. Whatever the commodity, however, there was still considerable differentiation among the slaves.

The drivers and the skilled slaves were thus treated differently from the rest of the enslaved. Slave owners gave them more provisions, provided them with better housing, and ensured that they were better clothed. On the Codrington estates of Barbados, skilled slaves were especially well treated. For example, a mid-eighteenth-century account book included a pair of shoes for the slave blacksmith, Sandy. Sandy also received £4 to replace goods stolen by other slaves, indicating special concern for this artisan slave as well as the degree of his own personal wealth. Towards the end of the century, two first gang drivers received cash rewards of 6s. 3d. each, and their successors in the nineteenth century received annual awards of £20 and two pairs of shoes. Moreover, it was common practice for visiting absentee owners to give each headman a special gift. In Cuba, such slaves were known as *contramayorales* or assistants to the whites; these posts carried with them considerable prestige and authority.

The authority of the head slaves was reflected in their relations with less elite slaves. Head slaves in St. Vincent and Trinidad, for example, maintained their social distance from the rest of the enslaved community. A nineteenth-century observer of these societies, Mrs Carmichael, reported 'an abundance of nominal ladies and gentlemen among slaves':

> Drivers (that is, black overseers), head boilermen, head coopers, carpenters or masons, head servants, these are all Mr. so and so: a field negro, if asked to go and tell a boilerman to come to his master, returns and says – 'Massa, Mr. _____ will be here directly.' They say, 'Ma'am,' to a domestic servant; or if a servant be sent on a message from another family tells you, 'there is a good lady wishes to speak wid you.' Second boilermen, etc. etc.

are not quite gentlemen, but stand in a middle rank, between the first, or gentlemen, and the third, or common field negro and under domestics.[7]

The enslaved thus helped to reinforce the categories established by their masters, although slaves undoubtedly had their own hierarchies as well. Differences of occupation, origin and colour were all significant within the enslaved communities; moreover, it was far more likely that members of the elite group would either be manumitted or be able to purchase their own freedom. While the overwhelming majority of the enslaved never enjoyed these possibilities, it was the coloured, the skilled, and the favoured who often enjoyed special privileges within the context of the slave society.

## The slaves' internal economy

Although the enslaved spent most of their time working for their masters, there was still some time which was their own. In large parts of the Caribbean, much of this was spent producing their own food. This had begun in the early stages of plantation society, as planters realized the financial savings involved in having the enslaved largely feed themselves. Accordingly, planters often set aside land at the margins of their estates, land which was generally hilly or mountainous and not appropriate for producing sugar or other major export crops.

While planters saw the economic advantages of supplying provision grounds to the enslaved, the slaves regarded the land in a very different light. For the enslaved, the land not only created the possibility of a more varied diet but also of a considerably higher standard of living. Enslaved people traded and sold their produce in markets all over the region; in the process, they created what has become known as the 'internal economy' or the slaves' own economy. Moreover, this was not limited solely to agricultural produce: the enslaved kept livestock, made handicrafts and stole goods from their masters, much of which found its way into the internal markets.

In time, customary practice meant that the land belonged effectively to the enslaved. They were therefore able to pass it on to their relatives when they died. Moreover, planters were very reluctant to interfere with the provision grounds and the house gardens of their slaves. In Martinique, one planter complained to a visiting abolitionist about some manioc growing in the middle of one of his cane fields. The enslaved had planted the manioc when the field was fallow, and when the planter decided to cultivate the field, he offered to buy the slaves' crop from them. Since the enslaved had demanded too high a price, there was nothing more he could do. As he told the abolitionist, 'I'll have to wait six or seven months until that damned manioc is ripe'.[8]

The enslaved sometimes negotiated time to tend their provision grounds in exchange for less food from their masters. In St. Vincent, enslaved people bargained in just this way: they offered to forego food rations, apart from salted fish, if they could have Saturday afternoons to cultivate their provision grounds. The growth of the provision ground system was therefore in part a response to the expressed wishes of the enslaved themselves. However, planters saw advantages for themselves as well; they realized that slaves who had provision grounds were likely to be more attached to the estates and less prone to running away. Moreover, planters had to devote fewer resources to feeding their slaves.

External developments also played a part in the growth of this system. The American Revolution meant that significant parts of the Caribbean were deprived of their usual supply of foodstuffs from North America. As a result, there was starvation on some of the islands and serious loss of life among the enslaved. In response, planters turned increasingly to the provision ground system to minimize their dependence on external sources of food. Moreover, they increased the size of the grounds themselves: between 1750 and 1800, the average size of the grounds grew from nearly half an acre to almost three-quarters of an acre. Planters also gave their slaves more time to grow provisions; it became the norm for the enslaved to have Saturday as well as Sunday off to work the land. By the early nineteenth century, the system had become so widespread that in the British West Indies, three-fourths of all enslaved people grew their own food.[9]

The slave markets which developed alongside the provision ground system became highly significant institutions. The enslaved did not just trade with other slaves; they sold goods to their masters, to free blacks and coloureds and to other whites. Indeed, as in

Martinique, many colonists came to depend on the markets for a substantial part of their food. The markets could be huge: by the late eighteenth century, 10,000 Jamaican slaves participated in the market at Kingston and 15,000 in Saint Domingue's main market in Cap François.

Although most transactions were undoubtedly small, some of the enslaved managed to accumulate savings. They did so not only from trading but also from payments from their masters. Planters understood that they generally had to negotiate with their slaves for work done in the slaves' own time. For example, the enslaved were compensated for work they did on Sundays, either by payment or by free time off on another day. While it was not possible for most enslaved people to save anything, the Jamaican historian and planter, Edward Long, knew of slaves who were worth between £50 and £200 at the time of their death, an amount equal to the estates of small artisans or farmers. Long also estimated that the enslaved had in their possession one-fifth of all the currency circulating in the island, most of it in the form of small coins.[10]

Market days were not just about trading and making money. They were also social occasions, and the enslaved usually dressed in their best clothes. Once the trading was over, there were also other activities, including religious practices and rituals, drinking and socializing. When the slaves met, there was always the possibility of making trouble, even hatching plots, which is why planters sought to regulate the markets and the independent trading associated with them.

The independent economic activities of the enslaved highlighted another aspect of their lives: the importance of the family. Family members often had specific roles on the provision grounds. For example, the grounds themselves were frequently worked by the older and younger members of the family. Women were generally involved in marketing while men reportedly laid out the grounds. These family roles in the provision grounds and in the markets testify to the centrality of the slave family, an aspect of slavery which has recently been the subject of intense debate. What has become clear is the resilience of the family, despite the difficulties of family formation and stability in Caribbean slave societies. Family patterns varied and included both nuclear and extended forms; indeed, family life often meant wide networks of relationships rather than restriction to the nuclear household.

But just as the slave family was under considerable pressure, the independent economic life of the enslaved also created serious problems. One was the exploitation of less fortunate enslaved people. Newly arrived Africans, for example, were sometimes given to creole slaves to work their provision grounds and their gardens. In return, the creoles fed the Africans until they could establish their own grounds, but creoles were known to have taken advantage of the Africans. Privileged slaves sometimes had larger grounds and hired field slaves to work for them, but often at a pittance.

There was an additional problem of the provision ground system: possible shortfalls in the production of food. Drought or disease could affect the grounds just as they could damage the staple crops of the plantations. In the end, there was no correlation between the production of food by the enslaved and their own health. In fact, it appears that the enslaved may have been better off when they were fed by their masters rather than when they produced their own food. One of the few Caribbean colonies in which the enslaved population was able to increase naturally was Barbados; yet it was one of the only places in the region where masters provided food for their slaves.

Despite these problems, it is clear that the economic activities of the enslaved provided them with more control of important aspects of their lives. They chose what to grow in their grounds, they marketed the produce and they participated in the wider slave economy. The world of work for enslaved people was not just confined to labouring for their masters; they worked for themselves and their families and, in the process, gained an important measure of independence.

# CHAPTER FOUR

# Neither black nor white

Slavery was a complicated institution. It involved the importation of millions of Africans to the Caribbean and the incorporation of these enslaved people and their descendants into Caribbean society. Moreover, relations between whites and black were not simple. Of course, whites sought to control blacks, but it is clear from the discussion of the slaves' economy in Chapter 3 that this was not a simple or an easy process. In addition, relationships developed between whites and blacks that resulted in a new class of people, the free people of colour.[1]

The free coloureds consisted initially of manumitted slaves. Privileged or elite slaves were the most likely to be freed or to have the ability to purchase their freedom. There was another possibility: the state manumitted some of the enslaved who revealed potential rebellions or discovered foreign conspiracies. However, the number of freedpeople in early Caribbean slave society was very small. There were just over 500 of them in Martinique in 1696 compared to over 13,000 slaves. As in Guadeloupe, where there were 275 free people of colour and nearly 5,000 slaves, the figure for freedpeople included Caribs as well. In French Guiana at about the same time, there were only four free coloureds in the whole colony. Yet across the region, the free coloured population would grow significantly, especially during the late eighteenth and the early nineteenth centuries.

Free coloureds were an unintended by-product of slave society. As Arnold Sio has put it, they were 'a third party in a system built for two'.[2] Many free people of colour were the offspring of liaisons between white males and black (and subsequently brown) females, and whites sometimes freed their brown children as well as the enslaved women who produced them. This pattern of manumissions contributed to the numerical growth of the free people of colour and helped to make them the only consistently self-sustaining group in Caribbean slave society.

These sexual relationships also reflected the curiously skewed demography of most slave societies in which a minority of whites controlled a large majority of black slaves. Since the white population was often predominately male, relationships between white and black, free and slave developed. With the addition of enslaved women freed by white men, the resulting free coloured population was heavily coloured and female. In Cuba, for example, 65 per cent of the enslaved who were freed were women. This was the case in seventeenth-century Cuba and continued in the nineteenth century as well.[3]

The proportions of freedpeople within the wider slave society varied considerably from colony to colony (see Table 4.1). At the end of the eighteenth century in Martinique and in the Danish West Indies, free coloureds constituted about one-third of the free population; in Saint Domingue just before the outbreak of the revolution, they formed nearly 40 per cent of this group. Yet in these societies, they were massively outnumbered by the enslaved:

TABLE 4.1 Free coloureds, whites and slaves at the end of the eighteenth century

| Year | Society | Freedpeople | Whites | Slaves | Total pop. |
|------|---------|-------------|--------|--------|------------|
| 1789 | Martinique | 5,235 | 10,636 | 83,414 | 96,158 |
| 1789 | St. Domingue | 24,848 | 30,831 | 434,424 | 490,108 |
| 1775 | Jamaica | 4,500 | 18,700 | 192,800 | 216,000 |
| 1786 | Barbados | 838 | 16,167 | 62,115 | 79,120 |
| 1774 | Cuba | 36,301 | 96,440 | 38,879 | 171,620 |
| 1775 | Puerto Rico | 34,510 | 29,263 | 7,487 | 71,260 |

Source: David W. Cohen and Jack P. Greene, eds, *Neither Slave Nor Free: The Freedmen of African Descent in the Slave Societies of the New World* (Baltimore, 1972), Appendix: Population Tables, pp. 335–9.

free coloureds were only 5 per cent of the total population in the French islands and less than 4 per cent in the Danish colonies. In two of the most significant colonies of the British Caribbean in the last quarter of the eighteenth century, free coloureds made up even less of the total population. In Jamaica, the free people of colour were just over 2 per cent of this group, while in Barbados, they formed about 1 per cent of the total population.

The Hispanic Caribbean provided a significant contrast to the British and French colonies. In Cuba and Puerto Rico, a long history of white settlement predated the development of plantation society at the end of the eighteenth and the beginning of the nineteenth centuries. There was a more racially mixed society and a less important slave sector during the pre-plantation period. For example, Puerto Rican free coloureds made up almost half of the total population in 1775 and more than 80 per cent of the non-white population. The figures for Cuba were less one-sided but still revealing: the free people of colour in Cuba were 20 per cent of the total population and 41 per cent of non-whites. Both Cuba and Puerto Rico were yet to feel the full impact of sugar and slavery which would alter these ratios as well as the position of the free coloureds in society.[4]

As with slaves, the free people of colour were internally highly differentiated. This group included recently manumitted blacks as well as light-coloured planters who mixed in white society. The gradations of colour among the free people of colour were often varied and potentially of considerable importance. It is unlikely that too much attention was paid to the twenty-five different categories of coloureds in the Spanish Caribbean, especially in the pre-plantation period, but the distinctions in parts of the British Caribbean were significant. There, the demarcations were: 'mulatto', the result of a union between black and white; 'sambo', between black and mulatto; 'quadroon', between mulatto and white; 'mustee', between quadroon and white; 'musteefino', between mustee and white. In Jamaica, the union of a musteefino and a white produced a 'quinteron' who was legally white and enjoyed all the rights of whites. However, this process of 'whitening' did not always produce legal equality, even within the British Caribbean. No matter what their colour, Barbadian free coloureds, for example, could not become the legal equals of whites until just before the abolition of slavery.

Colour was only one of the differentiating elements among the free people of colour; another important category was the nature of that freedom. Free-born and manumitted people of colour were often treated very differently in law as well as in custom. Those born free in Jamaica were subject to trial by jury, whereas manumitted coloureds were subject to slave courts. Manumitted people of colour were also unable to give evidence in court against free-born members of this group.

There were free coloureds in Jamaica who appealed against their legal disabilities and were granted privileges which were denied to other freedpeople. In some cases, as with a legislative enactment of 1733, this meant that the free coloureds in question and their families were granted all the rights of whites. The acts which followed this one were more demanding: they stipulated that the privileged person of colour marry a white if their children were to inherit these privileges.[5]

Jamaica was not alone in creating privileged coloureds: Curaçao also had a similar category known as *mesties*. These freedpeople were usually light in colour and had a fair amount of wealth and education. They were still considered freedpeople, but enjoyed certain privileges over the other members of this group. Although officially classified as 'burghers', they did not enjoy all the rights of whites.

The *soi-disant libres* of the French Antilles were also a distinct category of free people of colour, but not so fortunate as either the *mesties* or the specially privileged coloureds of Jamaica. The *soi-disant libres* were nominally free, having obtained their deeds of manumission abroad because of the difficulty of manumission in the French Antilles. But this was a highly precarious category of freedom below the status of ordinary free coloureds. Although *soi-disant libres* could become legally free, it was also possible for them to revert to slavery. For example, a woman named Marie-Ann from Martinique had been a *soi-disant libre* for thirty-six years. Despite her long period as a nominally free person, however, she was sold as a slave along with some of her children. Discussing her case, Léo Elisabeth concluded that

the fact that she has also been listed in the census as 'free' and has paid the poll tax required of all 'free' people, that her children had been inscribed as 'free' in the records of the civil authorities, and her sons had served as freedmen in the militia clearly shows how precarious this nominal freedom was and how weak a deed of liberty granted abroad was as a guarantee of free status.[6]

Marie-Ann`s situation dramatized the plight of particular groups of freedpeople; yet it was also true that free coloureds generally suffered a wide range of legal disabilities throughout the Caribbean. Although free, they usually could not vote, hold public office, give evidence in court against whites, or serve on juries. There were a whole series of economic restrictions as well. In many colonies, free people of colour were unable to serve in any of the supervisory posts on plantations and were barred from a large number of specific jobs. In the Danish West Indies, free coloureds could not plant cotton unless they owned land. From the early eighteenth century, the free people of colour in Martinique were forbidden to participate in the gold and silver trades. After the middle of the eighteenth century, the restrictions became even more severe in Martinique: free coloureds were not allowed to practice medicine or pharmacy or work in the offices of clerks of court or notaries.

The limitations on the free people of colour were particularly difficult to accept in the French Antilles. There the seventeenth-century legal code regulating slavery, the *Code Noir*, had enacted full citizenship rights to all manumitted slaves, although the legislation did not always reflect colonial realities. In any case, the increasing restrictions on the civil rights of the free coloureds in the course of the eighteenth century contradicted this earlier decree. In Saint Domingue, the eighteenth-century legislation against the freedpeople included outlawing white and free coloured marriages; it also meant that many free coloured landowners were deprived of their land. Resentment at these and other restrictions was widespread and helped to create a revolutionary situation in Saint Domingue.

While the results were less dramatic in other parts of the Caribbean, the legislation against freedpeople could be severe. Some laws went to extreme lengths to identify free people of colour. In the Danish West Indies, a law passed in 1768 made it obligatory for free coloureds to wear a cockade or badge at all times. There was also a long list of items freedpeople could not wear: this included silk stockings, clothing made of silk, chintz, and gold or silver brocade. The position of the free coloureds in the British Virgin Islands was even more circumscribed; after 1783, freedpeople were required to have a white patron who was responsible for them. This patron relationship had to be formally acknowledged in court, with stiff penalties if the obligation was ignored. Moreover, free coloureds in the Virgin Islands were not allowed to own more than eight acres of land and were effectively limited to having no more than fifteen slaves. The economic possibilities for Jamaican free people of colour were also sharply curtailed by legislation. In 1761, the Jamaican Assembly passed a measure making it illegal for whites to leave real or personal property worth more than £1,200 (sterling) to any coloured or black.

These laws suggest that freedpeople were making considerable economic progress in Caribbean slave society. The *gens du couleur* in Saint Domingue, for example, claimed to own one-quarter of all the enslaved in the colony and between a quarter and a half of its productive land in 1790. In Jamaica, the Assembly was responding to a report that property in the hands of the free people of colour already amounted to between £200,000 and £300,000. Much of this property had been left to them by their white fathers. However, by restricting bequests, the assemblymen in Jamaica were declaring that it was more important to keep the land in European hands than to follow their parental instincts. Elsewhere, unpropertied whites had become concerned about the economic competition of free coloureds. Laws against freedpeople working in shipping and navigating were designed to safeguard the jobs of whites in these areas.

Not all Caribbean colonies adopted the same measures against the free people of colour; indeed, some acts were notably less restrictive. For example, Antiguan free coloureds, who had the necessary property qualification, could vote. Freedpeople in Barbados were not legally prohibited from holding supervisory positions on the estates, and there was no legal limit on the amount of land or slaves they could own. In St. Kitts and Grenada, free coloureds could appear in court and give evidence against whites. However, none of these enactments affected the position of the freedpeople as a whole. Very few Antiguan free people of colour would have qualified for the vote, and customary practice would have excluded free coloureds from supervisory positions on Barbadian sugar plantations. Similarly, very little weight would have been given to the testimony of freedpeople in St. Kitts and Grenada. While there were thus a few exceptional statutes favouring the free coloureds, most were designed to limit their civil rights, restrict their economic possibilities and curtail their social interaction with the whites.

In light of the restrictions against the freedpeople, it was not surprising that they generally shunned the plantations and favoured living in more urban settlements. Apart from the problem of usually being denied posts on the estates, free coloureds sought to distance themselves from the most visible symbol of slavery, the sugar plantation. Those freedpeople who made their living from the land usually avoided growing sugar. Many free coloureds in Cuba therefore worked the land in the eastern part of the island, away from the main sugar-producing areas. This was also the case in Trinidad, where large numbers of free coloureds grew cocoa, coffee and provisions, generally on small plots of land with a few slaves. Some freedpeople in Grenada did own large estates. For instance, the leader of the 1795 rebellion in the island, Julien Fédon, had a 360-acre estate while his brother owned one that was 141 acres. Yet even in the case of Grenada, most free people of colour probably had little or no land. Like free coloureds in other parts of the Caribbean, they lived predominately in towns and were generally poor.

Once there, many freedpeople occupied a niche between the upper ranks of the urban enslaved and the lower echelons of whites. Male free coloureds worked primarily as artisans, and especially as carpenters, masons, tailors and shoemakers. In Havana, freedmen included cigar-makers, cooks, musicians, stonecutters, harness makers, small truck farmers, blacksmiths, tinsmiths, butchers and barbers. Freedwomen in Havana had a smaller range of possibilities: they worked as seamstresses, washerwomen, house servants, dressmakers, midwives and prostitutes. In St. Kitts, freedwomen were frequently hucksters or shopkeepers. Elsewhere, they gained considerable notoriety as tavern-keepers and brothel owners. One of them, Rachael Pringle-Polgreen, was a well-known figure in Bridgetown, Barbados. Her Royal Naval Hotel was frequently visited by Prince William Henry (later King William IV). An astute businesswoman, Pringle-Polgreen died a wealthy woman: she owned at least ten properties in Bridgetown as well as thirty-eight slaves, seven of whom she manumitted in her will (Figure 4.1).[7]

Rachael Pringle-Polgreen was exceptional in Barbadian society, but some Caribbean societies offered more economic scope for the free people of colour than others. For example, there were greater opportunities for freedpeople in Grenada than in St. Kitts. There was more land available in Grenada and also less competition from

**FIGURE 4.1** *Rachel Pringle-Polgreen of Barbados, by Thomas Rowlandson, 1796.*

*Source:* Public domain.

landless whites than in St. Kitts. Grenada relied on the free coloureds for supplying goods and services which were often provided by whites in St. Kitts. Similarly, the demography of Suriname, with an overwhelming slave population and a tiny white elite, ensured that freedpeople had an important place in that society. Curaçao, on the other hand, had more free coloureds than slaves and a larger proportion of whites. Consequently, free coloureds had a more difficult time economically in Curaçao than in Suriname.

By virtue of their occupations and the restrictions imposed on them, free people of colour tended to occupy a very different world from the whites. This was especially true in the period leading up to the Haitian Revolution, when free coloureds often made up a very small fraction of the population. Moreover, they were unable to socialize with whites on an equal basis. Many public institutions were segregated: for instance, whites had their special pews in church as did freedpeople. Theatres sometimes held separate performances for whites and free people of colour; when they attended the same performance, free coloureds entered by a different door than whites and sat apart from them. Each group often had its own burial ground.

Yet there was one area where these rules could not be enforced. Sexual relations between white men and black and brown women fell outside the usual conventions which affected this group as a whole. While some of these relationships were casual and informal, others were longer-term liaisons. One of the most prominent of these involved the governor general of the Danish West Indies, Peter von Scholten, and a freedwoman, Anna Heegard. Heegard lived with von Scholten for twenty years; moreover, she presided over gala evenings and other social occasions at Government House.[8]

These more permanent relationships were often formally recognized by contracts or rituals. Such relationships in Suriname were known as 'Surinamese marriages'. The marriage was accompanied by a ceremony in which the mother of the 'bride', accompanied by a female neighbour, brought her daughter into the bedroom of the 'groom'. After the 'husband' and 'wife' had left the next morning, the mother and neighbour again visited the room and then were able to announce that the 'marriage' had taken place. Such relationships often provided a measure of economic security for the 'wife' and any resulting children, even when the European 'husband' departed for home. Elsewhere in the Caribbean, such customary relationships could involve the payment of large sums of money to the brown or black mistress, if the white married or left the colony. The advantages for the freedwoman were quite apparent. She was able to better herself economically, far more so than in almost any legal marriage with a freedman. Moreover, her children would be light in colour, which was an important consideration in Caribbean slave society.

Although it was unusual, there were marriages between whites and browns. These could be between white men and brown women or brown men and white women. While such unions were illegal in the French Antilles and in British Guiana, they occurred in Jamaica, Grenada, Cuba and probably elsewhere as well. In some cases, lower-class whites may have married wealthy brown women for their fortunes. But in Grenada, the situation was more complicated. There well-placed local whites, such as the government secretary and the provost marshal, married free coloured women.

Apart from these marriages, some of which were kept secret, the informal relationships between white males and freedwomen did not improve the standing of the free coloureds generally. The freedwomen were not legally recognized and were never accepted in white society. They may have prospered personally, but their relationships stemmed from the social inferiority of the free people of colour and highlighted the general exclusion of free coloureds from white society.

Despite this situation, wealthy freed people of colour often sought to emphasize their affinity with the whites and to distance themselves from the blacks. They adopted the Euro-creole culture of the whites, attended church and sought to marry. Yet this group formed a small segment of the free coloureds as a whole. Most free people of colour were unable to acquire the wealth or education to maintain a lifestyle compatible with the whites.

Freedpeople were therefore more likely to interact with the world of the enslaved than with that of the whites. This was certainly the case in the towns where free people of colour and urban slaves mixed freely. They not only lived in close proximity to each other but also worked together as artisans, shopkeepers or hucksters. Free coloureds frequently participated in the slave social networks, attending slave funerals and religious activities as well as weekend dances. Both groups often had kin in common; some free people of colour owned slaves who were their kin and whom they were seeking to manumit.[9]

The line between free coloured and slave was considerably easier to cross than that between free coloured and white. Moreover, in making the transition from enslaved to free person of colour, the manumitted slave reinforced the links between the two sectors of the non-white population. The freed slave could therefore expect to find significant continuities in the culture of the free people of colour.

In the period up to the end of the eighteenth century, then, the free people of colour had become established in Caribbean slave society. Although their proportions in the population varied from colony to colony, free coloureds shared a series of legal restrictions which limited their economic and social progress. In the aftermath of the Haitian Revolution, they would be far less ready to accept their status in these societies and would begin to seek equality with the whites.

# CHAPTER FIVE

# The world the planters made

With the rise of sugar, white society changed dramatically. Most smaller planters could not afford the large capital requirements which sugar required. Instead, a different class of planter emerged in the Caribbean, prepared to invest heavily in slaves, land and equipment. By the end of the seventeenth century, a far more elaborate white social structure had replaced the simple division between masters and their indentured servants. The model for white society had become established which was to characterize the Caribbean for the next 200 years.

White plantation society was typified by a narrow concentration of wealth and slaveholding in relatively few hands. A small number of planters dominated landholding as well as the most important social and political offices in the colonies. These were the *grands blancs*, the resident whites who were at the top of white society. In this group, especially in the French and Spanish colonies, there would have been some noble families. Cuba, for example, had twenty-nine titled families in 1810, many of whose ancestors had settled in the island in the seventeenth century.

Many of the wealthier planters returned to Europe to live off the proceeds of their estates, leaving their plantations in the hands of planting attorneys. Often owners of estates themselves, attorneys could represent upwards of twenty estates and were among the richest residents in the Caribbean colonies. In the same class, and enjoying even higher social status, were the imperial administrators: the royal governors, the *intendants*, the admirals and the generals.

Absentee planters – those who could afford to leave their estates in the hands of planting attorneys and overseers – have been portrayed in highly negative terms. Cuban planters, for example, preferred city life in Cuba and spent much of the year away from their plantations. Absentee planters from other parts of the Caribbean were not content to remain in the region; they moved to Europe, where they were described as living in luxury in cities such as Bath and Bordeaux on the profits of their slave plantations. While this stereotype may have been accurate in some cases, planters who returned to Europe often did so to conduct the European part of their plantation business. Many worked as merchants who sold the sugar on the European markets and also advanced credit to their own estates as well as others.

Absentees also performed an important political function. From the seventeenth century onwards, groups of absentee owners and merchants met to conduct business as well as to influence policy. One of the earliest known groups consisted of merchants who established the Jamaica Coffee House; they were meeting as early as 1674 in London. At this early stage, planters had their own separate club but after the American Revolution, the two groups merged to form the Society of West Indian Planters and Merchants. This powerful lobby was influential in Parliament and strongly opposed moves to interfere in the slave trade and slavery.

There was another accusation against the absentee planters. In this view, estates in the hands of attorneys and overseers were badly managed; since planters' agents were paid on the gross yield of the estates, the aim of these representatives was to maximize short-term results. This meant harsh treatment of the enslaved and an unwillingness to deal with the long-term interests of the plantations. Yet the reality was sometimes very different: attorneys and overseers were often more professional than resident planters, who themselves could lead estates into debt and bankruptcy.[1]

For the wealthy planters who did reside in the Caribbean, there was little doubt about their generally lavish lifestyles. They could, of course, afford to do so. As Trevor Burnard has suggested, the wealth and influence of the Jamaican elite planter class was 'unprecedented for the eighteenth-century British Atlantic'.[2] For example, one of the wealthiest planters in Jamaica, Peter Beckford, owned eleven sugar estates and had an interest in five others. A medium-sized Jamaican plantation towards the end of the eighteenth century would have

**FIGURE 5.1** *A planter and his wife on a journey, 1810.*
*Source:* Public domain.

had at least two hundred slaves and would have consisted of approximately nine hundred acres. As a result, planters dined well, drank copiously and entertained magnificently. Samuel Long was one of them. A rich planter, he owned two mansions in Jamaica, one in the capital and the other on his estate. According to Richard Dunn:

> [Long's] house in Spanish Town [the capital], more expensively fitted than his plantation house, had a hall – the principal room – large enough to hold sixty chairs and seven tables. In his dining room Long had a dozen table cloths, twelve dozen napkins, and £76 worth of silver to dress his table. In the bed chambers he had four costly looking glasses and a best bed with hangings (valued at £100), which he bought on a trip to England. In his plantation house Long had another fifty-eight chairs, seven tables, and three looking glasses. All of the big planters kept dozens of chairs in their houses, suitable for large-scale entertainments.[3]

Although not as grand, one of the largest plantations in Puerto Rico, Las Vayas, was also impressive. It had 130 slaves and was valued at $150,000 in the 1830s. An American lawyer provided a description of the estate as well as the lifestyle of its owner:

> Here [in Ponce] I met with an old friend and schoolmate, who owns one of the best plantations on the Island. His house is one hundred feet in front, with porticos or galleries on both sides, and the rooms are papered and painted and handsomely furnished throughout... . The estate being under the direction of a Manager, the proprietor is at leisure & the accidental increase of the guests is always anticipated in the ordinary operations of the cook... .[4]

Such trappings of wealth were far beyond the next class of white society, the merchants and the professionals such as lawyers and doctors. This group would have also included estate-owners with middle-sized holdings. Many of these middle-ranking planters in eighteenth-century Saint Domingue produced coffee and resented the privileges of the wealthier and often absentee planters. This class tension among the whites was particularly marked in Saint Domingue. In turn, these middle-level whites were distinguished from the bottom rung of white society, the *petits blancs*.

The *petits blancs* consisted of the poorer whites in the society. Generally economically insecure, the *petits blancs* were often among the most racist elements among the whites. In this group were the lower-echelon employees on the estates: the overseers, bookkeepers and artisans. Overseers were responsible for the day-to-day management of the plantations, and bookkeepers, rather than keeping the estates' books, generally helped to supervise the enslaved in the fields and in the factories. In addition, school teachers and small shopkeepers would have numbered among the *petits blancs* class. Many Barbadian whites in this group migrated to South Carolina when they were squeezed off their small farms by wealthy planters or found they were unable to compete with slave labour. Yet the 1680 Barbadian census revealed 'thousands of them still hanging on, with a few acres and a few slaves apiece, repressed and voiceless like the submerged labouring class in England'.[5]

The *petits blancs* who worked on the estates – especially as overseers and bookkeepers – often did not remain on any single estate very long. For example, eighty-five white men worked on Worthy Park Estate in Jamaica between 1783 and 1796. Since there were usually less than ten whites (and often as few as five) on the estate at any one time, the figure of eighty-five whites over a thirteen-year period suggests a very rapid turnover. Most of the whites therefore remained on the plantation for a few months at most. Moreover, Jamaica was not unique; there was a similar succession of bookkeepers on plantations in the French Caribbean. This movement of whites contrasts with the relative stability of the slave population.

Whether it was *petits blancs* or prosperous planters, whites in the Caribbean had significant power over their black slaves. This was clearly the case in organizing the working lives of the enslaved. But it went far beyond this. White men often exercised sexual control over their female slaves, especially in the Caribbean, where there was frequently a paucity of white women. In the relative absence of white women, then, white men turned to their black slaves for sex. The development of a significant mixed-race population across the Caribbean was testimony to the sexual activities of the whites.

The eighteenth-century diary of an Englishman, Thomas Thistlewood, makes it possible to comprehend the power of white men over black women. Thistlewood was a planter in western Jamaica who kept a daily diary during his time in the island: he arrived in 1750 and died there aged sixty-five in 1786. In the diary, Thistlewood highlighted his sexual encounters with his enslaved women and makes it evident that he regarded his female slaves as available for sexual exploitation. He slept with many of his slaves, often in return for small gifts. Moreover, when Thistlewood had male guests, they, too, frequently expected to be able to have sexual relations with his enslaved women. Planters such as Thistlewood were surrounded on their plantations with women who could not resist their advances and for whom compensatory small gifts and presents were significant in a world of material deprivation. Thistlewood did have one enslaved woman, Phibbah, whom he considered as his wife. Yet most of Thistlewood's sexual relations were casual and fleeting. Most importantly, Thistlewood's exploitation of his female slaves ignored the women's feelings as well as their existing relationships within their own community.[6]

But it was not just white men who owned the enslaved; white women did as well. In Barbados, for example, one calculation suggests that in 1834, twenty-seven women owned sugar plantations, consisting of over 6,000 acres and nearly 4,000 slaves. Although the number of women owning estates over fifty acres was just over 10 per cent of the total of planters in this category, women made up half of the urban slave owners who had fewer than ten slaves. This is partly explained by their role in the urban economy: there, many white women had small businesses and properties and used the enslaved to help run these businesses. The figures in St. Lucia reflect a similar situation: women owned nearly half of the properties on that island with less than ten slaves but approximately the same percentage as Barbados of properties over fifty acres.[7]

The relationships between white women and their black slaves were complicated. This was especially the case with the domestic enslaved, as white women often spent much of their time with them. Inevitably, white women influenced their black slaves but it also worked the other way around: black enslaved domestics had a significant impact on their white mistresses. White women began to speak like their black slaves and also to behave like them. For example, Edward Long complained about the appearance of 'a very fine young woman, awkwardly dangling her arms, with the air of a Negroe-servant lolling almost the whole day upon beds or settees, her head muffled up with two or three handkerchiefs, her dress loose and without stays. At noon, we find her employed in gobbling pepper-pot, seated on the floor, with her sable hand-maids around her.'[8]

Like men, white women also abused their black slaves. In fact, there is no evidence that white women treated their slaves any better than men did on the plantations. Mary Prince, an enslaved woman who lived in Bermuda and Antigua, certainly had cause for complaint. In her slave narrative, Prince described her experiences at the hands of one of her mistresses:

> [She] … caused me to know the exact difference between the smart of the rope, the cart-whip, and the cow-skin, when applied to my naked body by her own cruel hand. And there was scarcely any punishment more dreadful than the blows I received on my face and head from her hard, heavy fist. She was a fearful woman, and a savage mistress to her slaves.[9]

Some of this behaviour may be explicable in light of what we know about white male and black female relations. In this context, women may have taken out their frustration on their enslaved women because of their resentment at such relationships. This was especially the case since the relations between white men and black women were often conducted openly, with the planters' coloured offspring sometimes living in the great house itself.

Yet whether it was white women or white men, there is no doubt that whites in the slave societies of the Caribbean had significant possibilities of advancement in colonial societies. Some were able to do so by acquiring slaves and hiring them out. Others moved up in the plantation hierarchy, starting out as bookkeepers, rising to become overseers, and ultimately purchasing their own properties. The effect of this process was to narrow the distance between the lower-class and more elite whites. Bryan Edwards described this situation and blamed the institution of slavery for a more egalitarian white society:

> The poorest white person seems to consider himself nearly on a level with the richest, and, emboldened by this idea, approaches his employer with extended hand, and a freedom which, in the countries of Europe, is seldom displayed by men in the lower orders of life towards their superiors. It is not difficult to trace the origin of this principle. It arises without doubt, from the preeminence and distinction which are necessarily attached even to the complexion of a white man, in a country where the complexion, generally speaking, distinguished freedom from slavery.[10]

By the end of the eighteenth century, it was clear that white society in many plantation colonies had become closer and more homogeneous in composition. As Elsa Goveia concluded for the British Leewards, 'the absenteeism of the richer whites and the improved position of the poorer whites combined to reduce the extremes of wealth and poverty which had once been evident among the white population'.[11]

Divisions within the white group nonetheless continued and could become serious. In Saint Domingue, the Haitian Revolution at the end of the eighteenth century was partly the result of splits between the *grands blancs* and the *petits blancs*. This revolution destroyed Haitian plantation society and led to the abolition of slavery in that colony. Yet it had other effects as well: elsewhere in the Caribbean, it served to unite the white population. Faced with the danger of revolution from below, the wealthier whites began to accommodate lower-class whites. In some of the Caribbean colonies, the nineteenth century witnessed a drawing together of the white population which would have been unimaginable in the course of the eighteenth century.

# The planter class in the nineteenth century

The whites in the Caribbean faced serious problems in the aftermath of the Haitian Revolution. A strong abolitionist movement developed in Britain which succeeded first in abolishing the slave trade in 1808 and ultimately slavery itself in 1834. Whites in the British colonies were thus on the defensive during the course of the early nineteenth century. Elsewhere in the region, the experience of the Haitian Revolution as well as the attacks of the abolitionists had serious implications. Saint Domingue itself emerged as independent Haiti in 1804; in the process, most whites either fled or were killed.[12] The abolition of slavery in the other French colonies as well as in the Danish West Indies occurred in 1848; the Dutch followed in 1863. But Cuba enjoyed a booming sugar economy in the nineteenth century and did not abolish slavery until 1886.

The result in much of the Caribbean was a declining planter class, at least numerically. The effect of this decline for the whites was to continue the process of consolidation which had been taking place since the end of the eighteenth century. Lower-class whites found they had more possibilities for social mobility. For example, in Suriname, many white planters left the colony as a result of its declining economy. This made room not only for immigrant whites but also for locally born Jews, some of whom became members of the planter class.

But the decline of the planter class was not a universal phenomenon in the Caribbean. In the late-developing sugar colonies of Cuba and Puerto Rico, the planter class flourished. This was partly because of the transfer of technology and, to some degree, planters themselves from the decaying areas of the region to the more flourishing ones. Some of the refugees from the Haitian Revolution, for example, settled in Puerto Rico along with their slaves. Other immigrants came to the colony as a result of the encouragement given to immigration and trade by the Cédula de Gracias of 1815, a royal decree designed to encourage plantation development. Many of these planters came from the eastern Caribbean colonies of Britain, France, Denmark and Holland.

The planters in Ponce, Puerto Rico's most important sugar-growing area, were thus a cosmopolitan group. Only 55 per cent of all the planters in Ponce were of Spanish origin (meaning either creole, peninsular Spaniards, or South Americans). The most numerous of the immigrant *hacendados* were French, but British, Dutch, Germans and Americans were also well represented. In fact, it was the immigrant planters who fared best in Puerto Rico. Because of better access to finance and technology, they profited most from the sugar revolution in nineteenth-century Puerto Rico. Creole planters did not have these advantages; as a result, their estates were the lowest in value of all the *hacendados*. It was also possible for artisans and others skilled in sugar technology to profit from the sugar revolution. In an expanding market, they came to Puerto Rico and found that they could prosper and acquire haciendas of their own.[13]

Cuba presents a comparable, although somewhat different picture. From the 1840s onwards, it enjoyed a significant increase in the white population, from more than 400,000 to well over 1,000,000 in 1887. This meant that whites in Cuba once again became the majority; by 1887, they made up 67.5 per cent of the total population. A large percentage of this increase came from immigration, especially from Spain and the Canary Islands but also from Latin America, other parts of the Caribbean and the United States.

The whites were divided by origin. *Criollos*, or locally born whites, and *peninsulares*, who came from Spain, often were at loggerheads. *Peninsulares* tended to dominate the colonial bureaucracy as well as the commercial sector of the Cuban economy. This group was ultra-Spanish in its outlook and sought to retain the connection with Spain, since it proved so economically advantageous to them. On the other hand, *criollos* were the principal landowners and planters in the colony. They resented Spanish control and the loss of free trade which was associated with that connection. They were also unhappy about their social and economic subordination to the *peninsulares*.[14]

In the face of a booming sugar economy and the threat of abolition of slavery, these two groups came together. Planters needed credit from the merchants, and the merchants were dependent on the planters for sugar. Moreover, both groups were strongly opposed to the ending of slavery. Ultimately, however, creole resentment against the domination of Spain overrode their desire to retain slavery.

As elsewhere in the Caribbean, whites in Cuba also had to give up the trappings of slavery. Whether it was as a result of abolitionist movements, internal pressure from the enslaved, external demands from other powers or contradictions in the system itself, slavery throughout the region ended by the late nineteenth century. But the plantation system, and much of its social structure and prevailing attitudes, continued to dominate most of the region well into the twentieth century.

# CHAPTER SIX

# Slave resistance: Africans, Maroons and women

Slave resistance was endemic in the Caribbean. As elsewhere in the Americas, it took a variety of forms, the most dramatic of which were revolts and conspiracies. Although frequent by comparison with slave revolts in the United States, violent resistance in the Caribbean was still a relatively rare event. On the other hand, day-to-day resistance has received far less notice but was probably more insidious. Since African-born slaves in the Caribbean participated in both rebellions and in day-to-day resistance and did so in ways which often differentiated them from creole slaves, this chapter will include a discussion of African-led resistance. The one successful slave revolt in the Caribbean (and in the Americas) was the Haitian Revolution; it helped to transform the patterns of slave resistance and will be dealt with in the next chapter.

The Caribbean colonies in their early stages of development, especially once sugar production got underway, inevitably had a majority of African-born slaves. The earliest slave revolts in the region were therefore led by Africans and shared some of the same characteristics. There were also similar conditions in these colonies which resulted in the outbreak of slave conspiracies. Where the enslaved significantly outnumbered whites, for example, revolts were more likely, especially before the whites had fully developed the institutional mechanisms to control the slaves. It was also the case that slave uprisings were more frequent when the forces of control were weakened or distracted by internal difficulties or depleted during times of war. In addition, geography mattered. There were far more uprisings in a colony like Jamaica which had an extensive and mountainous interior than in a small, relatively flat island such as Barbados where the enslaved had no place to hide or easily regroup.

Yet the enslaved did not wait until they arrived in the Caribbean to resist slavery. All along the route, from their initial capture to the Middle Passage, enslaved people sought to escape from slavery. On the long marches from the interior of Africa to the coast, the enslaved were carefully guarded and proceeded in coffles to minimize the number of slaves who were able to flee. The same was true in the forts and barracoons on the coast of Africa, where the enslaved were kept before being put aboard ships bounds for the Americas. The slaves there developed frightening images of what awaited them on board the ships of the Middle Passage and in the colonies of the New World, which only served to increase their resistance to leaving Africa. Expanding on this theme, one observer involved in the trade noted:

> We are sometimes sufficiently plagued with a parcel of slaves which come from a far in-land country who very innocently persuade one another that we buy them only to fatten and afterwards eat them ... they resolve ... to run away from the ship, kill the Europeans and set the vessel ashore.[1]

The most difficult time to maintain control of the enslaved was at the point before the ships left the coast of Africa or relatively soon afterwards. Where it was possible, slaves jumped overboard in a desperate attempt to return to their homes. Moreover, these were not the only times the enslaved sought to escape from the ships. Since slaves believed that they would return to their homelands after their deaths, many tried to commit suicide by drowning or by starving themselves. There were also many mutinies aboard the ships, despite efforts to rigorously control the enslaved. David Richardson has calculated that revolts occurred on possibly as many as one in ten of all transatlantic voyages, half of which took place while ships were still moored on the African coast. Yet nearly all the ships which experienced revolts nonetheless managed to reach the Americas, with most of their captives on board.[2]

Once in the Caribbean, the enslaved had more opportunities to rebel. When they did so, African slaves had specific aims. Inevitably, they were seeking freedom for themselves, but enslaved Africans were also often intent on recreating their African societies. They were seeking to separate themselves from the whites; this sometimes meant making treaties with the whites, and it could mean enslaving either creole slaves or other African ethnic groups.

It is possible to point to several examples of African-led uprisings. One occurred on St. John in the Danish Virgin Islands in 1733–34. Prior to the rebellion, St. John had only recently been opened up to sugar production, and there had been a significant number of African slaves brought to the island in the previous decade. The majority of the enslaved were from Akan kingdoms of the Gold Coast, and they heavily outnumbered the whites on St. John. Moreover, the slaves were badly treated and also suffered from a series of natural disasters, such as drought and a hurricane, which affected their provision grounds. In 1733, the authorities also passed some draconian legislation against the enslaved.

In response, the African slaves planned a conspiracy in November 1733, first taking over the small fort on the island and then setting off the cannons to announce the general uprising. The rest of the slaves responded, killed the whites who were unable to escape and burnt the canes and many of the plantation buildings. Short of troops, the authorities appealed for help, especially for armed forces from Martinique. Yet it was only after a month-long campaign against the enslaved that the whites were able to end the rebellion. They did so in a particularly horrific fashion, much like the colonists of nearby St. Croix who responded brutally when faced with a possible conspiracy several years later. As the historian of the Danish Virgin Islands put it, 'gibbet, stake, wheel, noose, glowing tong – all were employed to impress upon the community the sinfulness of rebellion'.[3]

Less than thirty years later, in 1760, African slaves in Jamaica led one of the largest revolts in the eighteenth-century Caribbean. This was an example of the colonial forces being distracted elsewhere, as Britain was heavily involved in the Seven Years' War against France and Spain. Apart from weakening the imperial forces, the war resulted in a significant reduction in the export of Jamaican sugar and in a doubling of the cost of imported provisions. As in the case of St. John, it was 'Akan' slaves who were involved in the rebellion. According to Edward Long, the leader of the revolt was an 'Akan' slave named Tacky who was intent on 'the entire extirpation of the white inhabitants; the enslaving of all such Negroes as might refuse to

join them; and the partition of the island into small principalities in the
African mode; to be distributed among their leaders and head men'.[4]

The revolt broke out in St. Mary's parish, possibly because of
the high concentration of 'Akan' slaves in the district. On the night
of Easter, 1760, between fifty and one hundred of the enslaved
from several estates attacked the fort in the capital of the parish,
Port Maria, killed the man in charge of munitions and seized the
muskets and gunpowder stored there. The rebellion spread across
much of the country and may have involved as many as 30,000
slaves. In Kingston, Jamaica's chief town, there were reports that a
female slave had been made queen of Kingston; she was described
as wearing a crown and sitting under a canopy. This may well
have been an example of a West African custom, with the enslaved
woman assuming the title of Queen Mother of the Ashanti.

Although the Jamaican government eventually suppressed the
rebellion, it took well over a year to do so. The cost was enormous.
Sixty whites were killed as well as an equal number of free
coloureds and free blacks. Between 300 and 400 slaves were killed,
another 100 executed and at least 500 transported off the island.
The monetary cost exceeded £100,000, a huge sum in eighteenth-
century terms.[5]

Yet not all eighteenth-century revolts were led solely by Africans
or were intent on recreating an African past. In 1736, a conspiracy
involving creoles and Africans in Antigua had a more complicated
background than either the revolt in St. John or in Jamaica. A year
before the conspiracy, a group of 'Coromantee' slaves had hatched a
plan to kill all the whites and establish an African kingdom with an
enslaved named Court (alias Tackey) as the King. A 'Coromantee'
himself, Tackey was owned by Antigua's Speaker of the Assembly.
However, Tackey and the other leaders of the conspiracy realized
that they needed the help of creoles. They therefore enlisted the
aid of Tomboy, a creole master-carpenter and several other elite
creole slaves.

Their plan was to blow up the governor and other whites who
would be attending a ball in the capital of Antigua, St. John's, on the
night of 11 October 1736. This would also provide the signal for
the enslaved all over the island to revolt on their individual estates
and then converge on the capital. However, the ball was delayed,
and the planters learned of the plot. Their investigations uncovered
the ringleaders almost immediately but also gradually the names of

conspirators across the island. As in the case of the other revolts, the authorities acted with enormous ferocity. Of eighty-eight slaves executed, five were broken on the wheel, six starved to death and seventy-seven burnt alive. Many others were banished off the island. A significant proportion of those involved in the conspiracy were elite slaves: drivers, skilled slaves and domestics, not the type of the enslaved the planters expected to lead a conspiracy. And worryingly for the planters, the overwhelming majority were creoles.[6]

There seem to have been differences in the aims of the creoles and the Africans. The Africans were apparently intent on killing the whites and setting up an autocracy on African lines. On the other hand, creoles were less committed to a war against the whites and may have been considering the continued enslavement of the Africans. At the same time, there were African overtones to the conspiracy. As in the Jamaican case, it was likely that a woman named Queen was to be a traditional Akan Queen-Mother. Her role would have been to advise Tackey and act as his principal confidant. Moreover, in advance of the conspiracy, there had been an African ceremony to crown the King of the 'Coromantees' and to prepare the rebels for the intended war against the whites. African patterns were therefore significant in this conspiracy, but the role of elite creoles was also crucial.

## Other forms of resistance

Yet it should be remembered that slave revolts and conspiracies were not the only ways in which the enslaved resisted slavery. In spite of the relative frequency of slave uprisings in the Caribbean, rebellions affected only a small minority of the enslaved. If we are seeking to understand the forms of resistance which directly impinged on the lives of the enslaved and their masters, we need to examine day-to-day patterns of resistance.

This type of resistance was a feature of all slave societies. It included acts of sabotage against plantation equipment and machinery, insolence, malingering, negligence, arson and escape. Recently, historians have been devoting more attention to the role of women and resistance and have found that women were responsible for much of this everyday resistance. It was certainly the case that women were often described as more troublesome than men; indeed, they were far more likely to be accused of insolence, disobedience and quarrelling than male slaves. While plantation managers therefore reported a great deal of female insubordination on their estates, there was also a wider issue involving women: that of cultural resistance.

This was particularly significant over issues such as the weaning of children and reproduction. Caribbean enslaved women tended to follow the African pattern of late weaning, despite the attempts by planters to cut down on extended suckling of children. While planters described this behaviour as another form of idling, enslaved women saw it as a rational response to the problems of high infant mortality. Moreover, it was evidence of the strength of African cultural practices. This was also the case regarding contraception and abortion; again, women made use of African practices in their attempts to resist planter demands to produce more children.[7]

Some historians have gone further and argued that women, as mothers, were the principal transmitters of culture. In this capacity, women were largely responsible for shaping the culture of resistance. This could be significant in specific areas such as reproduction, but it also had an impact in other aspects of resistance. Since enslaved women served as domestics and, especially as cooks, they were sometimes accused of attempting to poison their masters. In Martinique, for example, there were stringent measures against the use of poison by the enslaved. Women were also involved in obeah, an African-derived use of supernatural practices largely for healing and protection, but which planters believed could be used against them and, indeed, to help foment insurrection.[8]

Yet, in another important aspect of day-to-day resistance, enslaved women were less likely to run away than enslaved men. This type of running away, known as *petit marronage*, referred to temporary absences as opposed to *grand marronage*, in which the enslaved attempted to run away permanently or set up communities of runaway slaves. When women ran away, they tended to do so temporarily rather than permanently and also took their children with them far more frequently than men. Indeed, it may have been that women refrained from running away in larger numbers because of the strength of family ties which kept them attached to a particular plantation or a particular area.

The evidence on *petit marronage* generally suggests that many of the enslaved ran away to visit family or friends or sought to merge into free black and free brown urban communities. These slaves were trying to pass as free people rather than resist the system as a whole. As a result, they were more likely to be creole slaves who spoke the language of the colony and were often skilled tradesmen or craftsmen. Coloured and creole slaves therefore had a better chance of eluding capture, while African-born slaves were more easily and quickly captured. This may have been partly because Africans often ran away in groups, while creoles tended to desert individually. Some newly landed Africans ran away to get back to Africa. For example, an advertisement in the Jamaican press reported on the flight of four newly arrived Africans; they told their shipmates 'that they would proceed to the sea by night and remain in the bush through the day, and the first canoe they found, they would set sail for their country'.[9]

Once away, the enslaved were harboured by a variety of people. The kin of runaways were prominent among the harbourers, but so were whites, free coloureds and free blacks. Those who protected runaway slaves did so for a variety of reasons: family considerations were, of course, important, but the prospects of employing runaways could also be crucial. Across the Caribbean, the enslaved ran away to other owners; in some cases, especially at times of labour scarcity, owners may have enticed the enslaved with offers of better conditions of work. There is also some evidence of runaways working for slaves.

Equally as intriguing is the evidence that some of the enslaved ran away for a different reason: they were seeking to put pressure on their masters, either to sell them or to improve their conditions. In Barbados, runaways were sometimes promised freedom to choose new owners, if they returned of their own accord. For example, the owner of a runaway slave named Phill wished to sell him but also noted that 'should [Phill] voluntarily return, the privilege of choosing an owner will be granted to him'.[10] This is suggestive about the power that the enslaved had in controlling or at least affecting important aspects of their lives.[11]

By contrast, *grand marronage* posed a very different threat to the societies of the Caribbean. In establishing independent communities across the region, Maroons cast doubt on the foundations of the plantation system. Since Maroons were effectively at war with the colonial societies, they posed real military and economic problems for the white settler communities.[12]

Yet many of the Maroon communities were short-lived and disappeared after a few years. In the seventeenth century, for example, there were Maroon communities briefly in St. Kitts, Barbados and Antigua, but the development of sugar in each of these colonies destroyed any possibility of these communities surviving. Elsewhere, there were small numbers of Maroons in Martinique, Guadeloupe, Dominica and St. Thomas. Puerto Rico also had Maroons and became a prime destination for the enslaved from the Lesser Antilles. These slaves, who escaped by sea, added to the Maroons from Puerto Rico to form several communities in the island, especially in the 1820s. In Saint Domingue, the Maroons of Le Manuel lived near the Spanish border with Santo Domingo and traded with Spanish settlers who often protected them against the French.

On the other hand, in Cuba from the 1530s onwards, there were Maroon settlements known as *palenques*; one report claimed that there were sixty-two such communities across the island. Although the numbers in each *palenque* were small, rarely exceeding fifty people, some of them continued to exist through the sugar boom of the nineteenth century. However, the longest surviving Maroon communities were those in Jamaica and Suriname: each had significant topographical advantages, and each developed a political relationship with the colonial power which helped to ensure their continuity.

In the case of Jamaica, the first Maroons were the slaves of the Spanish settlers who were freed when the English invaded Jamaica in 1655. These enslaved people eventually settled in the remote mountainous interior of the island and were augmented during the last half of the seventeenth century by African slaves who rebelled against their masters. One group, which came to be known as the Leeward Maroons, established itself in the western part of Jamaica. There, in the 'Cockpit Country', which was characterized by deep canyons and limestone sinkholes, they formed a tightly knit band under the leadership of an Akan-speaking slave named Cudjoe. The other major group of Maroons in Jamaica, the Windward Maroons, were located in the high mountains in the eastern part of the island where they formed a federation of individual communities.

The Maroons of Suriname had even greater geographical advantages. They fled the coastal plantations bordering the Caribbean in favour of settlements deep in the interior of Suriname,

**FIGURE 6.1** *An armed Maroon in Suriname.*

*Source:* Courtesy of the Special Collections Library at the University of Virginia, Charlottesville, Virginia.

reachable only along the rivers which run through the colony. In this situation, the Surinamese Maroons were able to develop their communities in relative freedom and formed clans in different parts of the interior. Unlike the Jamaican Maroons, who were limited by the mountainous terrain of the island and by the encroaching sugar plantations, those in Suriname had the huge continental expanse of mainland Latin America as their backdrop.

These Maroon communities had a high proportion of African-born slaves, most of whom were males. They made good use of the terrain to hide themselves away from the white settlers and also developed skills in guerrilla warfare against the soldiers and militia forces who sought to destroy them. European troops therefore often had great difficulties against the Maroons; accustomed to battles in open countryside, European troops were vulnerable to marksmen hiding in the bush who would fire and then disappear into the mountains or jungle.

Heavily outnumbered, the Maroons also developed magical ideas about their own invincibility. For example, Nanny, an obeah woman and one of the leaders of the Windward Maroons of Jamaica, was said to be able to attract and catch bullets, making them harmless in the process. Similarly, another Jamaican Maroon leader, Tacky, could catch bullets and hurl them back against the enemy. It was not just Maroon leaders who had these skills: Maroons in Suriname went through complex rituals and wore amulets to make themselves bulletproof.

In the hostile environments of the mountains of Jamaica or the forests of Suriname, Maroons had to learn to subsist. Accordingly, they developed sophisticated gardens, capable of producing a wide range of crops. But while the Maroons were highly skilled at subsisting in alien and often very difficult locations, there were items they could not produce. Maroons could not create guns or pots; they needed manufactured goods of all kinds; and they also needed women. Maroons were therefore dependent on the plantation societies they were seeking to flee. Moreover, in raiding for enslaved women, they made relations with slaves highly problematic.

Although the Maroon communities consisted predominately of Africans, they were not re-creations of African society. This was exemplified by the stance taken by the leader of the Leeward Maroons in the early decades of the eighteenth century, Cudjoe. Cudjoe, a Maroon-born creole, was the son of the founder of the Leeward Maroons; he insisted that English be spoken in the community as a way of promoting a shared Maroon identity among Maroons of different African ethnicities. For the Maroons, leadership meant being able to deal with the white community as well as understanding fellow Maroons.

These characteristics became especially significant in the 1730s, when there was a rise in the number of the enslaved escaping to the Maroons and also an increase in Maroon raids on plantations. In response, the whites increased their efforts to destroy the Maroons and brought in troops and auxiliary forces to deal with them. By 1739, with neither side able to claim victory, the British decided to negotiate a treaty with Cudjoe recognizing the freedom of the Maroons. This treaty was subsequently the model for the Windward Maroons and, in the 1760s, for the Surinamese Maroons as well.

The treaties offered the Maroons considerable advantages. It granted them their freedom and provided the Maroons with legal recognition of their status as well as specific grants of land for their own use. In return, the Maroons promised to help catch all subsequent runaway slaves, either returning the enslaved to their owners or providing proof that they had killed the runaways. Crucially, the treaties meant that the Maroons were no longer at war with the whites; they could concentrate on the development of their own communities without the constant fear of harassment and attack by the whites.

Yet, ultimately, the treaties had profoundly negative implications for the Maroons. In the case of the Jamaican Maroons, the British insisted that white superintendents take control of the Maroon communities. This significantly limited the power of the Maroon leaders and undercut their authority. The Second Maroon War of 1795, which developed because of a series of local grievances involving one of the Leeward Maroon communities, Trelawny Town, was in reality a response to the treaty of 1739. The Maroons felt restricted in terms of the land they could occupy as a result of the treaty; in addition, they clearly resented the loss of their independence. When the Maroons of Trelawny Town agreed to surrender on condition that they would not be deported, the British none the less went back on their promise. They sent the Maroons first to Nova Scotia, where the Maroons suffered badly from the bitter winters and then, after several years, to Sierra Leone.

The Second Maroon War took place in the middle of the 1790s, a decade in which the slave rebellion in Saint Domingue broke out and caused enormous consternation across the Caribbean as well as in Europe. The governor of Jamaica at the time, the Earl of Balcarres, was prompted to take action against the Maroons, in part because he had heard that French agents from Saint Domingue were inciting the Maroons to revolt and create another Saint Domingue. The story of Saint Domingue and the consequences of the revolution are therefore a crucial part of any study of slave resistance.

# CHAPTER SEVEN

# The Haitian Revolution

In 1789, on the eve of the French Revolution, Saint Domingue (later to become Haiti) was the richest colony in the Caribbean. It had over 8,000 plantations and 500,000 slaves, who produced nearly half of the world's sugar and coffee in addition to a range of other commodities, including indigo and cotton. Saint Domingue's economic value to France was enormous: it generated about two-fifths of France's foreign trade.

Yet when France acquired Saint Domingue from the Spanish in 1697, sugar production had hardly begun in the colony. By 1715, however, there were already 120 sugar plantations, many of which were established in the first few years of French settlement. The growth of the enslaved population was equally rapid; in the thirty years after 1690, the number of the enslaved rose from 3,000 to 47,000. This number continued to increase during the course of the eighteenth century and was particularly marked in the five years from 1785 to 1790. During that period, 30,000 African slaves were imported each year to Saint Domingue, a development which would have a significant effect on the course of the Haitian Revolution.

Saint Domingue's white community was massively outnumbered by the enslaved. Totalling about 40,000 people, the whites formed less than 10 per cent of the population. Even more importantly, the whites were bitterly divided among themselves, especially along class lines. The most significant differences were between the *grands blancs* and the *petits blancs*; this pitted prosperous planters and merchants against artisans, plantations managers, clerks and shopkeepers. But there were divisions within these groups as well: sugar and coffee planters were divided as were planters and merchants. As in the case of Jamaica, there was a sizeable absentee planter class but also a very significant resident planter class in Saint Domingue producing coffee, indigo and cotton.

The free coloured community was different from the rest of the Caribbean: it was considerably wealthier and owned more land and slaves than its counterparts elsewhere in the region. In 1789, there were 30,000 free people of colour in Saint Domingue, owning about 100,000 enslaved people. Although the free coloured population was smaller than that of the whites, free coloureds outnumbered whites in two of the three provinces of the colony. Moreover, it was a rapidly growing population, many of whom had a significant role in coffee production.

At the same time, free coloureds in Saint Domingue faced increasingly severe legal restrictions during the last half of the eighteenth century. For example, from the 1760s onwards, free coloured men were forbidden to carry arms or to take as their surname that of a white. Free people of colour were also forbidden to use titles of respect such as 'Sieur' and 'Dame' when addressing each other. Furthermore, sumptuary legislation, probably directed more towards women than men, prevented free people of colour from dressing like whites, wearing their hair like whites or wearing jewellery or fine fabrics. Such regulations galled the free coloureds, especially as they had been promised legal equality with the whites in the *Code Noir*, the late seventeenth-century French imperial legislation dealing with slavery.

Yet it was not the free coloureds or the enslaved who were responsible for beginning the revolution in Saint Domingue. Rather, it was the whites, largely because they were bitterly opposed to France's restrictive mercantile policy towards Saint Domingue and also because they wanted more control over the internal politics of the colony. The whites saw their opportunity to bring about such changes through representation in the Estates General in the metropolis, the consultative body that met at Versailles in June 1789. In this way, the French Revolution created the possibility for delegates from Saint Domingue to be represented in the metropolitan Assembly and also to develop their own Colonial Assembly in the colony.

A Colonial Assembly met in Saint Domingue during 1790 and produced a constitution which sought to limit French control over the colony's affairs. Its most radical members, known as the Patriot Party, even called for virtual independence from France. Although the delegates argued about the degree of autonomy they should seek, the representatives generally agreed on two issues:

> No one should tamper with the institution of slavery, and that the system of white supremacy should be rigorously maintained. Increasingly, however, the revolution in France came to be seen as a threat to both these pillars of colonial society.[1]

One threat came from the abolitionists in France, the society of the Amis des Noirs. This group did not attack the institution of slavery but instead campaigned for the abolition of the slave trade and for equality for the free people of colour. Yet white colonists in Saint Domingue were alarmed by its activities. Since they regarded racial discrimination 'as an essential bulwark of slavery, such action endangered white lives in the West Indies.'[2]

Whites in Saint Domingue were consequently unwilling to improve the legal position of the free coloureds. In response, the free coloureds began to resist their persecution in the colony. They were aided by the return to Saint Domingue of wealthy free coloureds from France, such as Vincent Ogé, who had been a leading figure among the free coloureds in Paris. Along with another prominent free coloured leader, Jean-Baptiste Chavannes, Ogé organized an army of over 300 free coloureds. The free coloureds were seeking an end to racial discrimination and demanded changes in their treatment. However, their short-lived rebellion was crushed, and the two leaders brutally executed.

Politicians in Paris were shocked by the news of these executions. The National Assembly in Paris therefore decided to enact a compromise gesture towards the free coloureds: it passed legislation in May 1791 declaring that free coloureds born of free parents would be legally equal with the whites. Although this measure affected only a few hundred people of colour, it nonetheless aroused great anger in Saint Domingue. Whites in the colony vowed to resist this decree and talked openly of secession. It was in this context of a possible civil war between whites and free coloureds that the enslaved decided to act: at the end of August 1791, they began a massive rebellion in the north of the colony.

The rebellion broke out in the area around Le Cap and spread quickly throughout the northern parishes. Moving from estate to estate and killing many whites, the enslaved destroyed over 200 sugar plantations as well as nearly 1,200 coffee estates within the first month of the rebellion. One account suggested that all of the plantations within fifty miles of Le Cap were burnt to the ground. Upwards of 100,000 slaves were involved in the rebellion.

A rebellion on such a scale clearly required organization. At a meeting over a week before the outbreak, 200 members of the slave elite, including enslaved drivers, coachmen and others, met on an estate in the north of the colony. They decided to rebel. However, some slaves who attempted to burn a plantation well in advance of the scheduled date of the outbreak were caught and interrogated. News of the rebellion spread to the planters, forcing the rebels to begin the rebellion early. One of the leaders of the rebellion, Boukman, feared that the slaves' plans were becoming known and may therefore have been forced to take precipitate action.

A second meeting also took place in advance of the rebellion. This one, at the Bois-Caïman in the same general area as the first one, was described as a *Vodun* ceremony which confirmed the call to arms at the previous meeting and 'committed the participants to utmost secrecy, solidarity, and a vow of revenge.' For one of the historians of the Haitian Revolution, Carolyn Fick, *Vodun* provided 'a medium for the political organisation of the slaves'.[3]

There is some debate about when the gathering at Bois-Caïman took place. The most measured account of the ceremony suggests that it may have occurred just ahead of the outbreak of the rebellion. It now seems likely that this ceremony served 'to sacralize a political movement that was then reaching fruition'. For David Geggus, this ceremony provided an opportunity for the enslaved leaders to communicate their decision to rebel to the mass of field slaves.[4]

Whatever the immediate precedents of the rebellion, there is little doubt about the existence of a rumour that the king had granted the enslaved three free days and that the masters had withheld this information. It was not just that the king was on the side of the enslaved; in their view, royalist troops were on their way to Saint Domingue to enforce the decree. Slaves were therefore not rebelling in the name of the French Revolution but in support of the king and the church and in the belief that they had already been partly freed. This also happened in several subsequent rebellions elsewhere in the Caribbean; again, the enslaved believed that they had been freed and that their masters or the local government officials were preventing their emancipation.

Faced with chaos in its colony, the National Assembly in France believed that only the free people of colour could create stability in this situation. In April 1792, it passed legislation granting full rights to the free coloureds in the hope that they would help restore authority in the colony. The French government also appointed civil commissioners to enforce this decree, the most famous of whom was Léger-Félicité Sonthonax.

A young radical lawyer, Sonthonax proved indifferent to white colonial opinion; he dissolved the Colonial Assembly and appointed free coloureds to offices formerly held by the whites. With the 6,000 troops who accompanied them, the civil commissioners also dealt with the remnants of the slave rebellion. One of the slave leaders, Boukman, had already been killed early in the rebellion and the French troops then attacked slave forces led by the two other major leaders, Jean-François and Biassou. Thousands of the enslaved were forced to surrender.

The whites, and especially the *petits blancs*, were furious about the legislation on behalf of the free people of colour and about the dissolution of their Colonial Assembly. When the whites then revolted against the civil commissioners and against the moves towards racial equality, Sonthonax armed the free coloureds and the enslaved against the whites. In the process, slaves burnt down the capital of the North, Le Cap, and killed many thousands of whites. As a result, 10,000 whites fled from the island, many taking their slaves as they went to other islands in the Caribbean and to the United States. The destruction of Le Cap meant the end of white supremacy in Saint Domingue.

External events and external powers now began to impinge on Saint Domingue. With the outbreak of war with Spain and England, France had to confront Spanish and British troops invading Saint Domingue. The Spanish, coming from their base in Santo Domingo, also had the support of some of the leading black slave rebels, including the future leader of the colony, Toussaint Louverture. The rebel leaders, who received money and their personal freedom from the Spanish, maintained that they were still fighting for the king against the godless French Republic. Confronted, then, with attacks by the Spanish from the west and the English from the east, Sonthonax increasingly turned to the enslaved to defend his regime. He liberalized the work arrangements on the plantations and recruited slaves to fight on the side of the French. In August 1793, he declared the abolition of slavery in the colony. The National Assembly ratified this decision in February 1794.

The ending of slavery was one of Toussaint Louverture's goals and formed part of his rationale for turning against the Spanish and supporting the French. For David Geggus, this 'was the turning point of the Haitian Revolution'.[5] Toussaint's decision to abandon the Spanish meant the end of the alliance between slave owners in Saint Domingue and the Spanish and English invaders who were intent on maintaining the slave system. By supporting the French, Toussaint guaranteed French rule in the colony for another ten years.

Toussaint Louverture, who was known until 1793 as Toussaint Breda, had been a creole slave (Figure 7.1). He was born about 1744 and worked on the Breda estate as a coachman and in charge of the livestock and therefore was a member of the enslaved elite. A Catholic, he could read and speak French as well as the African language of his father's ethnic group. It was therefore possible for Toussaint to move between the worlds of the enslaved Africans as well as that of the whites. At about the age of thirty, he was freed and, by 1789, he himself owned slaves and was a small proprietor.

Toussaint's role in the slave rebellion of 1791 is unclear. Although he may have had very little to do with the uprising itself, he had become an adviser to one of the enslaved leaders, Biassou, within three months of the beginning of the rebellion. Toussaint joined the Spanish forces and soon made himself invaluable to them. He proved to be a brilliant military commander, good at strategy and adept in the field. When he switched sides and supported the French, he was able to repeatedly defeat his former allies. The Spanish withdrew from the war in 1795, followed three years later by the English. Both the English and the French forces suffered huge losses in Saint Domingue. Part of this was attributable to the ravages of yellow fever among the European troops, but it was also the case that Toussaint's forces were deployed skilfully and proved highly resilient. It may have helped that many of the enslaved had served in African armies prior to their enslavement and were themselves

**FIGURE 7.1** *Toussaint Louverture.*

*Source:* © Photo 12 / Alamy Stock Photo.

war veterans who had been taken as prisoners and then sold in the slave trade.[6]

Toussaint had made himself invaluable to the French and was made Deputy Governor of Saint Domingue in 1796. His main rival for power in the colony was the mulatto leader, André Rigaud, who controlled much of the south of Saint Domingue and who had fought with Toussaint against the English. But Toussaint invaded the South and, in a brutal campaign with Dessalines, the governor of the South, he instituted a wave of terror against the people of colour. It was a battle between the predominately brown middle class against the black military officers represented by Toussaint and Dessalines. Toussaint triumphed, and Rigaud and many of the other leading people of colour fled the colony. The victory not only made Toussaint dominant in Saint Domingue; it also was a harbinger of the racial divide between blacks and mulattoes which would characterize the modern history of Haiti.

In 1800, Toussaint became governor of Saint Domingue. As leader of the colony, Toussaint sought to revive the plantation economy. He therefore instituted a system of forced labour in which ex-slaves had to work on the plantations in return for a share of the proceeds. As Laurent Dubois has suggested, Toussaint was faced with the difficult problem of dealing with the transition from slavery to freedom:

> Intent on maintaining and rebuilding the production of sugar and coffee, [Toussaint] sought to limit the liberty of the ex-slaves, responding to their attempts to move freely, acquire land, and escape plantation labor by constructing a coercive legal order. His administration marked the beginning of a longer story of how emancipation ultimately failed to bring true equality and independence to former slaves.[7]

Toussaint also invited white plantation owners to return to their estates and appointed whites and people of colour to offices in the government. But the system of forced labour under Toussaint suffered from a serious contradiction: ex-slaves did not want to remain on the estates but preferred to till small plots of land on their own account. The people of Saint Domingue increasingly saw their leader as distant and detached.

A year later, Toussaint proclaimed himself governor for life, with the power to choose his own successor. Effectively, although Saint Domingue was still nominally French, Toussaint had taken control of the colony. When he then annexed what had become the French territory of Santo Domingo, Napoleon, already angered by Toussaint's rise, decided to end Toussaint's regime. He despatched a force of 10,000 soldiers headed by his brother-in-law, General LeClerc, to invade the colony and re-establish French rule over Saint Domingue.

Along with some of his leading generals, Toussaint resisted the French advance. He fought a largely guerrilla campaign against LeClerc but eventually surrendered and retired to one of his estates. However, Toussaint was subsequently accused of plotting a rebellion against the French, then kidnapped and deported to France where he died as a prisoner in the Jura mountains nearly a year later. On his departure from Saint Domingue, he warned the French that

> in overthrowing me, you have cut down in Saint-Domingue only the truck of the tree of the liberty of the blacks; it will grow back from the roots, because they are deep and numerous.[8]

Toussaint proved correct. In the summer of 1802, the French declared that slavery would be re-imposed in all of their colonies. This was met with enormous resistance in Saint Domingue and united the non-white population of the colony. Jean-Jacques Dessalines, a former ally of Toussaint and a senior general, was chosen leader of the campaign against the French. Despite incredible brutality on the part of the French, LeClerc was unable to defeat Dessalines. Moreover, the ravages of yellow fever not only decimated LeClerc's forces but, ultimately, LeClerc himself who died of the disease. In the end, Napoleon had to concede that his attempt to restore slavery had failed. The remaining French forces left Saint Domingue in November 1803, and Dessalines was able to declare the independence of Saint Domingue on 1 January 1804. He gave it the Amerindian name of Haiti.

News of the Haitian Revolution spread rapidly across the Americas. Seamen, travellers, planters, slaves, all helped to inform plantation America that the enslaved and the free coloureds had not only overturned slavery but also had created an independent nation. Within a month of the 1791 uprising, slaves in nearby Jamaica were already singing songs about the revolt. For slave owners in the Caribbean and the Americas, this was a deeply worrying development and one which was bound to have ramifications across the region.

The most immediate repercussions occurred in the eastern Caribbean. France declared war on Britain in 1793, and a year later, the British launched an attack on the French colonies of Martinique, Guadeloupe and St. Lucia. The British were able to occupy Martinique and temporarily St. Lucia, but were eventually dislodged from Guadeloupe by forces led by a young republican French commissioner, Victor Hugues. Hugues then made use of Guadeloupe as a base to spread the message of the Haitian and French Revolutions to the enslaved and free coloureds of the Windward Islands, especially in St. Lucia, Grenada and St. Vincent.[9]

In St. Lucia, the British were able to occupy the island for a year from the spring of 1794. But resistance against the British was spurred on by the forces of Victor Hugues and by the knowledge that the French had freed their slaves. Hundreds of blacks therefore opposed the British; they called themselves 'l'armeé français au bois'. For David Barry Gaspar, they were 'anti-British, pro-republican freedom fighters' and, in 1795, they dislodged the British from St. Lucia. Victor Hugues' agent in St. Lucia was therefore able to abolish slavery, although only briefly. The British reinstated slavery when they retook St. Lucia in 1796.[10]

In the case of Grenada, which the French had ceded to the British in 1763 as a result of the Seven Years' War, there was still a significant French-speaking minority on the island in the 1790s. Rather than the equality which the free coloureds of Saint Domingue enjoyed after 1792, the people of colour in Grenada faced increasingly restrictive measures. With the support of Hugues and led by a French-speaking coloured planter, Julien Fédon, the free coloureds rose against the whites in a rebellion in 1795 which lasted sixteen months. Although the British were able in the end to put down the uprising, there is little doubt that the ideas of the French and Haitian revolutions were highly significant in encouraging the rebellion.

This was also the case in St. Vincent, which had become part of the British Empire in 1783 as a consequence of the settlement between Britain and France after the American Revolution. There the Black Caribs, descendants of escaped slaves from neighbouring islands who had intermixed with the native Amerindians, rebelled against the British with the support of the Francophone free coloured minority on the island. In the initial campaign a few days after news of Fédon's rebellion reached St. Vincent, Black Caribs and French-speaking free coloureds wore revolutionary cockades symbolic of their links to the French and Haitian revolutions. After a lengthy campaign, the British were able to defeat the Black Caribs; they subsequently transported the Black Caribs to Rattan, an island off the coast of Honduras.

The Haitian Revolution also had an impact on Cuba and, particularly, on a conspiracy organized by José Antonio Aponte in 1812. A free black carpenter and a priest of Shango (an African-derived religion), Aponte had portraits of leading Haitian figures such as Toussaint and Dessalines in his home and was clearly inspired by their example. As in the case of the Saint Domingue revolt, Aponte spread rumours that the enslaved in Cuba had been freed and also claimed that Haiti would support them in their uprising.

While the Haitian Revolution had immediate repercussions in the region, it also had more long-term effects. Slave rebels during subsequent decades of the nineteenth century, and especially those in Barbados in 1816, Demerara in 1823 and Jamaica in 1831, were aware of developments in Haiti. Moreover, Haiti emerged at a time when slavery and the slave trade was growing rather than diminishing. Although it had been ravaged by years of warfare and its population decimated, Haiti was still 'a great experiment, a crucial test case for ideas about race, slavery, and the future of the Caribbean'.[11]

The abolition of slavery in Haiti was a direct consequence of the massive slave rebellion of 1791. But it also took place within the context of the particular divisions within the slave society of Saint Domingue as well as the impact of the French Revolution. In addition, it would be difficult to imagine the Haitian Revolution without the leadership of Toussaint Louverture. But elsewhere in the region, the abolition first of the slave trade and then of slavery was a much more gradual development. Haiti had begun a process which would sweep across the Caribbean and liberate its slaves.

# CHAPTER EIGHT

# The abolition debates

In 1783, slavery was the dominant labour system across the Caribbean. It was a well-established institution, dating from the early sixteenth century in the Hispanic Caribbean and from a century later for the other major colonial powers. Apart from the resistance of the enslaved themselves, anti-slavery sentiment was almost non-existent. Yet within a little over a century, slavery would be abolished throughout the Caribbean; even more surprisingly, slavery in the British Caribbean would end within fifty years. In light of the importance of the British case for the rest of the region, this chapter deals primarily with the British campaign to abolish the slave trade and slavery before touching on abolition elsewhere.

The traditional explanation for the abolition of the British slave trade and slavery rested on the role of the humanitarians and the philanthropy of the British. In this view, Britain was sacrificing considerable wealth in abolishing first the trade in slaves and then slavery itself. The motivation was clear: the British were acting out of humanitarian concern for the misery caused by the trade and by the exploitation of Africans.

In the 1940s, a young Trinidadian scholar, Eric Williams, turned this argument on its head. For Williams, it was not humanitarianism which explained abolition but rather economics. In his book, *Capitalism and Slavery*, Williams argued that slavery and the slave trade were abolished because they were no longer economically profitable. As Williams wrote:

> The commercial capitalism of the eighteenth century developed the wealth of Europe by means of slavery and monopoly. But

in so doing it helped to create the industrial capitalism of the nineteenth century, which turned round and destroyed the power of commercial capitalism, slavery, and all its works. Without a grasp of these economic changes, the history of the period is meaningless.[1]

In underlining the importance of economic factors, Williams maintained that the role of the humanitarians had been misunderstood and exaggerated.

For many years, Williams' arguments replaced those of the traditionalists who had emphasized the importance of the humanitarians. In time, however, Williams' point of view was also criticized, especially by the historians Roger Anstey and Seymour Drescher. Among other issues, Anstey demonstrated that Williams had exaggerated the profits of the slave trade. This was not just a statistical error; it undermined Williams' claim that the profits of the slave trade and slavery had helped to provide the basis for Britain's Industrial Revolution.[2]

Seymour Drescher weighed in on another aspect of Williams' argument. In his book, *Econocide*, Drescher criticized Williams for arguing that the British West Indian colonies were experiencing severe economic decline at the end of the eighteenth century. For Williams, this decline theory helped to explain abolition itself. But Drescher convincingly demonstrated that the British Caribbean colonies were in fact prospering at the time Williams claimed they were declining. Not least, Drescher was able to point to the colonies' success in taking over the sugar production which was lost because of the devastating effects of the Haitian Revolution. The abolitionists were therefore attacking a system which was gaining in strength rather than faltering or on the verge of collapse.[3]

Yet apart from the often-intense historiographical debate on the Williams' thesis and on the relative importance of humanitarianism and economics, there were also other significant factors in the abolition of the slave trade. Among these was religion and, more specifically, the role of the Quakers. It was the Quakers who submitted the first petition to abolish the trade in slaves in 1783, and they dominated the Abolition Society which was founded four years later. Moreover, the Abolition Society was able early on to attract important recruits to its cause. These included Thomas Clarkson, whose research helped to undermine the arguments in favour of the slave trade and who served as a full-time organizer of the Society. More politically significant was William Wilberforce, a member of Parliament and close friend of the prime minister, who led the abolition campaign in Parliament.

The Abolition Society nearly managed to get an abolition bill through the Commons in the first few years of its existence. It organized a highly influential petitioning campaign and established local committees in various parts of the country. Although its initial attempts in 1789 and again in 1791 to get an abolition bill through the Commons did not succeed, the Society persevered. By 1792, the number of signatories on abolitionist petitions had risen to nearly 400,000, and pressure on Parliament was increasing. When Wilberforce presented another abolition bill to the Commons in the spring of 1792, legislators there voted to end the trade by 1796. But the Lords delayed consideration of the bill and effectively vetoed it. Thereafter and for over a decade, the abolition campaign was hampered by the French Revolution and the war with France as well as by the perception in England of abolition as potentially subversive.

The abolitionists therefore altered their strategy in the early years of the nineteenth century. They began to argue that it was in Britain's interest to abolish the slave trade, initially to newly acquired territories since this would allow these territories to acquire slaves and thereby compete with the existing British colonies. The abolitionists also maintained that the continued importation of African slaves posed a grave threat to the security of the colonies.[4] These arguments for abolition on the basis of national interest and security rather than solely on the grounds of humanitarianism, coupled with a new, more abolitionist British government in 1806, eventually carried the day. Passed in the Commons by a vote of 283 against 16 in 1807, the abolition bill prohibited British ships from any involvement in the slave trade after 1 January 1808.

Yet in spite of their success in abolishing the slave trade, British humanitarians continued to monitor developments in their Caribbean colonies. Since they feared the possibility of illegal slave trading, the humanitarians succeeded in enforcing a system of public registration on the slave colonies. Beginning in 1817 and usually repeated every three years, the registration of slaves revealed that conditions for the enslaved had not improved after 1808. As low birth rates and high mortality rates continued to characterize the British West Indian colonies, the abolitionists concluded that the planters were continuing their old patterns of mistreating their slaves and working them to death.

The abolitionists therefore decided to establish a new organization and a new policy to deal with the problem of colonial slavery. In the spring of 1823, they founded the Anti-Slavery Society; its leading members included prominent figures such as Wilberforce and Clarkson who had been active in the campaign to abolish the slave trade. Thomas Fowell Buxton replaced Wilberforce in 1824 as leader and parliamentary spokesman. Although the Anti-Slavery Society sought to develop a gradual plan for the ultimate abolition of slavery, it also favoured an immediate improvement in the condition of the enslaved.

Accordingly, Buxton presented proposals to Parliament in May 1823 to accomplish these objectives. They included the emancipation at birth of all children as well as measures to ameliorate the condition of the enslaved. In response, the government submitted an alternate set of proposals which had been agreed with representatives of the West Indian planters. These measures were designed to provide the enslaved with more opportunity for religious instruction, prevent the break-up of slave families, end the flogging of women, and make possible compulsory manumission. Most importantly, the measures did not involve emancipation and were to be formulated and implemented in the legislative colonies by the colonists themselves.

Yet even this moderate stance was too much for the colonists in the British Caribbean. In Jamaica, the response was particularly defiant. A committee of the Jamaican House of Assembly accused the government of accepting the 'principles laid down by the enemies of the colonies'. The reaction in Barbados was more direct. A mob there destroyed the Methodist chapel of the missionary, William Shrewsbury, believing that Shrewsbury sympathized with the government's proposals. The colonists' resistance set the pattern for the next several years: the British government provided suggestions for amelioration which were met by strong opposition in the colonies.[5]

Angered by these delays, more radical members of the Anti-Slavery Society decided in 1831 to seek immediate emancipation. They established the Agency Committee, which was designed to mobilize popular support for their cause. The committee also sought pledges from parliamentary candidates to back emancipation and urged voters to support only those candidates who supported the abolition of slavery. In the face of this renewed pressure, the government revived an earlier Order in Council which recognized the enslaved as legal witnesses. To ensure compliance in the legislative colonies, the government promised a considerable reduction in the sugar duties if the order was adopted in its entirety.

When news of the renewed anti-slavery drive and the intentions of the government reached the British West Indies in the late spring and summer in 1831, the whites immediately protested. As in 1823, the protests in Jamaica were especially vehement. Colonists were not just objecting to the Order in Council; because of the actions of the abolitionists, whites now feared a slave rebellion. Since the government was prepared to expose the whites to this risk, colonists even threatened to reconsider their allegiance to the Crown.

The problem for the whites was that the enslaved were aware of the activities of the Anti-Slavery Society and the local resistance to it. This had already led to serious outbreaks elsewhere in the region. In 1816, Barbadian slaves had become agitated about the Assembly's resistance to imperial legislation seeking the registration of slaves. Reports at the time equated the registration act with a plan for the emancipation of the enslaved, and some slaves believed that freedom was being withheld from them. One literate domestic slave, Nanny Grigg, claimed that the enslaved were to be freed on Easter Monday, 1816, but 'the only way to get it was to fight for it, otherwise they would not get it; and the way they were to do, was to set fire, as that was the way they did in Saint Domingo'.[6] When the slave rebellion did break out on Easter Sunday, it spread to a third of the island. The leaders of the rebellion timed it to coincide with the peak of the harvest season, and the enslaved made use of arson in an attempt to obtain their freedom. However, the rebellion – subsequently known as 'Bussa's Rebellion' after the name of one of its alleged leaders – proved short-lived and the repression was savage.

There was a similar backdrop to the Demerara slave rebellion in 1823. Again, the enslaved believed that local whites were withholding their freedom; in this case, the imperial context of the rebellion was the formation of the Anti-Slavery Society and the beginning of the abolitionists' campaign in Britain. The rebellion broke out in August, involving thousands of the enslaved. Like the Barbados uprising, it was repressed severely, with the death of about 250 slaves. The planters linked the rebellion to the work of the humanitarians and, more specifically, to the chapel in Demerara of Rev. John Smith, a missionary for the London Missionary Society. He was found guilty of complicity in the rebellion and died in prison while awaiting a reprieve from the Crown.

As in Barbados and in Demerara, the enslaved in Jamaica in 1831 concluded that they, too, had been freed, in part because of the whites' resistance to the 1831 Order in Council. When the rebellion broke out just after Christmas, 1831, it was the largest outbreak Jamaica had seen. One report claimed that 20,000 slaves were involved in the uprising; it spread throughout western Jamaica and 226 estates sustained damages involving more than £1,000,000 sterling. As in Demerara, missionaries were implicated; the rebel, Sam Sharpe, was a class leader in the Baptist Church as well as a 'Daddy' in the Native Baptist Church. In the aftermath of the rebellion, which the authorities suppressed ferociously, whites attacked missionaries and tore down their chapels, blaming them for the rebellion. Indeed, the rebellion was called 'The Baptist War'.

The Jamaican slave rebellion made it clear to many in Britain that slavery could not continue. The abolitionists were now seeking immediate emancipation, and after 1832, the reformed House of Commons was likely to be more responsive to popular pressure. One of the Baptist missionaries attacked in Jamaica after the rebellion, William Knibb, toured England, recounting the horrors of slavery and seeking its abolition. Since emancipation was now very much on the political agenda, ministers and officials began to think seriously about how to achieve emancipation.

**FIGURE 8.1** *Emancipation Statue by Karl Broodhagen – Barbados.*
*Source:* AA World Travel Library / Alamy Stock Photo.

Officials in the Colonial Office were struck by the need to free the enslaved while still retaining the basic structure of plantation society in their colonies. In their minds, one of the potential dangers for the enslaved was a reversion to 'barbarism', once they became free. Henry Taylor, the senior clerk in the West India Department of the Colonial Office, therefore devised a plan based on the Spanish model of *coartación*. Under this system, the British government would declare the enslaved free for one day; thereafter, slaves could use the proceeds of working on that day to buy further days of freedom. Taylor's superior, Lord Howick, the Under-Secretary of State for the Colonies, sought to solve the problem of labour in a different manner. His solution was to impose a tax on the ex-slaves' provision grounds, which would force the freedmen to work for wages on the estates to pay the tax. Although neither scheme was ever adopted, the rationale in each case was clear: freedom and continued sugar cultivation on the plantations were inextricably linked.

The final act to emancipate the enslaved was a compromise, worked out by the government with representatives of the Anti-Slavery Society and the West Indian planters. At its heart was the establishment of an Apprenticeship system: the enslaved would be freed but become apprentices. They would work for their former masters for up to forty-five hours a week, and less for those who maintained themselves by provision grounds. The legislation separated field and skilled slaves, with skilled slaves ending their Apprenticeship after four years while field slaves would do so after six. Children under the age of six were to be freed immediately, and special magistrates were to be appointed to oversee the workings of the system. Most important from the planters' point of view was a grant of £20 million compensation for the loss of their slaves. Two colonies, Antigua and Bermuda, decided to opt for full freedom immediately. In Antigua, planters believed they could control their ex-slaves without the intervening Apprenticeship; in Bermuda, the enslaved worked in maritime occupations and Apprenticeship was therefore less applicable. At midnight on 31 July 1834, three quarters of a million former enslaved people in the British West Indies (and slaves elsewhere in the British Empire) celebrated their freedom. But elsewhere in the region, abolition was slower in coming.[7]

In the French colonies of the Caribbean, slavery continued until 1848. French liberals favoured emancipation, although leading

**FIGURE 8.2** *Celebrating Emancipation.*

*Source:* © National Maritime Museum, Greenwich, London.

abolitionists such as Victor Schoelcher envisioned the creation of a modern wage labour force rather than a peasant-dominated agricultural system. When the liberal revolutionaries of 1848 overthrew the July monarchy, one of their aims was to abolish slavery. However, there were delays in implementing abolition while politicians debated issues such as compensation for slave owners.

The enslaved in Martinique and Guadeloupe responded by taking action on their own. They ceased work on the plantations and marched on the towns demanding freedom. One confrontation with the authorities led to the death of thirty-five slaves. To avoid further loss of life and a possible rebellion, the municipal authorities of Martinique and Guadeloupe abolished slavery well before the enabling legislation from Paris could arrive.

The action of the enslaved in Martinique and Guadeloupe and the revolutions in Europe had a direct effect on the slaves in the Danish Virgin Islands. On the island of St. Croix, there was an uprising of the enslaved in July 1848, followed by a refusal to work and a general march on the capital. In response, the governor, Peter von Scholten, issued a decree abolishing slavery immediately. Although Von Scholten later obtained the approval of the Danish king for his actions, there were difficulties about the stringent labour contracts the Danish authorities imposed on ex-slaves. Nonetheless, in both the French and Danish colonies, the enslaved had a significant role in their own emancipation.[8]

While there was a history of slave resistance in the Dutch colony of Suriname, emancipation was more a product of metropolitan legislation than action by the enslaved themselves. Like the British government, the Dutch believed that some form of enforced labour would be essential for the continuation of the plantation system. The Dutch authorities as well as the planters in Suriname maintained that, once freed, the ex-slaves would be unlikely to continue working on the estates. The Emancipation Act of July 1863 therefore included a ten-year Apprenticeship scheme involving a system of enforced labour by the ex-slaves.

Slavery in the Spanish Caribbean lasted the longest. In Puerto Rico, slavery was not abolished until 1873 and, in Cuba, slavery lasted until 1886. In the case of Puerto Rico, there were many slave revolts during the nineteenth century, the period when sugar production on the island flourished. Planters in Puerto Rico concluded that they could manage more successfully with a labour force consisting of local free blacks and imported workers rather than having to deal with a problematical enslaved labour force.

Slave resistance was also a problem in Cuba, where like Puerto Rico, sugar production expanded massively in the nineteenth century. The 1844 slave conspiracy known as *La Escalera* – which involved free coloureds as well as the enslaved – was suppressed ferociously. With the ending of the slave trade in the middle of the century, Cuban planters turned to alternative forms of labour, including large numbers of Chinese indentured labourers. The leaders of the Ten Years' War in 1868 proclaimed slave emancipation, but their struggle for independence as well as emancipation failed. Yet Cuban planters could see that the end of slavery was coming and, in

1880, enacted an Apprenticeship scheme known as the *patronato*. Scheduled to last for eight years, it ended prematurely with the final abolition of slavery in 1886.[9]

Abolition of the slave trade and of slavery was therefore a complicated development. While the enslaved were important in their own emancipation across the region, other forces were also significant. Despite the criticisms of the Williams' thesis, the role of economics could not be overlooked or that of the humanitarians or of popular politics. Indeed, the newly developed methods of petitioning and mass campaigning were to prove significant in other political campaigns as well in the course of the nineteenth century. Moreover, emancipation was not the end of the story: although slaves were now legally free, they still faced the prospect of a continuing struggle to make their freedom a meaningful one.

# CHAPTER NINE

# Race, racism and equality

By the beginning of the nineteenth century, the free people of colour across the Caribbean were becoming a significant element in their respective societies. Although hindered by legal, economic and social restrictions, the free coloureds were determined to improve their condition. The differing economies of the Caribbean in the nineteenth century clearly affected their chances of success. In Cuba, for example, the sugar boom in the nineteenth century provided increased economic opportunities for members of this group. Yet at the same time, the prosperity Cuba experienced during this period brought in its wake further restrictions and limitations for this group.

One problem for the people of colour was the increased difficulty of manumission. Once sugar took hold in Cuba, slave labour was far more valuable than it had been during the pre-plantation period. Planters were therefore far more reluctant to free their slaves voluntarily. Another recognized avenue of mobility in Cuba, *coartación*, which allowed the enslaved to buy their freedom gradually, was reduced in scope. In this system, the enslaved and the master agreed a fixed purchase price; once the enslaved had made a down payment, he or she could not be sold or transferred. Interestingly, enslaved women constituted 68 per cent of the slaves involved in *coartación*.[1]

It was not only the possibilities of manumission which affected the freedmen. As elsewhere in the Caribbean, various occupations were closed to them. They could not aspire to the law, to medicine, or to the church. Free people of colour were barred from becoming businessmen or members of the bureaucracy. During the course of the nineteenth century, it became more difficult for them to acquire land, and they were prevented from holding jobs which would compete with lower-class whites. In the 1840s, when whites became frightened about the predominance of non-whites in Cuba, legal restrictions against the freedmen multiplied. Moreover, they were blamed for *La Escalera*, a slave conspiracy in 1844. Many free people of colour were executed or exiled during the course of the repression which followed the discovery of the alleged rebellion. This included one of the leading free coloured poets in the island, Plácido (Gabriel de la Concepción Valdés). The advent of sugar in Cuba thus brought with it severe restrictions for the freedmen as a whole.[2]

In spite of these restrictions, however, the free black and free coloured population of Cuba grew substantially in the course of the nineteenth century (see Table 9.1). Numbering almost 55,000 in 1792, freedmen by 1841 totalled well over 150,000, a threefold rise. Their numbers continued to increase at this rate over the next four decades.[3] This pattern of growth for the free people of colour was not unusual in the rest of the Caribbean. The early nineteenth century witnessed comparable proportional increases in Martinique, Jamaica, Grenada and Barbados, although the actual number of freedmen in these societies was much smaller. Part of this growth was due to manumissions, but much of it reflected the ability of the free people of colour to increase their own population naturally, a phenomenon which neither whites nor blacks in much of the Caribbean were able to replicate.

An important difference between Cuba and the rest of the Caribbean was the proportion of freedmen to whites. In Cuba, the number of free non-whites amounted to only about a third of the white population, while elsewhere the free people of colour were already outnumbering whites early in the nineteenth century. By 1835 in Martinique, there were three times as many freedmen as whites, while the comparable ratio in Grenada at the about the same time was five freedmen for every one white. The numerical importance of the free coloureds and free blacks in these non-Hispanic colonies was crucial in the struggle to improve their rights.

In Martinique and in many of the British colonies, free coloureds thus began to protest against the restrictions imposed on them. The free people of colour in Martinique started early: their first-known

TABLE 9.1 Growth of freedmen population in the nineteenth century.

| Year | Freedmen |
|------|----------|
| **CUBA** | |
| 1792 | 54,154 |
| 1841 | 154,546 |
| 1887 | 528,798 |
| **MARTINIQUE** | |
| 1802 | 6,578 |
| 1835 | 29,955 |
| 1848 | 36,420 |
| **JAMAICA** | |
| 1789 | 10,000 |
| 1825 | 38,800 |
| 1834 | 42,000 |
| **GRENADA** | |
| 1812 | 1,688 |
| 1820 | 2,742 |
| 1830 | 4,033 |
| **BARBADOS** | |
| 1801–02 | 2,229 |
| 1825 | 4,534 |
| 1834 | 6,584 |

David W. Cohen and Jack P. Greene, *Neither Slave Nor Free: The Freedmen of African Descent in the Slave Societies of the New World* (Baltimore: Johns Hopkins University Press, 1972), pp. 337–9; Gad J. Heuman, *Between Black and White: Race, Politics and the Free Coloreds in Jamaica, 1792-1865* (Westport, CT: Greenwood Press, 1981), p. 7; Edward L. Cox, *Free Coloreds in the Slave Societies of St. Kitts and Grenada, 1763-1833* (Knoxville, TN: University of Tennessee Press, 1984), pp. 30–1.

petition against a poll tax was submitted in 1727. Later in the century, free coloureds in Saint Domingue were seeking to organize their community in the colony and to generate support in France. Their efforts were overtaken by the Haitian Revolution, and their activities foundered, partly because they were unwilling to ally with the enslaved. In Martinique, free coloured petitions in 1820 met with considerable hostility by the local whites. A few years later, one of their leaders in Paris, Cyrille Bissette, published a pamphlet arguing for an improvement in the rights of the people of colour. However, the local whites interpreted his appeal as the basis of a plot and used it to attack the freedmen.

Free coloureds in the British Caribbean were ultimately more successful in their campaigns to improve their rights than their counterparts in Martinique. However, their early attempts in this direction also met with considerable resistance. In Jamaica, a group of coloureds circulated a petition to the local legislature in 1792. In it, the people of colour complained about the laws directed against them. More specifically, they appealed against their inability to give evidence in court, against the different punishments handed out to whites and browns, and to the limitations on the amount they could inherit. The Jamaican assemblymen were in no mood to grant any of these requests in 1792. Worried about the slave rebellion in neighbouring Haiti, they turned down the free coloured petition which they believed was 'expressed in the language of fanaticism'. The assemblymen were concerned about the dangers posed by the free coloureds:

> From what has happened at Hispaniola [Saint Domingue], we have every reason to believe that these free people of colour have it in their power to lead our Slaves into rebellion by false representations. Their object would not be to make them free but to distress us and thereby oblige us to comply with their demand to be put upon an equal footing with the White Inhabitants.

For the whites, it was clearly too early to consider granting concessions to the free coloureds.[4]

The next major free coloured petition was signed by more than 2,400 freedmen and submitted to the Jamaican Assembly in 1813. It made many of the same requests as the earlier petition, but this time the assemblymen were prepared to make concessions to the coloureds. Yet, the legislators would not consider granting the coloureds any political rights: they resolved that 'the free people of colour in this Island have no right or claim whatever to political power, or to interfere in the administration of the Government'.[5]

The Jamaican free coloureds were not alone in their petitions. In the Danish West Indies, freedmen first submitted a petition in 1810; six years later, in another petition, they sought full legal equality with the whites. In 1813, sixty free coloureds in Montserrat petitioned the legislature against their inability to vote at a recent election. At about the same time, the people of colour in the Virgin Islands sought the repeal of earlier legislation which prohibited them from owning more than eight acres of land or more than fifteen slaves. Barbadian free coloureds were also making similar requests; in 1811, they sought the right of testifying in court. Thus, free coloureds in different parts of the Caribbean were seeking to improve their legal position in the early years of the nineteenth century.

This process continued in the 1820s. During that decade, free coloureds in most of the British Caribbean colonies organized new campaigns for their rights. In Jamaica, a committee of coloureds was established to hold meetings around the island and prepare a draft petition to the legislature. The committee forged links with abolitionists in England and sought to influence officials in the Colonial Office as well. Yet the reaction of many whites was, if anything, more virulent than it had been earlier. The Rev. George Bridges, an Anglican minister and strong ally of the plantocracy, claimed that the coloureds could not have such rights 'while the blood of pagan Africa still flowed thick and darkly in their veins'. Even their major supporter in the Assembly, Richard Barrett, agreed that the free coloureds were not yet ready for full equality.[6]

By 1833, however, just one year before the abolition of slavery, freedmen in all the British colonies in the Caribbean had attained their full civil rights. This was largely due to pressure from Britain, although many whites in the Caribbean realized that it was in their interest to unite with the free people of colour against the enslaved. Yet, ironically, the free coloureds did not generally side politically with the whites after 1833. They adopted a humanitarian and often abolitionist stance which differentiated them from the local plantocracy. Moreover, they were unable to gain acceptance in white society, even after they had attained their rights. In general, freedmen found that caste lines proved difficult to cross, despite their being the legal equals of the whites.

While the people of colour continued to experience discrimination, their prospects after emancipation improved considerably. Brown men not only entered politics but also moved into jobs that had formerly been limited almost entirely to whites. In part, this was because many whites were attracted to more prosperous areas of the British Empire, thereby creating openings for the people of colour. Moreover, as the labour supply from Europe dwindled, planters began to hire more men of colour as bookkeepers, tradesmen and overseers.

Coloureds were branching out into new areas as well, especially in business. Before the 1830s, people of colour had enjoyed little prospect of rising above a clerkship in a white-owned company. After emancipation, the people of colour became more independent of the whites. As the considerably larger and more diverse freed population developed different needs, brown merchants were able to import goods directly for themselves rather than being dependent on traditional patterns of doing business. As a result, many of them prospered and helped to form a mainly new middle class.

Observers noted that the people of colour were also playing a prominent part in government service. Although they complained about the lack of government posts in the early 1830s, coloureds served in the stipendiary magistracy during the Apprenticeship period and advanced to the highest levels of local government after 1838. In Jamaica, in the 1860s, for example, the Attorney-General, the Speaker of the House and the chairman of the Quarter Sessions were all men of colour.

Yet not all the free coloureds enjoyed this improvement in their fortunes. The worst sufferers seem to have been the brown women who had lived with whites during slavery and who had often received a little property and some slaves to support them. After emancipation, these women often had a difficult time economically. Similarly, the large majority of the people of colour who had been poor before the 1830s did not necessarily fare that much better after emancipation. Urban coloureds continued to work as porters, servants, hucksters and artisans. Moreover, emancipation did not alter the attitude of many whites towards the people of colour. Coloureds could aspire to the most important political positions in these societies, but they were not usually admitted to white society. Whites continued to draw the line almost exclusively on the basis of colour.

These attitudes towards the freedmen were expressed in a variety of ways. For example, whites tended to forego the polite forms of social intercourse when dealing with free coloureds and free blacks. They did not use the usual titles of Mr, Mrs or Miss when addressing freedmen and adopted first names instead. The titles were thus reserved for whites and were a further mark of distinction between whites and freedmen. Furthermore, whites generally sought to avoid any contact with the people of colour which could imply social equality. As two visitors to the Caribbean reported in the 1830s, 'to visit the houses [of high-ranking freedmen] ... and especially to sit down at their tables, would have been a loss of caste'.[7]

**FIGURE 9.1** *Agostino Brunias'* Free Women of Color with Their Children and Servants in a Landscape, *ca. 1770–96.*

*Source:* Brooklyn Museum, Gift of Mrs Carll H. de Silver in memory of her husband, by exchange and gift of George S. Hellman, by exchange. Photo: Brooklyn Museum.

Privately, whites generally refused to have any contact with the people of colour, a policy that some observers believed to be unwise. For instance, Henry Morson, a member of the West India Association, was concerned about the whites' lack of foresight in refusing to mix with the coloureds. Writing in 1841, Morson warned the planters to modify their views because brown men would inevitably become one of the most important groups in the Caribbean. But relations between whites and coloureds did not improve significantly. Although brown people were invited to public gatherings, observers noted that many whites feared and disliked the people of colour. In this context, emancipation seems to have done little to affect the attitudes established during slavery.

Coloureds themselves were guilty of some of the same behaviour towards the enslaved and towards free blacks. During slavery, coloureds sought to avoid being identified with the enslaved and refused to do manual labour on the estates. In the case of Cuba, Verena Martinez-Alier confirmed the coloureds' aspirations to avoid any association with slaves as well as their adoption of white racial attitudes. Martinez-Alier was therefore surprised by the reaction of a mulatto woman, Angela Carpos, who rejected a white suitor wishing to live with her daughter. Carpos turned down the white man because 'her daughter was a virgin [and] she [wished] that she marry one of her own class'.[8]

Racial distinctions were also important in the free coloureds' campaign for their rights. In their petitions, the free coloureds therefore sought to distance themselves from the free blacks. In Belize, the free coloureds did not complain when they, and not the free blacks, were accorded full civil rights. As Nigel Bolland has suggested, 'the racist ideology of the whites had so permeated the free coloured sense of identity that the free coloured were glad to have finally achieved social differentiation from the blacks'.[9]

As in the case of white racial attitudes after emancipation, the views of the coloureds did not alter substantially. Browns continued to look down on the blacks and refused to work with them in the fields. But Anthony Trollope was aware that coloureds as well as blacks had negative stereotypes of each other. For Trollope, coloureds were 'imperious to the black men, and determined on that side to exhibit and use their superiority'. Yet blacks viewed coloureds as 'sly and cunning; that they cannot be trusted as masters; that they tyrannize, bully, and deceive'.[10]

Such racial views had ramifications for Caribbean society. Excluded from white society, the coloureds often staged their own entertainments. For example, they organized balls and dinners, some of which were for browns only.[11] However, white men were frequently invited, since brown women sought to form relationships with them. Racial stereotypes thus broke down over sexual relations. Just as white–brown relations were common, brown men mating with black women was also a feature of Caribbean slave society. Yet such relationships did not overturn the prevailing racial stereotypes of the society as a whole.

Neither the enfranchisement of the people of colour nor emancipation itself seems to have fundamentally altered either the place of browns in Caribbean society or the racial attitudes of the majority of the population. Coloureds found that they could not generally associate on an equal basis with whites and were often unwilling to do so with the blacks. While considerations of class enabled a small number of browns to become part of white society, colour continued to restrict the social mobility of most people of mixed race.

The free coloureds in the nineteenth century had thus advanced considerably. With some exceptions, such as Cuba, free coloureds had become the legal equals of the whites and were able to vie for high political office. But considerations of colour did not disappear with legal equality. Coloureds remained the object of social discrimination and, in turn, abused other groups lower down on the social hierarchy. Much of the structure of plantation slave society continued, even though slavery ended.

# CHAPTER TEN

# From slavery to freedom

The ending of slavery and the development of free societies proceeded very differently across the Caribbean. As discussed in Chapter 8, in some parts of the Caribbean, the enslaved became fully free once slavery ended. However, this did not happen in Cuba and the British Caribbean; there the authorities instituted an intermediate system – Apprenticeship – between slavery and full freedom. In both cases, however, the system did not work as planned and ended prematurely.

The Apprenticeship system in the British Caribbean, which began when slavery was legally abolished in 1834, meant that the enslaved were freed but became apprentices. They were obligated to work for their former owners for up to forty-five hours a week without pay, although the apprentices would be paid for any work they did beyond this stipulated amount. The officials responsible for the creation of the Apprenticeship system saw it as a necessary bridge between slavery and freedom. For them, it was important that there was a gradual transition to full freedom. Not surprisingly, many apprentices across the British Caribbean found this a difficult concept to accept.

Apprentices on St. Kitts reacted particularly strongly to the idea of an Apprenticeship system. At the onset of emancipation on 1 August 1834, labourers on the island's plantations resolved not to return to work without pay. Some of the apprentices said that 'they would give their souls to hell and their bodies to the sharks rather than be bound to work as apprentices'. The authorities declared martial law, rounded up the striking apprentices who had fled and forced all the apprentices back to work.[1]

Further afield in the Caribbean, there were also serious difficulties among the apprentices. In Trinidad, the apprentices vowed to strike and reiterated some of the same themes as those in St. Kitts. According to one report, the Trinidad apprentices believed that the king had freed them outright and that Apprenticeship was a plan hatched by their masters and the governor. For the apprentices, the planters were 'dam tief' and the governor 'an old rogue'; after all, the king had enough money to buy them fully out of slavery and was not such a fool as to only make them half free.[2] Again, there was a problem with the logic of Apprenticeship. The apprentices could not understand how the king could call them 'free', and yet force them to work for their former owners. Parodying the concept of Apprenticeship, the apprentices also claimed that they already knew their work sufficiently and did not need an 'Apprenticeship' of any kind.[3]

Apprentices in Jamaica shared these views and also reacted negatively to the Apprenticeship system. In the parish of St. Ann, apprentices went on strike, vowing not to work unless they were paid. Elsewhere on the island, the apprentices were disappointed by the behaviour of the planters who withdrew many of the privileges which the apprentices had enjoyed as slaves. These included forcing back into the work gangs women who had formerly been excused from field labour because of old age or because they had produced six children; not allowing mothers to nurse their children in the fields; and taking away all field cooks and nurses to watch the children in the fields. The governor of Jamaica, Lord Sligo, was disturbed about the behaviour of the whites: he saw it as 'outrageous and oppressive' and believed that it was producing very negative effects among the apprentices.

The reaction of the apprentices in the first year of the Apprenticeship was highly revealing. Their image of freedom differed substantially from those of the policymakers in the Colonial Office as well as their former masters. For those in authority, it was critical to maintain the established order and the existing hierarchies. While there was a recognized need to protect the apprentices, it was also important to ensure the continuity of the plantation system and the production of sugar.

For the apprentices, and especially those who resisted the establishment of Apprenticeship, it was difficult to comprehend the new system. Like the apprentices in Trinidad, they felt that they needed no 'Apprenticeship'; they needed no training for freedom or for their work on the plantations. In fact, the nature of the slaves' own economy in the Caribbean, with its extensive provision ground system and highly developed markets, meant that the enslaved were probably better prepared for freedom than their former masters. At the onset of Apprenticeship, ex-slaves wanted to be fully free; they sought 'unrestricted freedom' and not a system of forced labour, even for part of the week. Apprentices were prepared to work for wages, but many also believed that their houses and their provision grounds belonged to them and not to the planters.

One of the most noticeable aspects of the apprentices' resistance to the system was the role of women. They were prominent in the march on Government House in Trinidad and in several of the disturbances in Jamaica. The authorities repeatedly complained about the women apprentices; for example, Governor Sligo wrote home that 'it is notorious that they [the women] are all over the Island the most troublesome'.[4] There were good reasons why women were so prominent in the resistance to Apprenticeship. As Thomas Holt has pointed out, female apprentices formed the bulk of the field labouring force on the plantations, just as they had during slavery. Regulations about hours and about working practices would therefore have affected women more directly than men.[5]

However, the explanation for the role of women as ringleaders against Apprenticeship is more complicated than simply numerical predominance. In a perceptive treatment of this issue, Mimi Sheller discusses women's role in Jamaica during this period as both workers and mothers. As Sheller suggests, 'unlike their male counterparts, female field labourers could make claims for improved working conditions not simply as free workers, but specifically as mothers who were struggling to support their families'. The planters' withdrawal of privileges during Apprenticeship and, specifically, those affecting pregnant women, women with children and the role of elderly matriarchs impinged directly on women. 'Female apprentices were punished in large numbers for trying to assert and protect the limited rights they had won as mothers of the slave labour force.' In the end, the harsh treatment of women rebounded against the planters and helped to discredit the whole Apprenticeship scheme and led to its premature abolition in 1838.[6]

Abolitionists in Britain, who had opposed the establishment of the Apprenticeship system, were aware of its problems and began

**FIGURE 10.1** *An Interior View of a Jamaican House of Correction.*
*Source:* © National Maritime Museum, Greenwich, London.

an anti-apprenticeship campaign. Led by a wealthy merchant, Joseph Sturge, it gathered momentum after Sturge and one of his associates, Thomas Harvey, visited the West Indies and published an attack on the system, *The West Indies in 1837*. Although the government sought to improve the workings of the system in early 1838, the campaign against the Apprenticeship system continued. Bowing to this pressure, the assemblies in the West Indies ended the system prematurely on 1 August 1838. Yet even in its abbreviated form, the Apprenticeship system was not successful: it did not establish a useful basis for a free society. Instead, it frequently led to bitterness and controversy and made the working out of freedom that much more difficult.

More than forty years later, Cuba also had an Apprenticeship system. Established in 1880 and known as the *patronato*, it too was designed to end slavery gradually. Yet in the case of Cuba, Spanish legislators had already envisioned the ending of slavery even before the establishment of the *patronato*. In 1870, they passed the Moret Law, which freed elderly slaves and also young children and meant that slavery would eventually disappear. Planters in Cuba therefore turned to other types of labour well before the end of slavery. While slavery still existed, Cuban plantations were characterized by an unusually diverse labour force, consisting of Chinese indentured labourers, black, white and brown wage workers and the enslaved.

As with Apprenticeship in the British Caribbean, the *patronato* was a system of forced labour. Ex-slaves, known as *patrocinados*, had to work for their former masters and could not leave the plantations without permission. Nor could the *patrocinados* change masters without the approval of their former owners. At the same time, the masters also had certain obligations: they were required to feed and clothe their apprentices, and they could not separate families. Masters were also required to pay the *patrocinados* a meagre wage. For Rebecca Scott, the system was in some ways reminiscent of 'a liberal slave code'.[7]

One of the most significant aspects of the *patronato* was the requirement that one-quarter of the apprentices were to be freed each year from 1884. By 1888, then, the *patronato* would come to an end. The system also established regional boards to oversee the operation of the *patronato* and gave apprentices the right to buy themselves out of the system. In practice, apprentices quickly learned how to successfully appeal to the regional boards and gain their freedom. They did so on a number of grounds, including age, status and harsh treatment. The result was a dramatic decline in the population of the apprentices. Although there were nearly 200,000 slaves in 1877, by 1886 only 25,000 apprentices remained in the system, and the Spanish government in consultation with Cuban planters abolished the *patronato*.

There were important differences between the *patronato* and the Apprenticeship system in the British Caribbean. Unlike planters in the British West Indies, Cuban planters did not feel the need to get rid of the holidays and indulgences which had characterized slavery. There was less bitterness, then, between many of the former masters and ex-slaves in Cuba. The rapid exodus of so many Cuban apprentices out of the Apprenticeship system also helped to change the relationship between ex-slaves and masters. The legislation establishing the *patronato* had brought in a third party – the state – which often protected the apprentices. Apprentices could appeal to the local boards, they were protected against certain forms of punishment and they had the right to buy themselves out of the system. Although planters would seek to control the labour of their ex-slaves after the end of the Apprenticeship system, the *patronato* had altered the relationship between the former owners and ex-slaves. The onset of full freedom would further test that relationship not just in Cuba but across the Caribbean.

## Post-emancipation developments

Although the planters were willing to end the Apprenticeship system early in Cuba and the British West Indies, they did not envision emancipation altering either the hierarchical nature of society or their political dominance. More importantly, they sought to ensure a steady and cheap supply of labour. Faced with the possibility that ex-slaves might leave the estates, former masters turned to a variety of coercive measures to retain their labour. The most common method in the British West Indies, known as the tenancy-at-will system, combined rents with wages and led to exorbitant charges for the rental of houses and grounds, often exceeding the wages paid to the labourers.

The governor of Jamaica pointed out some of the consequences of these excessive charges. He had heard of many cases in which a labourer earned five shillings a week for his work but was charged eight shillings for rent, leaving him in debt to the plantation and with nothing to maintain his family. A further problem arose when planters simply ejected their former slaves from the plantations. These 'ejectments' could arise over trivial offences. In Barbados, Betsy Cleaver, a labourer, was thrown off the plantation, had her house destroyed and her possessions thrown into the road because she had chosen to have her sugar cane processed at another estate.

In Martinique and Guadeloupe, planters imposed a head tax on every inhabitant. Since the tax was higher in the cities and lower in the countryside, the aim was to keep labourers on the plantations. Moreover, the tax would force blacks to work on the estates to raise enough money to pay the charge. In addition, the authorities levied a tax on land producing commodities other than sugar or coffee to limit the development of provision grounds and the production of alternative crops. The government also instituted a pass system, seeking to limit the mobility of the ex-slaves and to force them to accept contractual labour on the estates.

Freed men and women reacted to these measures, often by leaving the plantations when it was possible to do so. This was precisely what the planters had most feared. In Guadeloupe, there was a significant exodus from the plantations just before emancipation and immediately after it. By 1853, five years after the end of slavery, Guadeloupe and Martinique had lost one-fifth of their plantation workers. In the case of Jamaica, where there was abundant land not controlled by the estates, thousands of ex-slaves left the plantations to establish freeholds and independent villages. Thomas Holt calculated that by 1845, seven years after full emancipation, over 20,000 freeholds of less than ten acres had been registered, encompassing a population of over 60,000 people. Over 20 per cent of the ex-slave population had settled on small freeholds. While many of these free people continued to work at least part-time on the estates, their freeholds provided them with a significant degree of independence from the planters. Other colonies also reported significant losses of labourers from the plantations. In Dominica, a survey of forty-one estates for the six-month period after the onset of full freedom revealed a decrease in the plantation labour force of 39 per cent.[8]

Such mobility after emancipation was not always possible. In Cuba, ex-slaves were faced with an aggressive and expanding plantation system and did not have the possibility of becoming small-scale cultivators. Yet even there, some freed people managed to migrate to the eastern part of Cuba to establish small holdings. While it was not possible in many cases for free people to purchase freeholds, they nonetheless made clear their views about the meaning of freedom. A magistrate in Jamaica writing about events in the western part of the island just over six months after emancipation complained about the labourers. They began work late, finished earlier than in the past, and had the idea that freedom meant they should work less than during slavery. As the magistrate put it, 'a foolish idea having got into the negroes' head that (to use his own words) he must not sell 'his free' and he thinks that freedom ought at all events to produce a diminution of his manual labor, or he would be undeserving such a boon'.[9]

Other free people elsewhere in the Caribbean expressed similar ideas about labour and freedom. When a magistrate visited some of the largest estates in Dominica soon after emancipation, he asked the ex-slaves for their views. One woman said that she 'had been a slave all her life, and would not work for anybody again'. Another asked if she could go to town for a week or two and then return to work on the estate. When the magistrate told her that she needed permission, she responded, 'Is this what you call free?' Writing nearly two months after emancipation, another magistrate on the island reported that the people had done little or no work on the plantations since 1 August. According to the magistrate, the free people believed that they had two months to rest and, as they put it, 'to refresh themselves'.[10]

Issues of gender and labour were also highly significant to the ex-slaves. After emancipation, women often withdrew from plantation labour in large numbers. Since women had formed the majority of the field labour force during slavery, this could have dramatic effects. Swithin Wilmot has detailed the decline in the female labour force on Golden Grove Estate in Jamaica: he found that of the 137 women working on the estate up to emancipation, only nineteen were at work in October 1838. Across the island in St. James parish, three-fifths of the workers on estates were women up to the end of the Apprenticeship system; less than six months into full freedom, only one-third of the labourers were women.[11]

Although European ideas of gender had a role in the withdrawal of female labour from the plantations, there were also more important factors at work. Bridget Brereton has emphasized the family strategies pursued by many ex-slaves after emancipation. Rather than working on the plantations, women chose to work in the provision grounds and in marketing their produce. This decision made economic sense, but it also provided a greater degree of autonomy for ex-slaves after emancipation. Independence from the plantation meant more than just autonomy; as Brereton has argued, freedom also included 'the right to control one's own body, the right to be free of violation and abuse'. This right extended to children as well: it was part of the family strategy after emancipation to keep young children out of field work and, if possible, to send them to school or to use the older children in household production.[12]

The ex-slaves' views about gender and labour as well as about freedom led to a series of strikes and riots in the immediate aftermath of emancipation. Across the region, free men and women resisted low wages and high rents. For example, in St. Lucia, one report soon after emancipation claimed that 'two-thirds of the labouring population refused to work on the estates'. There were frequent strikes on the island and many clashes with the authorities. In Grenada, the authorities sought to eject an ex-slave from his house because he refused to accept the wages offered and also would not leave his home. But the attempt failed, as a large group of free men and women attacked the constables who sought to serve a warrant. The men and women regarded the houses as their own, 'given them by the Queen; and said, with violent oaths, they were determined to keep possession of [them]'.[13]

Strikes and riots were one form of response of the ex-slaves to emancipation; another was challenging the political domination of the planters. This took the form of electing black and brown representatives to the local assemblies. Although not forming a single political bloc, black and brown assemblymen generally supported government policies. Moreover, they could be significant: in Dominica, for example, coloured representatives formed a majority in the Assembly. Their presence prevented the passage of harsh legislation against the ex-slaves which characterized many other West Indian colonies.

In Jamaica, the coloured and black members of the Assembly united to form the Town Party, a faction which opposed the predominately planters' Country Party. The coloureds favoured funds being spent on education, resisted expensive immigration schemes and sought to counter planter attempts to restrict the franchise. Moreover, the coloureds also voted against measures to shift the burden of taxation almost entirely on small settlers. Brown and black representatives did remain a minority in the Jamaican House of Assembly, but as their numbers increased, the planters became increasingly alarmed about the possibility of being outnumbered.

Coloured and black politicians were not the only group to oppose the planters. European missionaries, and especially the Baptists, were concerned about the plight of the ex-slaves. They attacked the harsh legislation emanating from the Jamaican Assembly and also wished to sever the connection between church and state in the colony. Led by William Knibb, the Baptists sought to organize the small settler vote; they wanted to elect assemblymen committed to their programme. The Baptists therefore attempted to register large numbers of freeholders who would return suitable candidates to the Assembly. In the early 1840s, they were becoming a potentially important political force: Governor Charles Metcalfe regarded them as a political party with great influence over the ex-slave population.

However, when his successor, Lord Elgin, called a surprise election in 1844, the Baptists were unable to affect the results significantly and they declined thereafter as a political force in Jamaica.

Missionaries also aided the process of setting up free villages after emancipation. Often helped by British philanthropists, missionaries bought land from the planters for the purpose. Some of the Jamaican free villages were established during the Apprenticeship period: the first such village, Sligoville, was founded in 1835. During the next six years, Baptist missionaries settled more than 3,000 people in Baptist villages, some with evocative names such as Buxton, Wilberforce, and Victoria.[14]

It was not only missionaries who organized free villages; ex-slaves did so as well. In British Guiana, former plantation headmen bought up estates on behalf of a larger group of freed people. For example, in November 1839, sixty-three people, many of whom were headmen, bought Northbrook Estate for $10,000; this was subsequently subdivided. A few years later, four headmen purchased Den Amstel estate on behalf of seventy field workers. Villages were also established in some of the smaller colonies: in Antigua, by 1842, there were twenty-seven independent villages containing over 1,000 homes and 3,600 people.

The establishment of free villages and the withdrawal of labour generally from the estates meant that planters looked abroad for a new supply of labour. The most fruitful source of that labour proved to be India, and the number of Indian immigrants was significant. Nearly 250,000 went to British Guiana, almost 150,000 to Trinidad, and over 36,000 to Jamaica. From the point of view of providing labourers, India had significant advantages: it was largely British, and it had millions of people often close to starvation, who could be attracted to work outside of India. It is important to recall that there was a global diaspora of Indians in the nineteenth century, who travelled not only to the Caribbean but also to other parts of the world, including South-East Asia, East Africa, South Africa and Mauritius.

The Indians came to the Caribbean as indentured labourers; in general, they agreed to a five-year indenture. This meant that during that time, they could not leave their employer or refuse to do the work they were assigned. Indentured labourers were paid at appallingly low rates: the minimum wage in Trinidad after 1872 was just twenty-five cents a day (a little over one shilling), and many employers did not even provide that amount. After their five-year indenture was over, Indian labourers could choose other employers but were not entitled to a free passage back to India until they had worked for ten years in the colony.

The nature of the indenture was harsh, and the punishments were severe. Employers could prosecute indentured labourers for a variety of offences and even minor infractions of the rules, such as using threatening language or carelessness at work, could lead to a jail sentence. The result, as Bridget Brereton has suggested, was that the planters had 'a core group of resident, unfree labourers whose work was completely dependable'.[15] But there was also the problem of the gender disparity among indentured labourers. Since there was a scarcity of indentured women on the plantations, this often led to violence, especially towards women. As Gaiutra Bahadur has pointed out, one of the significant problems of the indenture system was the despair of many newly arrived indentured men resulting in attacks on women as well as in suicides.[16]

In addition, because indentured labourers had to do the least attractive jobs on the sugar plantations, freed blacks looked down on them. As a result, the host societies in the Caribbean, both white and black, developed a series of negative stereotypes of the Indians. Yet although they formed a largely separate group from the rest of the population, at least during the nineteenth century, the overwhelming majority of Indians chose to remain in the Caribbean. Once their indenture was over, they formed the basis of an Indian peasantry which helped to diversify the region's economy by producing rice and other food crops.

Immigration was also significant in Martinique and Guadeloupe, where, as in the British Caribbean, it was used to force down the wages of the ex-slaves. In Cuba, the immigrants after emancipation were largely Spanish: there were roughly 60,000 Spaniards who came to Cuba between 1889 and 1894. Whatever their origin, however, immigrants had a significant effect in maintaining sugar production in the Caribbean and also in keeping wages low. But in the post-emancipation period, ex-slaves would seek to resist these low wages as well as their continued exploitation.

# CHAPTER ELEVEN

# Riots and resistance in the aftermath of emancipation

The post-emancipation Caribbean experienced a large number of riots and other disturbances. Frequently violent, these outbreaks occurred across the region and often recurred in individual colonies. They were evidence that ex-slaves did not passively accept the terms of their freedom or their conditions in the aftermath of emancipation. The protests also made it clear that ex-slaves' hopes for freedom had often not been realized. Instead of controlling their own labour and gaining access to land, ex-slaves struggled against low wages, high rents for their lands and houses and even a fear that they might be re-enslaved.

One of the most significant of the post-emancipation outbreaks, the 'Guerre Negre', took place in Dominica in 1844. There, freed men and women protested violently against the taking of a census in 1844. Initially, enumerators were assaulted, but the protest developed into attacks on estate property and managers. In restoring order, the militia killed four people and arrested 300.

The ex-slaves of Dominica were motivated by a fear of re-enslavement. For many freed people on the island, this was the explanation for the enumerators taking down their names. While some Dominicans regarded re-enslavement as implausible, others, such as a freedman named Saint Louis, argued that it could happen:

> I think that our freedom can be taken away from us, because it was once done in another country near to us; it was the French

who gave their people free, and afterwards made them slaves again; my parents told me so when I was quite a child, and I have remembered it ever since; what is done once can be done again, and we all know that liberty is good; I don't know but what the English will do like the French one of these days; it is only for the Queen to send a Gazette, and say 'make them slaves again,' and they will be all made slaves; if a man pays money, and does not get a receipt, he can be made to pay the money again; so it is with freedom; if we have been made free and have not paper to show for it, we can be made slaves again.[1]

Freed people in Jamaica shared these concerns. Rumours of re-enslavement helped to spark several conspiracies and disturbances which broke out in 1848. In the case of Jamaica, the threat of re-enslavement was often associated with the possibility of Jamaica joining the United States as a slave state. During the riots in 1848, the ex-slaves regarded 1 August as the day the whites would choose to re-enslave the blacks. The date was particularly significant, as the tenth anniversary of full freedom. In addition, the planters were experiencing a severe economic crisis; as a consequence, they sought to reduce wages on the estates, often by as much as 25 per cent. However, many ex-slaves regarded this loss of wages as a first step towards the reintroduction of slavery.

A decade later, in 1859, two serious riots again broke out in Jamaica. The first, in February, was directed against the toll-gates in several parts of Westmoreland. Residents tore down the toll-gates in at least four different places in the parish, suggesting a concerted campaign against them. Public feeling against the tolls had been vented in a petition sent to the governor six months earlier, but he had ignored it. When some of the offenders were tried for their part in the toll-gate assault, people attacked the police station. Peace was ultimately restored when troops arrived from Port Royal.

The second major riot in 1859 originated in a property dispute at Florence Hall Estate near the town of Falmouth. The controversy was between a coloured man, Theodore Buie, and his Scottish aunt who sought to evict him from the property. Buie and about sixty others were arrested, but before they could be brought to trial, a large crowd attacked the police station and freed them. As the crowd stoned the police station, the police fired on the crowd. They killed two women and severely wounded eight or nine others, one of whom died a few days later. In the process, the crowd set fire to the police station and prevented anyone from extinguishing it. They also sought to burn down other parts of the town and succeeded in destroying the Falmouth wharf. Jamaica thus experienced a significant number of outbreaks in the post-emancipation period.

Three years later, in 1862, a labour strike in St. Vincent became a riot: freed people assaulted estate managers and plundered planters' houses and shops over a considerable area. The authorities killed four people and wounded at least seven others in putting down the riot; many other people were sentenced to terms of imprisonment and flogged for their part in the outbreak. Labourers in St. Vincent were particularly incensed at the withdrawal of their allowances of sugar and rum in 1862, which formed part of their remuneration. Although these allowances were not protected by law, the workers considered them sanctified by custom. The 'vox populi' statement of the labourers on Mt. Bentinck estate made their grievances quite clear:

> We, the inhabitants of Mount Bentinck estate, have been monthly employed to work on the above estate, some at $4, others at $3, etc., along with our privileges (viz) our sugar, rum and provision grounds, *and we never received any notice that these were to be stopped, until when we came to receive them we found that the sugar and rum were stopped; we were all annoyed about it. ... We then said that at the expiration of the month, we must make other arrangements, during which time they went to the mountains and took away our provision grounds that we have worked in our time, without giving us notice to take out our provision; they have taken it out; and both manager and overseer are feeding upon labour; the month is up, and they will not pay us our money, and we will not work.*

As Woodville Marshall has pointed out, the labourers on Mt. Bentinck estate considered their allowances as a 'right'. This was not only because of tradition; the molasses allowance formed part of the workers' wages and was important in itself or could be exchanged for cash or provisions. When the allowance was withheld, the labourers considered it a hardship. Marshall concluded that the workers faced wage reductions of at least 25 per cent during 1862. Moreover, labourers on the island faced a form of debt peonage, since planters ran estate shops and the amount owed to the shop was generally deducted from the workers' wages. Disputes could easily arise but 'labourers were ever on the losing end because the shopkeeper was often the pay-master'. Lack of payment of wages did not make these problems any easier.[2]

Similar problems about wages also help to explain an outbreak in Tobago in April 1876. It occurred on Roxborough estate, which was owned by a Barbadian who employed many Barbadian workers, some of whom were apparently involved in arson attacks on the estate. When a party of policemen were sent to arrest the alleged arsonists, a crowd resisted the police. One of the policemen, Corporal Belmanna, fired into the crowd, killing a Barbadian woman and injuring a Barbadian man. The incident triggered a major riot; the police retreated to the estate's court house which the crowd surrounded and attacked. They demanded that Belmanna be handed over to them; instead, he eventually agreed to leave the court house as a prisoner and to be tried later in court for murder. However, the crowd managed to pry him away from his escort and beat him severely. Belmanna subsequently died from his injuries.

Workers were incensed at the continuing low wages on the island. Rates of pay after emancipation remained low, averaging ten pence a day for resident labourers and one shilling for those not living on the estate. Indeed, efforts to reduce these rates of pay in 1847–48 had led to strikes and emigration to Trinidad. An additional irritant for workers was a pattern of irregular payment and arbitrary stoppages of pay. As in St. Vincent, workers also faced a system of wage deduction to pay for debts contracted at estate shops, a further grievance among estate workers in Tobago.[3]

Low wages were also an element in the serious riots which developed in Barbados in 1876. The question was whether Barbados would be joined politically in a federation with the Windward colonies; however, the Barbadian planter class was strongly opposed to this plan. Confederation would have resulted in Barbados becoming a Crown Colony and losing its House of Assembly and representative form of government which it had possessed since the seventeenth century. For the planters, this would have meant a loss of power. Workers, on the other hand, saw distinct advantages in such a change: for example, they believed that wages would be raised under the proposed scheme. Initially, there was a riot in which blacks sought to break up a meeting of those opposed to federation, which led to stone throwing and some pistol shots. Subsequently, more threatening riots developed, in which freed people plundered estates and, especially, the estates' provision grounds. The riots were suppressed, and eight of the rioters were killed. Although the confederation issue had sparked the riots, traditional concerns about low and irregular wages were crucial. Moreover, the attack on the estates' provision grounds suggested that the rioters were lacking food and were ultimately seeking a living wage.

Similar issues helped to spark an agricultural labourers' revolt in St. Croix two years later. It broke out on 1 October, the day that the workers' yearly contracts began. Because of the nature of the annual contract, workers could be forced to work for an estate against their wishes. October 1 was therefore an emotive day for labourers in St. Croix, made worse by rumours that emigration for work elsewhere was being blocked. Moreover, wages actually fell below what was stipulated in the labour ordinance and were significantly lower than wages at the central factory which was opened in early 1878. Workers in St. Croix were also unhappy about the power of managers to levy monetary fines for particular offences, especially since the fines formed part of the managers' income.

A serious riot developed in the town of Frederiksted in which shops were ransacked and the customs house and homes of the city's most prominent citizens were set alight. The rioters then attacked the plantations, causing enormous damage to the sugar mills, the great houses and the crops. During the outbreak, the loss of life was high: official figures put the number of blacks killed at eighty-four while the unofficial total was closer to 250. By contrast, three whites lost their lives.[4]

Women were among the leaders of this outbreak. Mary Thomas was one of them: she was known as 'Queen Mary' and called herself Captain. Another woman in the revolt, Axelline Salomon, was referred to as 'the black Amazon'. Moreover, St. Croix was not unique; women were also involved in other protests across the region. In the 'Guerre Negre' in Dominica, a crowd of women abused one of the local enumerators seeking to carry out the census. Elsewhere on the outskirts of the principal town, Roseau, women harassed enumerators. In the Tobago riots, women were among the most prominent of those brutally attacking Corporal Belmanna.

Women also played an important role in riots that broke out in Antigua in March 1858. These riots grew out of a confrontation

between dockworkers from Antigua and Barbuda. Antiguan dockworkers regarded the Barbudans as their economic competitors,
taking their jobs at a time of severe economic stagnation. Hundreds
of Antiguans in the capital of the island, St. John's, joined the riots:
they attacked Portuguese Madeirans who had been imported to
work in the sugar plantations after emancipation as well as white
planters and black and mixed-race policemen.

Black women were very involved in the riots. As Natasha Lightfoot
has observed, 'women allegedly led angered crowds about the
streets, brandished weapons, attacked their designated antagonists,
and appeared in their comportment and dress to be "like men"'.[5]
Antiguan women attacked Barbudan women and destroyed some
of their homes because the Antiguans were concerned about the
economic competition of the Barbudans in the markets and in
jobs as domestics. Like the men, the women also threw stones in
attacking the police station in an unsuccessful attempt to seize the
arms stored at the station. For Lightfoot, then, the women were not
bystanders in the Antiguan riots but essential to its spread. They
also paid a heavy price for their participation in the riots: women
were among the eight people killed in the riots and more than fifty
women were arrested during the riots. Moreover, the description of
women acting 'like men' was not unique to Antigua: this symbolic
masculinization of women was part of the gendered discourse of
slavery and the post-emancipation period.[6]

There were also common grievances in many of these post-
emancipation riots. One was the problem of low pay, made worse by
patterns of irregular payments and arbitrary work stoppages. When
linked to the truck system, in which estates had their own shops and
created a type of debt peonage among their workers, these practices
produced severe tensions. Another serious grievance centred around
the fear of re-enslavement; this was the motivating force behind the
Dominica riots and was a factor in several others. In addition, the
ex-slaves' desire for land was often an element in these disturbances.

Several of these factors were prominent in the Morant Bay
Rebellion in Jamaica, the most important post-emancipation
outbreak during this period. On 11 October 1865, several hundred
blacks marched into the town of Morant Bay, the principal town
in the sugar parish of St Thomas in the East. Led by Paul Bogle, a
native Baptist deacon, the crowd attacked the police station before
confronting the militia and the parish authorities. Firing erupted. In

**FIGURE 11.1** *Attack on the Court House, St. Thomas-in-the-East, Jamaica, during the Morant Bay Rebellion.*
*Source:* © Culture Club/Getty Images.

the subsequent mêlée, the crowd killed eighteen people. Over the next few days, local people killed two planters and attacked many plantations in the parish.

As in several other post-emancipation disturbances, women played a prominent role. At Morant Bay, the officials and the militia confronted a stone-throwing crowd in front of the court house. As the custos of the parish attempted to read the Riot Act, a member of the militia observed a woman he knew named Letitia Geoghegan throwing the first stone, followed by a hail of stones from other women in the crowd. The militia and the parish officials retreated into the court house, and eventually the crowd decided that the best method of attack was to burn the building down and force the volunteers and vestrymen to come out. It is likely that women were responsible for this plan. One witness claimed that a woman named Rosanna Finlayson 'said they must go and get a fire stick and trash, and set the school-room on fire. She said the white people were locked up in the court house, and if they set fire to the school room the whole people would be burnt up alive'. Five minutes later, the school house was on fire. It was adjacent to the court house and it was not long before that building began to burn as well.

The women in the crowd also encouraged the men to continue their attack on the court house. After the volunteers had fired at the crowd, some of the men had withdrawn. But women on one of the roads leading into the town reportedly told the men:

> Now, you men, this is not what you said in the mountain. You said you would come to the Bay and do so and so, and now you leave all this work to the women; go to the Parade and see what the Volunteers do to the men there.[7]

At Morant Bay, men and women were clearly responding to specific tensions in the parish of St. Thomas in the East. At the same time, many of the local problems were symptomatic of difficulties across Jamaica in the aftermath of emancipation. The common people were bitter about the continued political, social and economic domination of the whites. Among other things, this meant a lopsided and partial judicial structure. Since the magistracy was dominated by planters, many freed people believed that it was impossible to obtain justice in the local courts. Too often, the employers were judging the cases of their employees. High court fees also made it very difficult for labourers and small settlers to pursue cases in court. One of the grievances of the crowd at Morant Bay and in the rebellion generally was the lack of justice in the parish. For example, when asked the reason for the rebellion the day after the events at Morant Bay, one of the rioters at Bath claimed it had broken out 'because the poor black had no justice in St. Thomas in the East ... there was no other way to get satisfaction in St. Thomas in the East, only what they had done'.[8]

For the blacks in Jamaica, there was at least another alternative that some of them had tried. In several parts of St. Thomas in the East, blacks had organized their own courts. These people's courts were held in districts not far from Morant Bay, and offences were punished by fines and by flogging. Such alternative courts seem to have existed in other parts of the island as well and were further evidence of the dissatisfaction of the people with the administration of justice.

Another problem centred around land: the people believed that their provision grounds belonged to them and that they should not have to pay rent for those lands. It is likely that Augustus Hire, one of the planters killed in the days following the outbreak at Morant Bay, was a target of the crowd because of his stance on this issue. Hire was the planting attorney for Amity Hall estate. Acting for the owners of Amity Hall, Hire had authorized a survey on land near the estate known as Rowland's Field. Hire had been unable to collect rent from people he believed were squatting on this land. When the surveyor and Hire began work in July 1865, they were surrounded by an armed crowd of over a hundred blacks. The crowd seized the surveyor's chain, broke it, and became 'very violent'. Despite having the ringleaders arrested, Hire and his surveyor met considerable resistance when they tried again the following day. Hire recalled the precise words of one man, Henry Doyley, who grabbed the surveyor's chain. When Hire asked him what right he had to the land, Doyley responded, 'What God Almighty make land for? You have plenty; we have none'. The surveyor also reported that the crowd told him that 'if we wanted war, we should have war'. Hire's recourse was to bring the people involved in the scuffle before the Circuit Court; the case was scheduled to take place the week after Hire's murder.[9]

The government's response to the rebellion was swift and brutal. The governor, Edward John Eyre, declared martial law in the eastern part of Jamaica; he also despatched British troops to the parish as well as organizing the Maroons to deal with the outbreak. The month-long period of martial law resulted in the deaths of over 400 blacks. Because of the severity of the repression, the case became a *cause célèbre* in England. John Stuart Mill was among a group of radicals and nonconformists who organized a campaign to try the governor for his part in the suppression of the rebellion. In response, Thomas Carlyle, Charles Kingsley and Charles Dickens helped to establish an Eyre Defence Committee. Although Eyre was never committed for trial, the controversy surrounding his case raised important issues about the nature of colonial rule and governmental accountability.

In Jamaica, Governor Eyre made use of the rebellion to push for constitutional change. Since the Colonial Office had wanted for some time to abolish the House of Assembly, Eyre convinced a frightened House that they should opt for Crown Colony government. Although there was some opposition to this change, the legislators ultimately accepted it. This meant classic Crown Colony government, with a nominated council, consisting of six officials and three unofficial members and the abolition of the 200-year-old House of Assembly. Apart from Barbados, the other legislative colonies in the West Indies followed suit, although it took nearly a decade for colonies such as Grenada and Tobago to make the change. By the mid-1870s, and with the continuing exception of Barbados, Crown Colony government was fully established in the British West Indies.

Elsewhere in the Caribbean, there were different patterns of resistance in the aftermath of emancipation. In Martinique and Guadeloupe, the conditions for freed people were different than in the British Caribbean, in part because of the rapid onset of emancipation in 1848. The 1848 revolution in France brought into power Victor Schoelcher, the leader of the anti-slavery movement in France. Schoelcher became the Under-Secretary of State for the colonies in the provisional French government, and one of the first acts of the new government was to declare its intent to abolish slavery. In fact, news of the revolution led to a slave revolt in Martinique in May 1848, forcing the local authorities in the colonies to abolish slavery before the official decree arrived from France.

As a result, the planters of Martinique and Guadeloupe found themselves in economic difficulties, especially faced with the immediate need to bring in the sugar harvest in 1848. They therefore turned to sharecropping schemes to deal with the problem. Under these arrangements, freed workers received a portion of the proceeds of the sale of the crop in return for their labour. In essence, this was a means to harvest the crop without paying wages, since the workers usually received between a third and a half of the proceeds of the crop once it had been harvested.

Though there was a significant decline in the number of workers after emancipation in the French Caribbean, there was generally less overt resistance in Martinique and Guadeloupe than in the British Caribbean. In the French Caribbean, workers were concerned about continuing to occupy their houses and grounds. Moreover, they were opposed to direct supervision of their labour and to working regular hours. The resistance in Martinique and Guadeloupe therefore centred on workers seeking to control part of their time; for example, they often did not work on Fridays.

They also sought to maintain their provision grounds and to market their crops as well as continuing related activities such as fishing, charcoal burning and handicraft production. When the government subsequently imposed a pass system designed to force freed people to accept contractual labour, workers resisted accepting the passes and even threatened to kill the mayor of a district in Guadeloupe. The response of the French authorities in the wake of this resistance was to bring in more repressive labour codes.[10]

There was one major outbreak in Martinique in September 1870: the Insurrection of the South. It occurred immediately after the proclamation of the Third Republic. According to David Howard and Christine Chivallon, the 'timing is significant, since it indicates that those leading the revolt recognised that the ideals of the Republic, and the rights of all citizens, were incompatible with the maintenance of racialized inequality and "white man's injustice"'.[11] The immediate spark of the revolt was the sentencing in August of a young black man to five years in prison for hitting a white man who had humiliated him. The revolt itself involved between 300 and 600 rebels and, in ways that are reminiscent of the Morant Bay Rebellion, the rebels sought to uphold the ideals of the Republic while condemning the local plantocracy. Like Morant Bay, the Insurrection of the South was put down violently: eighteen people were killed and 500 men and women were brought to trial and imprisoned.

In Cuba, the end of slavery in 1886 did not bring an end to the racial divisions which had characterized the island during slavery, and Afro-Cubans continued to face discrimination in the aftermath of emancipation. In education, for example, blacks often had difficulties gaining access even to primary schools, and most secondary schools would not admit blacks. There was segregation in many public places, including theatres, and restrictions in the type of jobs blacks could hold.

Despite these practices, blacks eagerly supported the War of Liberation against the Spanish from 1895 to 1898. This was in part because of the leading role of the mulatto general, Antonio Maceo, but also as a response to José Martí's progressive ideology. Yet in spite of their importance in the war, blacks continued to be marginalized, especially once the Americans intervened. The Americans generally denigrated Afro-Cubans, portraying them in starkly negative terms. Cuba's first independent government in 1902 continued this pattern: it promoted the whitening of the country through immigration from Spain and sought to suppress African-based religions, such as *Santería*.

Afro-Cubans protested against this ideology of white supremacy and ultimately organized a black political party, the *Partido Independiente de Color*. While the party emphasized black pride, it sought to improve the condition of Afro-Cubans and did not advocate black separatism. The party called for full equality for Afro-Cubans, jobs for blacks in the public service and social reforms. Women of colour supported the party and established women's auxiliaries that helped to raise funds for the organization.[12] However, in 1910, the Cuban government banned the party on the grounds that it only represented the interests of blacks and therefore violated the Cuban Constitution. The government imprisoned some members of the party and also helped to spread rumours that party members were planning a national uprising.

The response of the *Partido Independiente de Color* was an armed protest in 1912 to relegalize the party. The actual threats of party members were minimal and the only serious protests took place in Oriente province in the east. However, the Cuban government interpreted the protests as a race war and as a threat to take over the country as a whole. It unleashed a wave of terror by the Cuban army against blacks, leading to massacres, atrocities and summary executions. Thousands of blacks were killed, with some estimates putting the number as high as 5,000 dead.

The historian, Aline Helg, has compared the 1912 massacre of blacks to the suppression of the Morant Bay Rebellion in Jamaica. Helg's view is that, in both cases, the governments 'decided to resort to violence because blacks seriously challenged the white-dominated social structure'.[13] In Cuba, it was not so much a problem of access to land, as was the case in Morant Bay; instead, Afro-Cubans were seeking a proportional share of jobs in the public service. In addition, their party posed an electoral threat to white power in the island. But the 1912 massacres in Cuba did not just kill the leadership of the *Partido Independiente de Color*; like the suppression of the Morant Bay Rebellion, it was aimed at terrifying the black population and making sure that it would not pose a threat to the ruling structure.

Across the Caribbean, then, freed people resisted the qualified nature of emancipation. The causes and patterns of resistance differed throughout the region, but the protests, riots and rebellions in the aftermath of emancipation revealed the people's discontent with the terms of their freedom. Subsequent movements, often reflecting an identification with Africa, would be another expression of opposition to the dominant power structure.

# CHAPTER TWELVE

# Black cultural nationalism in the Caribbean

In the late nineteenth-century Caribbean, there was a significant reaction to the continuing negative representations of blacks. Blacks had been portrayed in derogatory terms since Europeans first visited Africa and, subsequently, as a justification for the Atlantic slave trade. In the nineteenth century, however, European attitudes towards blacks hardened, partly as a consequence of the abolition of slavery. One strand of this thinking was reflected in the work of Thomas Carlyle, whose famous essay, 'Discourse on the Nigger Question', described blacks as an inferior race and emancipation as the ruin of the West Indies. The Morant Bay Rebellion in Jamaica helped to strengthen these views, and the emergence of Social Darwinian ideas reinforced this belief in white domination as well as the subordination of blacks. But not all blacks accepted these notions. A Trinidadian, J. J. Thomas, in a book entitled *Froudacity* published in 1889, called for united action to uplift blacks and for a recognition of the links between the New World and Africa. Although some middle-class blacks in Trinidad undoubtedly rejected their racial heritage, a significant number were strong proponents of race consciousness.[1]

In Jamaica, such views were reflected in a black colonizing scheme. In 1899, Dr Albert Thorne, a Barbadian living in Jamaica, held a meeting in which he proposed to settle West Indian settlers in Africa, with the intention of improving the status of Africans. Thorne had some influence on Marcus Garvey, a black Jamaican whose ideas about black capability and self-worth would be highly popular just after the First World War. It is important, therefore, to see that many of Garvey's ideas emerged out of the black intellectual milieu of the late nineteenth century.[2]

Another individual who prefigured Garvey was Robert Love, a Bahamian who lived in Jamaica from 1890 until his death in 1914. His biographer, Joy Lumsden, regards him as the outstanding black man in Jamaica at the end of the nineteenth century. According to Lumsden, Love had a vision of the future for blacks in the West Indies and also sought to highlight black accomplishments in the past. He lectured on topics such as the life of Toussaint Louverture and also established a weekly newspaper for the blacks in the island, the *Jamaica Advocate*. In addition, Love supported black candidates for seats on the Legislative Council and was himself elected to the Council in the early twentieth century.[3] Rupert Lewis, one of the leading scholars on Marcus Garvey, described Love as 'the most prominent radical figure in Jamaican politics at the turn of the century'.[4] Moreover, Garvey undoubtedly heard Love lecture and also read his newspaper.

Garvey, then, did not emerge in an intellectual vacuum. He was born in 1887 in the parish of St. Ann. His father was a stone mason and a 'village lawyer', acting informally for the people around him. His mother came from a family of small farmers; she was a petty trader, cook and housekeeper. The family suffered from the economic depression of the late nineteenth century and lost much of its land in the decade of the 1890s.

Garvey himself became a printer's apprentice, working first in St. Ann and then in Kingston. He was also involved in early union activity and published a short-lived newspaper. Like many other West Indians during this period, Garvey left Jamaica in 1910 for Central America, first travelling to Costa Rica where his uncle helped him find work as a time-keeper for the United Fruit Company. He also travelled to Panama, where he contributed to the local press and was outraged by the conditions of migrant workers. He returned to Jamaica but left for England in 1912. While in England, Garvey became associated with Duse Mohammed Ali, an Egyptian nationalist and journalist who published a journal, the *African Times and Orient Review*.

On his return from England in 1914, Garvey established the United Negro Improvement Association (UNIA), an organization dedicated to affirming race pride and racial solidarity among blacks.

**FIGURE 12.1** *Marcus Garvey.*
*Source:* © Bettmann/CORBIS.

Garvey's cofounder was his future wife, Amy Ashwood, a Jamaican who was raised in Panama but had returned to Jamaica. The aims of the UNIA included the following:

> To establish a Universal Confraternity among the race; to promote the spirit of pride and love; to reclaim the fallen; to administer to and assist the needy; to assist in civilizing the backward tribes of Africa … to establish a central nation for the race.[5]

This proved to be an opportune time to establish such an organization. Blacks would soon be radicalized by their involvement in the First World War, although less so in Jamaica and the Caribbean than in the United States.

Two years later and having failed to gain much support in Jamaica for the UNIA, Garvey travelled to the United States. His hope was to learn more about Booker T. Washington's Tuskegee Institute in Alabama, a school designed to improve the material and educational condition of blacks in the United States. Garvey also was intent on enlisting support in the United States for a Jamaican version of Tuskegee. However, Booker T. Washington died before Garvey reached the United States, and Garvey instead became converted to the idea of pursuing more direct political goals. Garvey was to remain in the United States until 1927.

Garvey's movement flourished in the United States. He became a leading black nationalist, who combined a belief in race pride with plans to exploit his ideas commercially. Accordingly, Garvey established the Black Star Line, a shipping company which was part of a programme of return to Africa. As with other companies Garvey established, he sold shares in the company; indeed, he was to sell over 150,000 shares of stock in the company. He published a leading black newspaper, the *Negro World*, held huge UNIA conventions in the United States and saw the organization swell to over 1,000 divisions, many of which were in the Caribbean and in Africa.

Yet some of his ideas were contradictory. Garvey proclaimed that Africa should be for Africans and should be developed as a homeland to which blacks elsewhere could return. At the same time, he also established relations with the Ku Klux Klan and other white supremacist organizations in the United States. Seen as a threat by the authorities, he was found guilty of mail fraud over shares in the Black Star Line and sent to jail in 1925. While Garvey was in jail, his second wife, Amy Jacques Garvey, helped to raise funds for his legal defence. When Garvey's sentence was commuted two years later, he and his wife returned to Jamaica in December 1927.

Garvey was met with enthusiastic crowds on his arrival in Jamaica. Despite his time in prison, he had become an internationally recognized figure, a symbol of the new black consciousness of the 1920s. Yet, by the end of the 1920s, Garvey faced serious problems. Garvey's influence in the United States had waned, the various UNIA business enterprises had collapsed and the UNIA was split by divisions and factional splits. In Jamaica, he would encounter considerable difficulties in attempting to stem the decline of the UNIA and also in pursuing a political career on the island.

Apart from moving the headquarters of the UNIA to Kingston, Garvey also established a new political party in Jamaica, the

People's Political Party. It not only supported local candidates for office in the island but also was the basis for his attempt to gain a seat on the Jamaica Legislative Council in the 1930 elections. The PPP's platform was reformist: it called for improvements in public health, public housing, more educational opportunities and legal reforms. One of Garvey's criticisms was directed at the Jamaican legal system and its justices, whom he accused of corruption. As a result, the Jamaica Supreme Court charged him with contempt of court, and he was found guilty and jailed for three months.

Despite his time in prison, Garvey was elected to the local municipal council in Kingston. However, he was less successful in gaining a seat on the island's Legislative Council; in an election where the number of voters was restricted by a high property requirement, Garvey had little chance against his opponent, a wealthy white politician and landowner. At this point, the Jamaican electorate included women who had been given the vote in 1919. But only elite women who were at least twenty-five years of age and owned property worth £2 could vote. As Dalea Bean suggests, granting elite women the vote was 'a strategy to undermine the burgeoning Pan-African and feminist civic aspirations'.[6] In the case of Garvey, this strategy clearly worked.

In addition to his running for office, Garvey had also begun publishing a newspaper in Jamaica in 1929, the *Blackman*, which he hoped would rival that of the leading newspaper on the island, the *Daily Gleaner*. But the *Blackman* foundered in 1932, as did an evening newspaper he established the same year. By 1935, he had lost his family home, his printing machinery and the UNIA headquarters' building to creditors. Having made no progress politically in Jamaica and bankrupt financially, Garvey moved to London.

His remaining years until his death in 1940 were difficult. He was isolated from his former supporters, and his views became more conservative and less in tune with the Pan-African movement. For example, Garvey was highly critical of Haile Selassie's performance during the Italo-Ethiopian War and its aftermath, at a time when Selassie had become a significant black figure in the West. He also underestimated the importance of the labour rebellions in the West Indies in the late 1930s and was unable to recognize their long-term significance. Garvey died in 1940 of a cerebral haemorrhage, largely forgotten politically.

But Garvey's reputation enjoyed a renaissance in the period after the Second World War. He became a cultural icon for the Rastafarians in Jamaica and for the Black Power Movement in the United States. As Robert A. Hill has suggested, he was 'again lauded as a visionary of African freedom and a symbol of Pan-African unity and strength'.[7] In 1964, Garvey was declared a National Hero in Jamaica, and his body was flown home to be reinterred in a permanent Marcus Garvey memorial in Kingston. Yet Garvey and the UNIA were only part of a revaluation of ideas about Africa; Garvey's political activity needs to be situated alongside other movements – especially, the Rastafarians – which also aimed to overturn the white value structure.

In November 1930, Ras Tafari was crowned emperor of Ethiopia in St. George's Cathedral in Addis Ababa. He took the name Haile Selassie and added to it the biblical appellations of 'King of Kings' and the 'Lion of the Tribe of Judah'. The coronation was covered by representatives of the world's press and, although not present at the ceremony, Marcus Garvey welcomed the coronation as a symbol of black pride. Others in Jamaica regarded it much more seriously, seeing it as the fulfilment of a biblical prophecy and Selassie as their Messiah.

Four men in Jamaica, Leonard Howell, Joseph Hibbert, Archibald Dunkley and Robert Hinds, were the first to preach the ideas of Rastafarianism. The most important of these was Howell, a former Garveyite who established a ministry in the slums of west Kingston. Born in 1898, Howell, like many Jamaicans, had lived in Panama where he worked for the US Army Transport Service as a cook. He went to New York in 1918, possibly coming under the influence there of the Trinidadian black nationalist, George Padmore. Howell returned to Jamaica in 1932, in the midst of the economic depression of the 1930s.

Joseph Hibbert had also lived in Central America before returning to Jamaica; he began preaching in St. Andrew but also moved to Kingston. The third member of the group, Archibald Dunkley, was a seaman who worked for the United Fruit Company and started his mission in Port Antonio and later moved to Kingston. The most successful of these early preachers was Robert Hinds another Garveyite who led an organization in Kingston of over 800 members. All of these preachers proclaimed the divinity of Haile Selassie, although the group adopted Selassie's former name, Ras Tafari. Moreover, they were preaching at a difficult time economically and politically for Jamaica; their ideas of a future millennium controlled by blacks offered hope to some of the more marginalized sectors of Jamaican society.

Early in 1933, Howell moved his operations to the parish of St. Thomas, an area of Jamaica known for its radical history and which proved to be receptive to the Rastafarians. However, it was here that Howell and Hinds ran into difficulties with the authorities. Seen as subversive, Howell and Hinds were arrested and imprisoned. At the time, Howell was advocating a platform which included hatred of the whites and the superiority of the blacks, preparation for a return to Africa, and the divinity of Selassie who was the only ruler of the blacks.

Following his release from prison, Howell returned to Kingston, where he and his followers survived by making and selling bread. Faced with harassment by the police, Howell decided to establish a community in the countryside, along the model of the Maroons. Known as Pinnacle and located in St. Catherine, the community lasted until 1954. The community maintained itself by selling ganja (marijuana), and it was here as well that self-sufficiency became the ideal for the Rastafarians. But Pinnacle suffered several raids by the police, and Howell and many of his followers were arrested and sent to prison during this period. In 1954, the police finally destroyed Pinnacle. Howell, who had begun to claim divinity himself, was eventually committed to the Kingston Mental Hospital.[8]

However, the other leaders, Hinds, Hibbert and Dunkley, continued their missions in the slums of west Kingston, which again became the main area for the Rastafarians. Many of the Rastafarians had begun to wear their hair in dreadlocks and were characterized by wild behaviour and by their defiance of the authorities. The Rastas increasingly called for repatriation to Africa, especially after Haile Selassie granted blacks of the New World 500 acres of land in Ethiopia. Moreover, by the late 1950s, the Rastas found themselves in direct conflict with the Jamaican state, largely due to the actions of Rev. Claudius Henry.

Henry had a long history of difficulties with the Jamaican government. In 1929, he was arrested for attacking the Anglican Church as an agent of British colonialism. Judged insane, Henry also had a number of religious visions before migrating to the United States during the Second World War. He returned to Jamaica in 1957, with pictures of a black Jesus and calling himself variously 'God's Approved Prophet and Israel's Leader' and 'Another Moses leading Israel's Scattered Slaves Back Home to Motherland Africa'. Settling in Kingston, Henry attracted about 200 followers and lived in a commune. In March 1959, he distributed thousands of cards promising a return to Africa later that year on 5 October. At least 500 potential emigrants turned up at Henry's residence ready for the journey, many of whom had sold their houses and lands. Henry was arrested and fined and, subsequently, the police searched his headquarters where they found a cache of dynamite and weapons and incriminating evidence of Henry's intention to undermine the government.

Rev. Henry was sentenced to ten years in prison, but worse was yet to come for the authorities. Claudius Henry's son, Ronald, was reported to be in the hills above Kingston, allegedly training a guerrilla band of Rastafarians. Ronald Henry had already killed two of his followers, apparently for disobedience, and in a confrontation with the army, shot two British soldiers. He and four of his followers were eventually caught and sentenced to death. As Richard Burton has aptly described the feeling at the time, 'the association between Rastafarianism, subversion, and savagery was complete'.[9]

However, the Jamaican government, seeking to calm the situation, commissioned a report on the Rastafarians by three academics from the University of the West Indies. Written by M. G. Smith, Roy Augier and Rex Nettleford, the report adopted a sympathetic approach to the Rastas. Among other recommendations, it suggested a mission to investigate possible immigration to Africa, with representatives of the Rastafarians included in the mission. The report also attempted to counter the negative stereotype of the Rastas, by pointing out that the majority of the group were peaceful. Responding positively to the report, the Jamaican government sought to implement its recommendations. Partly as a result, the history of the Rastafarians after 1960 proved to be much less confrontational than it had been previously.[10]

One significant change for the Rastafarians was a gradual shift in their idea about repatriation to Africa. This was no longer on the agenda as it had been in the early history of the Rastas; instead of physically transplanting themselves, some Rastas sought to transform Jamaica more in their image. One example of this was

Sam Brown, a Rastafarian who ran for office in west Kingston in the 1961 election under the banner of the Black Man's Party. Although this was contrary to Rastafarian beliefs, Brown's political platform signalled an emphasis on changing Jamaica rather than seeking repatriation. This was reinforced by the visit of Haile Selassie to Jamaica in 1966; during the visit, Selassie made clear his view that it was important for the Rastafarians to liberate Jamaica before seeking to emigrate to Africa.

The Rastafarians have also had a significant impact on Jamaican cultural life. From the 1960s onwards, their music, language and art have become part of Jamaican life. This is largely explained by the success of various forms of Jamaican popular music, especially reggae. Bob Marley was the leading figure in this movement, whose Rastafarian-reggae lyrics helped to popularize the Rastas far beyond the Caribbean. In addition, the distinctive language and lifestyle of the Rastafarians have also been diffused more widely in Jamaican society. As Richard Burton has argued, Jamaica has itself become partly Rastafarianized.[11]

Movements emphasizing race pride were also characteristic of other parts of the Caribbean. In the French Caribbean, the poet and politician, Aimé Césaire, coined the term *Négritude*, which he first used in his 1939 poem, *Cahier d'un Retour au Pays Natal* (*Notebook of a Return to My Native Land*). Like Garvey and the Rastafarians, Césaire was intent on affirming a strong belief in African culture. He was also using the concept to reject the assimilationist policy of the French government towards its former colonies. Ironically, Césaire developed the term in Paris, along with two other black intellectuals, Léon Damas from French Guiana and Léopold Senghor, the future president of Senegal. Césaire himself was to have a distinguished political career as mayor of the capital of Martinique, Fort-de-France, and deputy to the National Assembly in France.

In Cuba, the poet, Nicolás Guillén, was the most prominent representative of Afro-Cubanism. Much of Guillén's important work reflecting this tradition was published in the early 1930s. For example, his *Motivos de Son* was published in 1930, soon after he had met the African-American poet, Langston Hughes. Alistair Hennessy has described *Motivos de Son* as 'the first affirmation by a Cuban poet of an authentic black poetic voice'.[12] But Guillén was preceded by another Cuban, Fernando Ortiz, who had already drawn attention to the African legacy in Cuba and devoted much of time to studying Afro-Cuban culture in language, folklore and religion.

The early twentieth century, then, witnessed movements across the Caribbean which sought to recognize the importance of the African contribution to the culture of the Caribbean. Many individuals and groups went further than this; for example, Marcus Garvey and his UNIA emphasized race pride and racial solidarity among blacks. Some of Garvey's ideas were taken up by the Rastafarians, who believed in black superiority and repatriation to Africa. Throughout the region, there was an attempt to overturn the white value structure which had characterized the Caribbean since the sixteenth century. In the process, these movements played a very significant role in the development of race consciousness and black cultural nationalism in the Caribbean.

# CHAPTER THIRTEEN

# The American century

The twentieth century witnessed the emergence of the United States as the leading power in the Caribbean. Although other European powers continued to be interested in the region, none possessed the political will or strength to challenge the hegemony of the United States. The major colonial power of the nineteenth century, Great Britain, was increasingly concerned about the growing power of Germany and also faced serious colonial problems of its own in South Africa at the turn of the century. France's interest in the region was affected by the collapse of its plans to develop a canal across the isthmus of Panama, a scheme subsequently taken up and developed by the United States. The other major colonial power in the region, Spain, was to lose its Caribbean colonies, Cuba and Puerto Rico, in the Spanish-American War of 1898.

During the nineteenth century, the United States had already made clear its perception of the Americas as an area under its control. The Monroe Doctrine, promulgated in 1823 in the wake of the independence movements in Latin America, was designed to prevent any further extension of European domination in the Americas. In the early twentieth century, the American president, Theodore Roosevelt, became increasingly worried about possible European encroachment in the region as well as the chronic indebtedness of several Caribbean countries. Seeing this as a possible means by which European powers could gain control of these countries, Roosevelt promulgated the Roosevelt Corollary to the Monroe Doctrine. This corollary made clear that the United States had a responsibility to exercise police power in the region.

**FIGURE 13.1** *Roosevelt's big stick in the Caribbean.*
*Source:* © Bettmann/CORBIS.

The subsequent administration of President William Howard Taft added a further element to US intervention in the region, 'dollar diplomacy', which was designed to use financial controls to create greater stability in the Caribbean and lessen the possibility of European intervention.

As a result of these policies, the first three decades of the twentieth century would see frequent interventions by the United States. The use of gunboat and dollar diplomacy led to US military occupation of Cuba, Haiti and the Dominican Republic at various points during this period as well as its exercise of financial controls, especially in the Dominican Republic and Haiti. Although nominally independent, Cuba assumed a protectorate status, Puerto Rico was annexed to the United States, and Haiti and the Dominican Republic were subject to military occupation and customs house controls. In addition, the United States purchased the Virgin Islands in 1917 from Denmark. By examining specific instances of US intervention during this period, it should be possible to understand the different mechanisms which the United States used to maintain its hegemony in the region.

Cuba was especially important to the United States. Throughout the nineteenth century, the possibility of the United States annexing Cuba had remained a serious threat. At the same time, Cuba's ties to Spain were steadily weakening. The Ten Years' War, begun in 1868 when Carlos Manuel de Céspedes proclaimed the independence of Cuba, ended in a stalemate. A planter from Oriente province, Céspedes mounted a highly credible campaign against the Spanish, forcing them to send over 100,000 soldiers to Cuba to put down the rebellion. Although the Ten Years' War did not achieve its objective, new leaders such as the Dominican, Máximo Gómez, and the Cuban mulatto, Antonio Maceo, emerged as future military leaders. Moreover, there was another important consequence of the war: the conflict helped to heighten the sense of a national identity, a feeling of *Cubanidad* which had been growing throughout the nineteenth century. In addition, many members of the Cuban landed aristocracy were ruined by the struggle against Spain and forced to sell their plantations. American capitalists bought many of these plantations, marking the beginning of American economic penetration into Cuba.

Anti-Spanish sentiment did not die with the end of the Ten Years' War. Instead, it was kept alive by José Martí, a journalist, writer and poet born in Havana of Spanish parents. From New York, where he settled in 1881, Martí founded the Cuban Revolutionary Party and planned the Second War of Independence. It broke out in 1895, and although Martí was killed early in the struggle against Spain, the revolution was carried on by the heroes of the Ten Years' War, Gómez and Maceo. The success of the rebels meant that the Spanish resorted to increasingly harsh measures to put down the revolt, further infuriating the rebels and eliciting international protests. The press in the United States and Congress responded with calls to intervene on behalf of the Cubans. This reached a crescendo when the US ship, *Maine*, exploded in Havana harbour in February 1898 killing 260 members of the crew. In April, the official congressional declaration of war against Spain was signed.

The war was over quickly. The Americans were able to destroy the Spanish squadron at Santiago de Cuba and also at Manila in the Philippines. Defeated in Cuba and in the Philippines and with Puerto Rico under American control, the Spanish sued for peace.

The peace treaty, the Treaty of Paris, was signed in December 1898, ceding control over Cuba, Puerto Rico and the Philippines to the Americans. Yet no Cuban representatives were present at the signing of the treaty. Worse was to come for the Cubans: when the Spanish formally handed control to the Americans on 1 January 1899, the occasion belonged to the Americans. The retiring Spanish governor general turned Havana over to the American general, John R. Brooke. As the diplomatic historian, Lester Langley, aptly summarized the situation, 'Spain's formal surrender invested the United States, not the Cuban republic, with formal custody of the island.'[1] In the process, the Cubans were humiliated.

This was also to be the case with Cuban independence. From 1899 to 1902, the American military government in Cuba dealt with some of the major problems left over by the war. It improved public health in the island, began to develop a new educational system and promoted Cuba's economic recovery. At the same time, American capital expanded its hold on Cuba, not only in sugar but also in the public utilities, tobacco and minerals. Although there were calls for the annexation of Cuba, the Teller Amendment added by Congress to the proclamation of war, specifically ruled this out. Instead, Congress approved a resolution, introduced by Senator Orville Platt and known subsequently as the Platt Amendment, to be added to the Cuban Constitution. Its provisions included granting the United States the right to intervene to protect life, liberty and property; validating the acts of the American military government; and providing long-term naval leases to the Americans, which would lead to the American base at Guantanamó Bay. Although the Cubans protested, they had little choice but to agree. The Cuban Constitution, with the Platt Amendment and especially its provisions for interfering in Cuba's internal affairs, meant that Cuban independence was circumscribed at its birth.

For the first three decades of the Cuban Republic, the Americans repeatedly used the provisions of the Platt Amendment to interfere in Cuban affairs. In 1906, for example, the first president of the republic, Tomás Estrada Palma, had to deal with a rebellion against his re-election. Estrada Palma requested that the United States intervene, and faced with evidence that the Cuban government had ceased to function, Theodore Roosevelt sent in the troops. Although the American occupation only lasted until 1909, it had a profound impact on Cuban life. It made Cubans question their ability to run their own affairs. More significantly, as Luis Aguilar has written, 'It undermined Cuban nationalism and reinforced the "Plattist mentality" of relinquishing final political decisions to Washington.'[2]

Three years later, the Americans were back. On this occasion, it was a consequence of a rebellion by blacks largely in Oriente province, because of a law banning political parties based on religion or race. The *Partido Independiente de Color*, which was established in 1907, had accused the government of betraying the black population. When the blacks rebelled in 1912, the uprising led to panic in the island and again to the landing of marines.

American intervention in Cuba was not limited to military occupation or intervention. The Cuban-American relationship, and specifically the Platt Amendment, as well as Cuba's economic dependence on the United States meant that many Cubans sought to transform relations with the United States. This became evident in the late 1920s when the administration of the Cuban president, Gerardo Machado, ran into serious economic and political problems. Machado had begun to rule by using terror tactics and was seen as brutal and corrupt. In response, Cubans sought to create a new economic and political order based on social justice and less American domination.

Following the crash of 1929 and the subsequent economic problems, an opposition formed against Machado and his increasingly dictatorial methods of control. In 1933, as the opposition increased, the new American president, Franklin Roosevelt, despatched Sumner Welles to Cuba as Ambassador Extraordinary to resolve the problem. Opposed to the policy of military intervention and striving to develop a 'Good Neighbour' policy, Roosevelt and the American administration nonetheless continued to have an enormous impact on Cuba. Because of a general strike, Machado resigned and a revolutionary government, headed by a physician at the National University, Dr Ramón Grau San Martín, took over. The new government saw itself as carrying out the failed aspirations of 1898: it was nationalistic and anti-imperialist. Specifically, this meant that the government annulled the Platt Amendment, sought to demolish the colonial economic structure and granted women the right to vote. In the process, however, the government antagonized the Americans and their representative, Sumner Welles. Seeing this revolutionary government as endangering American economic interests in Cuba which at that point totalled $1.5 billion, Welles worked with army commander Fulgencio Batista to topple the Grau regime. It was replaced by a more moderate pro-American administration. The Americans had again determined the political fate of the Cubans, this time without the use of the marines. But the frustrated expectations of 1933 would lead nearly three decades later to a far more lasting revolution led by Fidel Castro.[3]

A very different pattern of American control was to emerge in Haiti, where the Americans intervened in 1915 and remained in control for nineteen years. The pretext for the American invasion was the chaos following the lynching of the Haitian president, Villubrun Guillaume Sam. Sam, who was the fourth president of Haiti to run the country since 1913, had all the political prisoners in the National Penitentiary murdered, then fled to the French Embassy for protection. An infuriated mob dragged him out of the embassy and killed him. The same day, the marines landed in the island at the request of the French and British legations. The invitation to restore stability became a military occupation which lasted until 1934.

The Americans maintained control through a system of martial law and through a client government with Haitians nominally in charge. The navy therefore chose the new president of the country, Henri Dartiguenave, who was the only candidate acceptable to the Americans. Soon after the occupation began, the American admiral in charge proclaimed martial law and imposed severe restrictions on the press. As a consequence, American military tribunals were alone responsible for dealing with political offences until the late 1920s.

The Americans were also responsible for drafting a Haitian-American treaty which authorized American control of the Haitian customs houses as well as the organization of a constabulary force. More controversially, the State Department effectively wrote the new Haitian Constitution. Although Haitian law had forbidden the ownership of property by foreigners since the Haitian Revolution, the Americans insisted on reversing this prohibition in the new constitution. As in the case of Cuba after the American military occupation, the Haitian Constitution validated the acts of the occupying forces.

Initially, the Haitians welcomed the Americans, but this soon changed as American racial attitudes towards the Haitians became clear. For example, one of the main commanders of the occupation forces, Col Littleton W.T. Waller, was a Virginian with strongly negative views of the Haitians. Writing to a friend, Waller commented that the Haitians 'are real niggers and no mistake… . What the people of Norfolk and Portsmouth would say if they saw me bowing and scraping to these coons, I do not know'. Accustomed to the deference of Europeans, Haitians reacted against the racism of the Americans. As Anthony Maingot suggests, Haitians 'made the Americans' generalized lack of respect for them individually and collectively the basis of a strong nationalist movement'.[4]

The Americans also generated opposition among the Haitian peasants. The American road building programme was based on the *corvée*, a forced labour system which required peasants to provide six days of voluntary labour to the state annually. In practice, the system proved to be brutal and inefficient: peasants were forced to labour under extremely harsh conditions, even being roped together in gangs on occasion. Peasant resentment against these practices was widespread and eventually broke out into open resistance. Known as the *caco* uprising, it began in 1918 and was led by an ex-soldier, Charlemagne Peralte, who created a provisional government in the interior of the island. Peralte claimed to have a 2,000-strong *caco* army, capable of resisting the Americans. Haitian women were also involved in this resistance: they were secret carriers of weapons and hid members of the *caco* army in their homes.[5] The American marines eventually killed Peralte, but made the mistake of circulating his picture after he had been shot, helping to make him a martyr. The revolt continued until 1920, with the marines killing over 3,000 Haitians suppressing the revolt.

The American occupation of Haiti ended in 1934, partly as a result of the 'Good Neighbour' policy of President Franklin Roosevelt which sought to end the era of military interventions. While in Haiti, the Americans contributed significantly to improving the infrastructure of the island and to the health of the Haitian people. But according to Anthony Maingot, the Americans failed to achieve anything of lasting value in Haiti, largely because of their racial antagonism towards the Haitians and their misunderstanding of the complex racial and social structure of Haitian society.[6] In the end, the occupation served to reinforce the existing structures of power in the island.

In the Dominican Republic, which shares the island of Hispaniola with Haiti, there were similarities with the Haitian intervention as well as significant differences. The initial US foray in the Dominican Republic reflected a concern about the financial condition of the country and consequently the possibility of other European powers gaining a foothold there. The subsequent military intervention in 1916 provoked a resistance movement similar to that of the Haitian *caco* uprising and also the development of a stronger Dominican nationalism.

Following the assassination in 1899 of the Dominican president and dictator, Ulysses Heureaux, the country was plunged into turmoil, aggravating further its already difficult financial condition. Theodore Roosevelt sought to forestall the danger of any European power intervening on behalf of its creditors by making the United States the collection agent of the country's revenues. The subsequent protocol with the Dominican Republic obligated the United States to put aside 55 per cent of the customs duties to deal with the external debt, the remaining 45 per cent going to the Dominican government. For Roosevelt, the idea of a customs receivership was intended to avoid a financial disaster for the Dominican Republic and allow it to repay its debts to foreign bondholders.

In the short term, this plan worked. The Dominicans elected a new president in 1906, Ramón Cáceres, and his regime proved popular and stable. However, Cáceres was assassinated in 1911, ushering in a period of political turmoil and economic stagnation. With the collapse of the political situation in 1916, American forces occupied the country. They were to remain in the Dominican Republic until 1924, less than half the time that they occupied Haiti. But as in the case of Haiti, there was considerable resistance to the occupation.

The military resistance to the Americans was organized by peasants and sugar workers in the east of the country. From 1917 to 1922, they prevented the American forces from controlling large areas of the eastern region, an important part of the Dominican Republic dominated by corporate sugar interests. Faced with a guerrilla insurgency, the marines were unable to put down these irregular forces. Moreover, the Americans also had to confront the nationalists' political-intellectual campaign of resistance as well. As Bruce Calder has concluded, 'Resistance to the occupation was a primary factor in bringing it to an end.'[7]

There are several reasons why the Americans left the Dominican Republic so much sooner than they departed from Haiti. The resistance movement against the Americans was significant in both countries, but the Americans were able to kill the leader of the Haitian insurgents and therefore weaken the military opposition to their presence. The Haitian intellectuals also lacked the international backing which their Dominican counterparts were able to muster. The Dominicans could count on support from Latin America and Spain, whereas the Haitians' principal ally was France, a country less likely to cause difficulties for the Americans. It is also important to understand the importance of racism in the making of American foreign policy. According to a prominent State Department official writing in 1921, there were significant differences in the American perception of the two countries:

> It is well to distinguish at once between the Dominicans and the Haitians. The former, while in many ways not advanced far enough for the highest type of self-government, yet have a preponderance of white blood and culture. The Haitians on the other hand are negro for the most part, and, barring a very few highly educated politicians, are almost in a state of savagery and complete ignorance. The two situations thus demand different treatment. In Haiti it is necessary to have as complete a rule within a rule by Americans as possible... . In the Dominican Republic, on the other hand, I believe, we should endeavor rather to counsel than control.[8]

American intervention in the Caribbean, then, took several different forms. For the first three decades of the twentieth century, military intervention was a common feature of the US relations with the Caribbean. Theodore Roosevelt had sought to make use of police powers to maintain stability in the region, while his successors used financial weapons as well as military occupations to accomplish the same aim. In the end, the United States succeeded in improving the infrastructure of Cuba, the Dominican Republic and Haiti but also engendered a nationalist response in all of these countries. In doing so, the United States helped to create the conditions for longer-term problems in the Caribbean for the remainder of the American Century.

# CHAPTER FOURTEEN

# Labour protests and the 1930s

The labour disturbances of the 1930s in the Anglophone Caribbean developed as a result of underlying economic and social problems which were already apparent in the 1880s. These included economic depression, increased unemployment, reduced wages and considerable suffering for the working people. Their response was a series of strikes and riots, beginning in the 1880s, continuing during and just after the First World War and culminating in the dramatic events of the 1930s.

The first of these periods, the late nineteenth century, was characterized by economic problems in the region and the reorganization of the sugar industry. This arose largely because of the effects of European beet sugar producers who increased their output substantially during the second half of the century. By 1870, they produced nearly one-third of the total world sugar output. When Germany, which was the world's major producer of beet sugar, doubled subsidies on its sugar exports in 1883–84, the effect on the British market was dramatic. There was a massive increase in the amount of beet sugar imported into Britain and, consequently, a collapse in the sugar price. The position of West Indian sugar worsened further when the French and Germans doubled their bounties on beet sugar in 1896, leading to another drop in sugar prices the following year. In the West Indies, the production of West Indian sugar was drastically affected: for example, Grenada's output of sugar dropped by more than a half as an immediate result of the crisis. In St. Vincent, two-thirds of the sugar cultivation in the island had been abandoned by 1886.

The prolonged economic depression in the late nineteenth century had repercussions for West Indian workers. In response to the crisis, planters reduced wages, which created considerable hardship for sugar cane workers. There were reports of widespread destitution and malnutrition after 1884 as well as an increase in the incidence of disease. As in the years following emancipation, the economic and social difficulties of the period were reflected in a large number of riots and disturbances.

Violence erupted in Grenada in 1895, in St. Vincent in 1891 and in 1893 in Dominica. In 1896 strikes and demonstrations over the issue of lowered wages marked the beginning of the harvest season in St. Kitts; during the subsequent riots, two people were killed and many others wounded. A plantation riot among Indian indentured workers in British Guiana later in the same year also led to the loss of life: five Indian workers were killed and another fifty-nine injured when the police opened fire on the crowd. These were not isolated incidents: between 1886 and 1903, there were over 200 strikes on the sugar estates of British Guiana. Since trade unions were illegal and the planters regarded these disturbances as riots, the strikes were usually resolved by bringing in the police or the armed forces.[1]

There were also outbreaks in the first few years of the twentieth century. In addition to smaller disturbances in Montserrat and Dominica, there were serious riots in Montego Bay, Jamaica in 1902, largely because of high taxes but also as a result of difficult economic conditions. Montego Bay was the target of the rioters for two days, and it took the arrival of British forces from across the island to end the riots. The 1905 riots in British Guiana linked urban workers and sugar estate labourers and were also a response to the declining living standards of the workers at the end of the century. As was the case in many of these outbreaks, women in British Guiana had a significant role in the riots. However, these riots mostly involved Afro-Guyanese; the racial split which characterized British Guiana affected the disturbances as well. The absence of Indians in the riots meant that they never developed into a wider general strike.[2]

The late nineteenth century also witnessed the first organized workingmen's associations in the West Indies. In Jamaica, skilled tradesmen created separate unions, beginning in 1898 with the establishment of the Artisans' Union. A decade later, two others, made up of cigar-makers and printers, were also formed. Elsewhere, the Trinidad Workingmen's Association sought to bring together various trades within one organization. Unlike the unions in Jamaica, the Trinidad union had political objectives, such as the reduction of taxes and constitutional reform. But most of these early unions either foundered after unsuccessful strikes or simply ceased to function.[3]

During the First World War, there were some demonstrations and strikes in the region, but the war-time atmosphere was not conducive to labour protests. The most prominent early labour figure in the Anglophone Caribbean, Herbert Critchlow, emerged during the war to become leader of the Guyanese workers. In 1918, he led a large demonstration of workers in the capital, Georgetown. The following year, Critchlow formed the British Guiana Labour Union, an organization which rapidly gained supporters and which continued to be significant in the 1930s and 1940s. The First World War also had another effect on labour: returning soldiers to the West Indies often came home to face unemployment, having dealt with racial discrimination while serving as soldiers during the war. Some of them were involved in disturbances in 1919, especially in Belize and Trinidad.

One of the returning soldiers who served in the British West India Regiment was Captain Arthur Cipriani, a white Trinidadian creole. He was a hero to his fellow soldiers because he had defended them against the racism they faced during the war. On his return to Trinidad, he joined the Trinidad Workingmen's Association and became its president in 1923. However, Cipriani's focus was on reforming the political system rather than pursuing trade union demands, and he became a member of the Legislative Council in 1925. In 1934, the Trinidad Workingmen's Association became the Trinidad Labour Party, reaffirming Cipriani's interest in constitutional and political reform. It was not until the riots of the 1930s that trade union activity and political parties would combine to permanently change the face of politics and labour in the Caribbean.

The first of what Nigel Bolland has called the West Indian labour rebellions broke out in Belize (then British Honduras) in 1934. Although located on the Central American mainland, Belize has long been considered part of the West Indies, largely because of its social, economic and political links to the rest of the Anglophone Caribbean. Its economy was centred largely on the export of timber products such as logwood and mahogany and latterly chicle, the basis of chewing gum. Like the rest of the region, Belize was badly affected by the Great Depression. It was made much worse by the effects of the hurricane which struck the colony in September 1931 and destroyed the capital, Belize Town. The hurricane killed more than 1,000 people and destroyed much of the housing in the capital.

The response by the colonial administration to the plight of the people of Belize proved woeful. Facing unemployment, poverty and inadequate housing, a group known as the 'Unemployed Brigade' marched through the capital in 1934. This movement was eventually taken over by Antonio Soberanis Gomez, a barber who created and led the Labourers and Unemployed Association. As Bolland has suggested, this 'soon became a significant political force in Belize and was the prototype of future trade unions and political parties'.[4] Soberanis led a series of marches, strikes and protests designed to improve the conditions of the working people. This included further marches of the unemployed, boycotts of stores who did not give donations to the poor and strikes of stevedores and other workers. Although Soberanis' organization did not last, his actions in seeking to organize the working class would be repeated by other leaders across the Anglophone Caribbean.

Unlike Belize, many of the other Caribbean colonies were largely plantation economies whose principal crop was sugar. With sugar prices badly affected by the Depression, colonies such as St. Kitts faced growing distress caused by falling wages and unemployment. For example, the pay for cutting cane had fallen to 8d per ton, the same wage as fifty years earlier. In January 1935, workers on a sugar estate near the capital, Basseterre, struck, seeking to get their wages back to the 1932 level of 11d per ton. The strike spread to other estates on the island, and one schoolteacher described the scene as the rioters passed the school:

The children immediately made a mad rush for the door, and in a minute the school was empty. Teachers and pupils alike could not miss this once-in-a-lifetime event. There were the rioters – hundreds of them, all in their working clothes, barefooted, with sticks, bills and other weapons in their hands, shouting: 'We strike for higher wages! Everybody mus' stap wok today!'[5]

The strike lasted for several days, but remained a non-violent action designed to improve wage rates. However, the armed forces and the police were used to disperse the strikers, and in the process, three rioters were killed. It was this overreaction by the authorities which helped to make the strike such a significant event for St. Kitts and for the wider working-class movement.

Two other colonies in the eastern Caribbean, St. Vincent and St. Lucia, were also affected by disturbances in 1935. The problem in St. Vincent was a decision to raise custom duties, particularly on necessities such as matches. However, demonstrators also complained about some of the same labour problems as the strikers in St. Lucia: unemployment and low wages. In the process of the riots and demonstrations during October, six people were killed.[6] In neighbouring St. Lucia, the problem was a strike in November of men who loaded coal onto ships in the capital, Castries. Partly because of the events in St. Vincent, the governor overreacted by declaring a state of emergency. The strike was quickly suppressed.

Two years later, in 1937, the wave of labour rebellions spread first to Trinidad and then to Barbados. Trinidad was a unique case: although sugar and cocoa were important exports, the economy of the island was dominated by oil. By the 1930s, it accounted for about 60 per cent of the colony's exports. Moreover, after the First World War, the dominant figure in the labour movement, Arthur Cipriani, was increasingly challenged by other leaders who sought to move beyond Cipriani's reformist politics.

The first of these was Uriah 'Buzz' Butler, a charismatic Grenadian who had served in the British West Indian regiment in the First World War. He worked in the Trinidad oil industry as a pipe fitter and was also chief pastor of the Butlerite Moravian Baptist Church. Butler organized the oil workers in southern Trinidad and had strong links with the leaders of the National Unemployed Movement, who were also strongly critical of Cipriani and had organized a series of hunger marches and demonstrations in the mid-1930s. The other major figure in the labour movement was Adrian Cola Rienzi, who had also become disillusioned with Cipriani. Rienzi, formerly Krishna Deonarine, was a lawyer who was particularly interested in Indian nationalism and socialism.

The real cause of the 1937 riots was the continuing effects of the Depression and the economic plight of many Trinidadians, in spite of the profits which the oil industry in the colony was making.

Butler turned to strike action against the oil companies, but he envisioned a peaceful sit-down action. The government's decision to crush the strike and to arrest Butler triggered serious violence, as the strike spread to the plantations and to the capital, Port of Spain, and escalated into a general strike. In the disturbances, fourteen people were killed, including two policemen, and hundreds arrested.

In the immediate wake of the labour rebellion in the summer of 1937, several trade unions were formed, including the Oilfield Workers' Trade Union. For Bolland, the development of trade unionism in Trinidad was the most important outcome of the labour rebellion. Rienzi had a very significant role in these developments and became president of the Oilfield Workers' Trade Union. While Butler was the more charismatic leader, it was Rienzi who was responsible for creating more lasting institutions. Trinidad was unique in the number of unions which were established between 1937 and 1939, but the riots in Trinidad also had an important effect on events in Barbados.[7]

The economic problems in Barbados were similar to those in other parts of the Caribbean. Largely dependent on sugar, Barbados experienced a dramatic fall in the price of its sugar as a result of the Depression. In 1823, Barbadian sugar sold for twenty-three shillings per hundredweight on the London market; the price fell to nine shillings in 1929 and then to less than five shillings in 1934. The effects were predictable: falling wages, unemployment and poverty. Wages for many plantation workers were much the same as they had been after emancipation; moreover, the situation was aggravated by the lack of trade unions and also by news of the disturbances in Trinidad.

The spark for the riots in Barbados was the deportation of Clement Payne, a labour organizer who was born in Trinidad of Barbadian parents. He worked with Butler and other members of the labour movement in Trinidad, and his intention in coming to Barbados was to establish a trade union. Yet in his speeches, Payne not only dwelt on labour problems but also referred to the difficult state of race relations in Barbados and pointed to the strikes and riots taking place elsewhere in the region. When Payne was deported, there was an immediate outcry and disturbances in Barbados, first among the waterfront workers but eventually across the island. As in Trinidad, the suppression of the riots was severe: police and armed volunteers killed fourteen people and wounded nearly fifty others. Over 600 people were charged with offences.

Grantley Adams, a future prime minister of Barbados, served as Payne's lawyer in the Court of Appeal and also appeared before the commissioners who investigated the riots. Adams highlighted some of the problems caused by the lack of trade unions in Barbados:

> There are no labour organizations in Barbados, no Trade Unions, by means of which out people can air their grievances.... . Many ... people, clerks, shop assistants and others are afraid to come before this Commission and express their grievances with regard to wages. They are afraid that if they do so they will be fired by their employers who will have no difficulty in getting others to take their places. That is why grievances are bottled up.[8]

To deal with some of these problems, Adams helped to found the Barbados Progressive League in 1938, an organization established to press for social legislation and a wider franchise. Adams became president of the League a year later, and the organization subsequently became the Barbados Labour Party. In a pattern which was replicated across the British Caribbean, the party was responsible for setting up the Barbados Workers' Union to provide itself with a trade union base. Similar developments would also occur in Jamaica.

Jamaica experienced some of the same economic problems which affected the rest of the Caribbean. As elsewhere in the region, the combination of low wages and casual employment led to poverty and economic insecurity for a large number of Jamaicans. This was exacerbated by the seasonal nature of employment on the sugar estates, which increased the levels of unemployment and underemployment. To make matters worse, the Depression forced many Jamaicans who had sought work abroad to return home, where they too competed for jobs.

There were also problems which were unique to Jamaica and which exacerbated the situation. The banana industry had become a very significant part of the island's economy. While sugar exports dropped from 44 per cent to 10 per cent between 1870 and 1900, bananas accounted for over 50 per cent of exports during that period. Bananas were produced by large multinational corporations, such as the United Fruit Company, as well as by small farmers. But in the 1930s, banana production was affected by disease, which particularly impacted on the small farmers. As a result, many of them were forced to seek wage labour at a time when little work was available. In addition, workers were politicized by the return of Marcus Garvey to Jamaica as well as by the emergence of the Rastafarians. The labour movement was also influenced by a group of Marxists who were involved in the formation of trade unions in the 1930s.

There were early labour protests in the mid-1930s involving both banana and dock workers. But the major event which sparked the labour rebellion in Jamaica took place at Frome Estate in western Jamaica in April 1938. The disturbances at Frome and the subsequent protests catapulted two men into prominence, who would dominate Jamaican politics for the next two decades. The first was Alexander Bustamante: he was born as Alexander Clarke and spent time in Cuba, Panama and the United States. When he returned to Jamaica in the early 1930s, he had changed his name, created some curious myths about his past and was able to set himself up as a moneylender in Kingston. Bustamante also became

**FIGURE 14.1** *Norman Washington Manley.*
*Source:* © Hulton-Deutsch Collection/CORBIS.

involved in the labour movement. His cousin, Norman Washington Manley, had a very different background. A Rhodes Scholar, Manley studied law at Oxford University and, by the late 1930s, was the leading barrister on the island.[9]

The apparent cause of the problems at Frome Estate was the slow payment of wages to the workers. However, what lay behind the riot and the subsequent strike was the establishment at Frome of a large new central factory under the auspices of the British company, Tate & Lyle. When workers heard rumours of the promise of high wages of up to four shillings or five shillings per day, hundreds of people flocked to the estate. Inevitably, there were many more applicants for work than jobs. The strike over the promised higher wages turned violent, and in the process of suppressing the disturbance, the police killed four people and wounded many others. A protest in Kingston about the events at Frome attracted 3,000 people.

Three weeks later, dock workers in Kingston struck. Facing a virtual insurrection, the government mobilized hundreds of police, troops and special constables. Bustamante supported the striking

FIGURE 14.2 *Sir Alexander Bustamante.*
*Source:* © Hulton-Deutsch Collection/CORBIS.

workers and was arrested for sedition; Manley worked to get Bustamante released and to negotiate on behalf of the workers. Strikes spread across the country and the governor declared a state of emergency. In the disturbances, eight other people were killed, in addition to those who lost their lives at Frome. The riots ended when concessions were made to the workers in Kingston and a land settlement scheme was devised in response to the demands of the small farmers and banana workers in the country.

The strikes also had more long-term effects. Most significantly, they helped to promote Bustamante and Manley as leaders of the labour and nationalist movement. Bustamante organized a union, the Bustamante Industrial Trade Union, with himself as president for life. Emerging from jail, Bustamante became the hero of the working classes but also a dictatorial union leader. Manley, on the other hand, established a political party, the People's National Party, a reformist party which sought to have Bustamante's union as its base. It was explicitly a nationalist party, aiming to prepare Jamaica for self-government as well as to raise the standard of living of the people of the island. Ultimately, Bustamante established his own political party, the Jamaica Labour Party, and split with Manley. The rivalry between Bustamante and Manley not only divided the labour and nationalist movements but also defined Jamaican politics for the next two decades.[10]

In the wake of the labour rebellions across the Caribbean, the British government established a Royal Commission to investigate conditions in the region. Headed by Lord Moyne, a future Colonial Secretary, its findings were so damning that the British government suppressed the report, fearing that it could be used as enemy propaganda during the Second World War. However, the government published the commission's recommendations, including the need for labour legislation protecting unions and regulating working conditions and for improving the social welfare of the people of the Caribbean. Although outside of its brief, the commission also suggested constitutional changes leading to universal adult suffrage and more self-government.

By the end of the Second World War, the main recommendations of the Moyne Commission were being implemented. Adult suffrage was introduced in Jamaica in 1944, followed by Trinidad and Tobago two years later and Barbados in 1950. The other colonies in the Anglophone Caribbean gradually followed in their wake.

The system of government was also transformed: Crown Colony government gave way to more democratic forms of government, leading eventually to political independence. The labour rebellions of the 1930s had therefore changed the political and social landscape of the region. They brought to the fore new leaders, initially in the labour movement, but ultimately as political leaders in the drive towards decolonization and independence. The consequence in the Anglophone Caribbean was often a very close connection between political parties and their affiliated trade unions. This was the case for Bustamante and Manley in Jamaica, Vere Bird in Antigua, Eric Gairy in Grenada, Grantley Adams and Errol Barrow in Barbados, and Cheddi Jagan in British Guiana.[11] Arising out of the labour rebellions of the 1930s, these figures would dominate politics in the post-independent era of the Caribbean.

# CHAPTER FIFTEEN

# The revolutionary Caribbean

The Cuban Revolution was a defining moment in the twentieth-century Caribbean. It had significant implications for the region as a whole and for the Americas generally. As a result of the revolution, Cuban-American relations were transformed; moreover, Cuba became an important part of the Cold War. For all its wider implications, the Cuban Revolution also impacted dramatically on its Caribbean neighbours.

The revolution grew out the frustrations associated with the leadership of Fulgencio Batista as well as the structural problems of Cuban society. Batista, who helped to oust the revolutionary government of 1933, had dominated Cuban politics since then. In 1952, he was standing in the presidential elections, but was running third. Rather than face defeat, he engineered a military coup three weeks before the elections were to take place. Since the previous decade in Cuban politics had been characterized by graft and corruption, there was only muted opposition to Batista's coup.

However, the coup dramatically affected the career of one young politician, Fidel Castro. Castro was a member of the left wing of the Ortodoxo Party, a party founded by Eduardo Chibás in 1947 as a protest against the corruption of Cuban politics. The Ortodoxos had an ambitious platform not only to end corruption but also to diversify Cuban agriculture and develop new industries to reduce the high levels of unemployment and underemployment. Castro, who had grown up in a prosperous family in Oriente province and studied law at the University of Havana, was standing as an Ortodoxo candidate for Congress from a Havana district.

Frustrated by the coup, Castro became a proponent of armed insurrection against the military government.

Castro's idea was to attack two barracks in Oriente province, the Moncada at Santiago and the Bayamo barracks, on 26 July 1953. Although the barracks held about 1,000 men, Castro believed that an attack to coincide with the Santiago carnival could succeed in surprising the troops. The plan was to seize the barracks and arm his own anti-Batista movement. Moreover, Castro hoped that the attack could spark a popular rising against Batista in Oriente province and potentially a national insurrection.

However, the attack proved to be a fiasco. Of the 165 young men who took part in the attack, most were captured and sixty-eight of the prisoners were killed, often brutally. Castro and a group of the rebels survived, but Castro was sentenced to fifteen years imprisonment on the Isle of Pines. During the trial, Castro gave his famous 'History will absolve me' speech, which was later smuggled out of jail and produced as a pamphlet. In the speech, Castro highlighted the problems facing Cuba and his programme for the future, repeatedly invoking the name of José Martí. He concluded:

I know that imprisonment will be as hard for me as it has ever been for anyone – filled with cowardly threats and wicked torture. But I do not fear prison, just as I do not fear the fury of the miserable tyrant who snuffed life out of seventy brothers of mine. Sentence me, I don't mind. History will absolve me.[1]

Less than two years later, Castro was out of prison. In May 1955, the government issued a general amnesty for all political prisoners; soon afterwards, Castro travelled to Mexico where he again began to organize an attack on Batista and his regime. While in Mexico, he also met Ernesto 'Che' Guevara, a radical Argentinian doctor, who joined Castro's forces. In November 1956, Castro and a total of about eighty men left in a small yacht, the *Granma*, headed for Oriente province. The landing in early December was a disaster: government forces overwhelmed the rebels and only eighteen of the original group of eighty survived. They sought refuge in the Sierra Maestra mountains of eastern Cuba.

Gradually, the rebels, who included Castro, his brother Raúl and Guevara, gained additional supporters. They were able to expand their base in the countryside, and there was also growing resistance to the Batista regime in the cities. In 1957, a daring attack on the presidential palace in Havana almost succeeded in assassinating Batista. Guerrilla warfare in the countryside was therefore accompanied by increased sabotage in the cities.

It was not surprising that Castro and his forces were able to gain adherents to their cause. The structural problems facing Cuba in the 1950s were severe and particularly impacted on the rural population. For example, sugar workers, who made up a quarter of the entire Cuban labour force, suffered from high levels of underemployment: 60 per cent of them were employed for only six months of the year or less. While 80 per cent of the urban population enjoyed running water in their homes, the figure for rural inhabitants was only 15 per cent. Education levels were also very different across the island: although the national illiteracy rate was 20 per cent, it was 40 per cent in the countryside and 50 per cent in Oriente. As Louis Pérez has suggested, 'The peasantry lived at the margins of society and outside the body politic.'[2]

The situation for Batista's government became more difficult in 1958. There was increased insurgency across Cuba, and there was also some resistance within the army. Moreover, the United States imposed an arms embargo on Cuba, indicating that its backing for Batista was wavering. Faced with a lack of support internally as well as externally, Batista and some of his leading officials fled Cuba in the early hours of 1 January 1959. Against all the odds, Castro and his forces marched into Havana seven days later to take control.

Castro and the 26th of July Movement which he led had clear aims at outset of the revolution. The new government was intent on removing the glaring inequalities between rural and urban Cuba; moreover, it sought to promote agricultural diversification and industrialization and also wanted to reduce the economic presence of the United States in the Cuban economy. Castro's initial steps were designed to achieve these objectives. The Agrarian Reform Act therefore reduced the maximum allowable holdings of land, with the idea of transferring land ownership to the tiller of the soil. This act put agriculture at the heart of the revolution. The Urban Reform Law of March 1959 sought to have similar effects in the cities: it halved rents and then abolished renting. These measures had very immediate results in shifting the national income towards wage earners and away from property owners. Moreover, such acts helped the revolution gain widespread support and commitment from the majority of the population.

At the same time, US relations with Cuba were becoming increasingly tense. The United States criticized the Castro government for putting on trial and executing many of the officials who had served with Batista. Relations were not helped by threats of expropriation of American-owned property and firms as well as concern about the influence of communists in the Cuban government. In 1960, relations deteriorated further. In June, the Cuban government requested foreign-owned petroleum companies to process the oil it received from the Soviet Union. When the companies refused, the government expropriated them. During the summer of 1960, the Castro government took control of all large US-owned industrial and agrarian businesses as well as the banks. The process of expropriation of American firms continued in the autumn, affecting wholesale and retail businesses. In response, the United States cancelled its sugar agreements with the Cuba and then withdrew its ambassador. In January 1961, the United States severed diplomatic relations with Cuba.

The radicalization of the revolution had predictable consequences for many middle and upper-class Cubans. Between 1960 and 1962, about 200,000 of them left Cuba, mostly going to the United States. Primarily from the economic and social elite of the island, they were disproportionately white and urban, and many of them held strongly anti-communist views. Some of them enlisted in the CIA trained and financed plan to invade Cuba and oust Castro. In April 1961, 1,200 *émigrés* landed at the Bay of Pigs in south-central Cuba, hoping to spark the internal opposition to Castro which they believed existed. Instead, Castro personally led his armed forces and militia against the invasion force and quickly defeated them, capturing over 1,000 prisoners. In their first major encounter, Castro had defeated the Americans and immeasurably strengthened his reputation.

While relations with the Americans soured, those with the Soviet Union improved significantly. Just as the United States was cutting its links and trading arrangements with the Cubans, the Soviet Union was offering aid and advantageous terms of trade. It is unlikely that the Cuban Revolution could have survived without these new arrangements and its new ally. As Perez has suggested, 'If the making of a radical revolution in Cuba required a break with the US, the defence of a radical revolution in the face of US attack demanded support from the Soviet Union.'[3] But the Soviet Union went further than merely supporting Cuba: in the autumn of 1962, it installed forty-two medium range ballistic missiles in Cuba capable of striking the United States with nuclear warheads. When President Kennedy demanded the withdrawal of these missiles and imposed a naval quarantine on the island, the world stood on the brink of nuclear warfare between the two major superpowers. In the end, the Soviet Union decided to remove its missiles, without consulting Castro, but with the promise from the United States that it would not invade the island. While Castro was sidelined, he nonetheless gained a significant advantage in knowing that Cuba was safe from an invasion from the United States.

Although the Soviet Union provided crucial support for the revolution, it could not prevent serious economic difficulties for the Cuban government. One of Castro's early priorities was to encourage agricultural diversification and promote industrialization. Castro therefore put Che Guevara in charge of the economy as Minister of Industries with a brief to seek rapid industrialization. But this policy failed and, at the same time, sugar output declined drastically. In response, the government imposed rationing and froze prices. It also shifted its attitude to sugar: the Cuban government decided to concentrate on sugar and made a huge commitment to produce ten million tons of sugar in 1970. This plan produced economic chaos, especially as it proved an impossible target to achieve. During the 1970s and 1980s, Cuba continued to depend largely on sugar production. There was a rise in sugar prices in the early 1970s which helped the economy but, in general, Cuba found itself continuing to depend on the Soviet Union for support. As Marifeli Pérez-Stable has pointed out, during the 1980s, sugar provided more than 75 per cent of the value of total exports, which was not very different from Cuba's experience in the 1950s. Moreover, in the same period, the Soviet Union accounted for roughly the same share of Cuba's trade as the United States had done in the 1950s.[4]

While the Cuban economy continued to experience problems, the Cuban people were partially shielded from these difficulties. The government's aim to redistribute wealth had significant effects: from the time of the revolution until the 1980s, the share of national income for the bottom 40 per cent of the population increased from less than 7 per cent to about 26 per cent. There was

**FIGURE 15.1** *Prints of Castro and Che Guevara for sale in a Cuban market, 2002.*

*Source:* © Pablo Corral Vega/CORBIS.

a dramatic reduction in the inequalities which had characterized pre-revolutionary Cuba. For example, the position of women improved considerably. The number of women in the labour force doubled from 1950 to the late 1970s, and many more women were involved in higher education. Health care improved significantly, literacy increased dramatically, and education was transformed.

But there were also problems: for example, Cuban jails held a large number of political prisoners. Moreover, discontent with the regime flared up in 1980. Faced with thousands of people seeking refuge in the Peruvian Embassy, Castro announced that any Cuban could leave the island from Mariel, a port west of Havana. When Castro stopped the emigration several months later, roughly 125,000 refugees had fled by boat to Florida.

The collapse of the Soviet Union in 1989 tested the government further and posed serious questions about the survival of the revolution. The inability of the Cuban government to exchange sugar for oil led to an enormous decline in oil imports, with all the predictable effects on the economy. Between 1989 and 1994, the prices of imported food and oil rose by 40 per cent while the exports of sugar fell by 20 per cent. Sugar production was badly affected: in 1991, Cuba produced 8.4 million tons but three years later, the total was 3.8 million tons. In the four-year period after 1989, the economy contracted by between 35 and 50 per cent, forcing severe rationing.[5] Inevitably, the Cuban government had to bring in economic reforms: these included a dollarization of the economy, market reforms and an emphasis on tourism and immigrant remittances. For Pérez-Stable, this has meant that Cuba has become more like the rest of the Caribbean.[6]

Fidel's resignation in 2008 and replacement by his brother, Raúl, has served to emphasize these changes. Fidel died in November 2016 aged ninety, and his death led to an outpouring of grief and nine days of official mourning in Cuba. By that time, however, Fidel no longer had an important role in shaping the future of Cuba. Eight months previously, President Barack Obama's visit to Havana in March 2016 offered hope for a significant rapprochement between the United States and Cuba. But reporting from Havana at the time, Ada Ferrer recorded the views of a Cuban woman who remarked 'that the U.S. president couldn't make Cuban policy, nor even change U.S. policy on his own – referring to the fact that the Republican-controlled U.S. Congress seems, for the moment at least, unwilling to end the embargo'.[7] With the election of Donald Trump as president of the United States in November 2016, the end of the embargo seemed even further away.

Yet Cuba's political trajectory since 1959 has made it unique in the Caribbean, not least because of its foreign policy. Despite the early links with the Soviet Union, Castro and his government often differed with the Russians on foreign relations. Cuba supported revolutionary movements in many Latin American countries, a policy which differed substantially from that of the Soviet Union. Cuba's involvement in Latin America led to the death of Che Guevara in 1967, who was seeking to foment a revolution in Bolivia. In the 1970s, Cuba supported those fighting for the independence of Angola and was also involved in Ethiopia. The Cuban government also had increasingly close relations with sympathetic governments in the Caribbean.

One of them was neighbouring Jamaica, especially during the 1970s. Jamaica had become independent in 1962 and, during the 1960s, experienced rapid economic growth based largely on bauxite, tourism and light manufacturing. But many of these enterprises, such as the bauxite companies and the large hotels, were foreign-owned; moreover, the island suffered from a highly uneven income distribution. In addition, there were increasing levels of unemployment and illiteracy, compounded by inadequate housing, especially in parts of west Kingston. There was also a racial divide in the country: while people of full or part African ancestry made up more than 90 per cent of the population, it was local whites, light-coloured browns, Jews, Lebanese and Chinese who dominated the economy.

In 1968, the island was rocked by demonstrations and violence in the wake of the banning of Walter Rodney in October 1968. A Guyanese and a radical African historian, Rodney had returned from his studies in London and a teaching stint in Tanzania to take up a post at the Jamaica campus of the University of the West Indies. In addition to his lectures at the university, Rodney gave talks on Black Power to the unemployed blacks from west Kingston. In a short time, he was able to gather around him the nucleus of a local Black Power Movement, consisting of students, the unemployed and Rastafarians.

However, the Jamaica Labour Party government led by Hugh Shearer saw these developments in a very different light. The government depicted Rodney as a communist and a revolutionary who had visited Cuba and who posed a grave threat to the country. When Rodney travelled to Canada for a conference in October, he was declared *persona non grata* and refused permission to re-enter Jamaica. Student demonstrations led to mob violence, as the poor and unemployed of downtown Kingston attacked property and businesses, many of them foreign-owned, causing damage estimated at £1 million. As Anthony Payne has suggested, the only response of the ruling government was increased coercion. The opposition People's National Party, on the other hand, expressed a desire for social and economic renewal. With its new leader, Michael Manley, who was a prominent trade unionist and the son of the former prime minister, Norman Manley, the party pledged that it would deal with the aspirations of the country's poor blacks.[8]

In 1972, Michael Manley was elected as prime minister of Jamaica. A self-proclaimed democratic socialist, his aims were very different from his more conservative predecessor. For example, Manley favoured a more equitable distribution of wealth in the country and promoted land reform and the creation of co-operative farms. Although rejecting the expropriation of property, Manley sought to create a more egalitarian society and therefore funded work programmes for the unemployed and put more resources into the health service. He disagreed with the Puerto Rican model of development, which in his view led to economic growth and foreign investment but at the cost of the social welfare of the people. Similarly, Manley was not an advocate of the Cuban economic model, despite its social achievements. Instead, he advocated the development of a Third World strategy, independent of the West and the East. In the case of Jamaica, this meant creating an organization for bauxite-exporting countries along the lines of OPEC.

In terms of foreign policy, Manley was prepared to establish relations with new partners. This included Cuba. Manley was largely responsible for the recognition of Cuba by the independent countries of the Commonwealth Caribbean (Jamaica, Barbados, Trinidad and Guyana) and was personally close to Castro. In 1975, Manley visited Cuba and also established joint programmes with the Cuban government in areas such as tourism, public health and foreign policy. Against the wishes of the United States, Manley supported Cuba's decision to send forces to Angola. Re-elected in 1976, Manley welcomed Castro to Jamaica a year later on a state visit.

But Manley's government ran into serious problems. The United States disapproved of Manley's relationship with Castro and also his democratic socialism. It promoted the destabilization of his government, largely by discouraging tourists to visit the island and by refusing aid and financial help to Jamaica. The result was an enormous credit squeeze and the flight of capital out of the island. Between 1974 and 1980, there was a fall of 16 per cent in the gross national product, a rise in the cost of living by 320 per cent and a significant devaluation of the Jamaican dollar. In 1980, Manley was defeated by the Jamaica Labour Party candidate, Edward Seaga, who, within a year of taking office, had severed relations with Cuba. Castro had lost a close ally.

But by 1980, Castro had another sympathetic government in the Commonwealth Caribbean – Grenada. In 1979, Maurice Bishop led a revolution in the island which ousted Prime Minister Eric Gairy. Bishop's People's Revolutionary Government lasted until 1983; during its short history, it helped to transform Grenada and also established close relations with Cuba. But it ended tragically four years after it had begun, with the death of its leader and invasion by the Americans.

Grenada, a small, relatively poor island in the eastern Caribbean, was dependent mostly on its exports of cocoa, bananas and nutmeg. In the 1950s, Eric Gairy, a Grenadian who had worked as a shop steward in Aruba, emerged as a popular trade union leader and politician. Regarded as a champion of the estate workers and rural population of Grenada, Gairy and his party won the first elections under universal suffrage in 1951. Within a decade, however, he and his government were characterized by corruption and repression. He also created a group of illegal thugs under his control, the Mongoose Gang, which he used to break up demonstrations and protests.

One of the targets of the Mongoose Gang was the New Jewel Movement. Formed by a group of young Grenadian professionals, many of whom had been educated abroad, the New Jewel Movement criticized Gairy's government for its failure to deal with high unemployment rates, lack of educational opportunities, and problems in health and transportation. Instead, it offered a manifesto to deal with the reconstruction of the island. In the elections of 1976 two years after Grenada had become independent, the head of the New Jewel Movement, Maurice Bishop, became leader of the opposition.

Bishop had trained as a lawyer in London, while another of his close associates, Bernard Coard, had studied economics in Britain. In 1979, tipped off that Gairy was planning to arrest the leadership of the New Jewel Movement, Bishop and his colleagues organized a coup, attacking the Defence Force Barracks and taking over the radio station. Twelve hours later, Bishop stood at the head of the People's Revolutionary Government, with Coard soon to be named deputy prime minister and in charge of Finance.[9]

Bishop's government immediately set to work implementing its manifesto. During the next four years, it was able to reduce unemployment from about 50 per cent to around 15 per cent. Health and education were significantly improved, including making secondary education free for all students and expanding the opportunities for Grenadians to study at university level. In addition to a literacy campaign, the government also promoted the use of Grenadian Creole in teaching. Under Bernard Coard's economic leadership, the government was able to achieve stable economic growth, as it moved slowly towards socialism.

The government's foreign policy objectives were to align itself with Cuba and the Soviet Union, with other socialist countries, and with the Non-Aligned Movement. Bishop was personally and ideologically very close to Castro, and Castro responded with extensive aid to help construct the new international airport at Point Salines, a project which was essential to Grenada's development as a modern tourist destination. Inevitably, Grenada's links with Cuba and with the socialist world meant a severing of relations with the United States. In reality, it meant much more than that. With a conservative administration headed by Ronald Reagan in the White House, it was clear that the United States regarded Grenada as a communist threat in its backyard. As with the Manley administration in Jamaica, the United States government sought to destabilize the revolution.

Ultimately, external and internal pressures on the People's Revolutionary Government led to its implosion. The revolutionary leadership split, eventually leading to Bishop's assassination in October 1983. In the wake of Bishop's murder, a Revolutionary Military Council sought to establish order. But the self-annihilation of the revolution allowed the United States to do what it had long planned: invade the island. The Grenada revolution was dead, and Fidel Castro had lost another sympathetic regime in the region.[10]

Apart from Jamaica and Grenada, Castro's other ally in the Commonwealth Caribbean was British Guiana. Divided along ethnic lines between descendants of East Indian indentured labourers and blacks, British Guiana had a majority Indian population. It was strategically important and also had significant reserves of bauxite. Its first major political leader, Cheddi Jagan, was a Marxist of Indian origin; he formed the People's Progressive Party and won the elections of 1953. However, because of concerns about the prominence of communists in the government, the British suspended the constitution, only restoring constitutional rule three years later. With an Indian population which voted along ethnic lines, Jagan was able to win the next two elections.[11]

Worried about the possibility that, under Jagan, British Guiana could become another Cuba, the American government persuaded the British to impose a system of proportional representation in the colony. As planned, the 1964 elections gave power to Forbes Burnham, the leader of the opposition party, the People's National Congress. Regarded as a moderate black politician, Burnham remained in power, largely through rigged elections, until his death in 1985. However, Burnham moved politically to the left, establishing close links with Cuba and the Soviet Union and nationalizing many of the leading companies in the country. In 1975, Cuba gave Burnham its highest national award.[12]

But Guyana, as it became known on independence in 1966, found itself in serious economic and ethnic difficulties in the Burnham era. Moreover, in 1980, Walter Rodney was assassinated. One of the foremost intellectuals in the region, Rodney had taught in Africa after his deportation from Jamaica and returned to Guyana in 1974. He became the leader of the Working People's Alliance, a small multi-racial party to the left of Burnham's People's National Congress. It is likely that the Burnham government was involved in Rodney's murder. Although Cheddi Jagan returned to power in 1992, he died in office five years later. However, Guyana has continued to be plagued by some of the same underlying problems which have characterized the country since independence.

Through all these changes, Fidel Castro remained in power. Manley, Bishop and Burnham sought to bring significant changes to their societies. But their regimes have either been toppled democratically, imploded from within or ended by death. The revolutionary Caribbean has carried on where it began: in Cuba.

# CHAPTER SIXTEEN

# Decolonization and independence in the Caribbean

The Caribbean has been one of the most colonized regions in the world. Each island and territory in the Caribbean has at one point or another in its history been a colony. Yet in the twentieth century, much of the region has become independent. This raises questions about the meaning of independence in a region characterized by political fragmentation, dependence on external economies and a geopolitical position in the backyard of the United States. It is therefore useful to review the political status of the different parts of the region before examining how they have dealt with the problems posed by independence and dependence.

We have already seen that parts of the Caribbean have been independent since the nineteenth century. When Haiti was established in 1804, it was only the second independent republic in the Americas and the first in the Caribbean. In the case of Haiti, independence was the outcome of a successful slave revolt and a revolution which ousted the French; however, economic conditions were very difficult in the wake of the revolution which decimated the country's sugar economy. Moreover, Haiti subsequently had to agree to compensate the French for their property losses, before the French would recognize the country. The indemnity of 150 million francs, agreed by the Haitians in 1825, was a crippling amount for a newly independent country. Haiti's island neighbour, the Dominican Republic, became independent in 1865, but only following Haitian domination for a twenty-year period ending in 1844 and re-annexation by Spain in 1861.

Cuba gained its independence in 1902 as a result of the Spanish-American War. However, Cuba's independence was circumscribed by the nature of its constitution, which allowed the United States to intervene repeatedly in the first three decades of the twentieth century. Like Cuba, Puerto Rico was occupied militarily by the United States after Spain had ceded the island to the Americans in 1898. In 1900, Puerto Rico became an unincorporated territory of the United States; it was given a civilian government but one controlled almost entirely by the Americans. In effect, Puerto Rico remained a non-self-governing colony well into the 1940s. But this changed with the arrival of Puerto Rico's leading twentieth-century politician, Luis Muñoz Marín. A poet and a journalist, Muñoz Marín became the first Puerto Rican to be elected as governor in 1948. Re-elected four more times, he helped transform the island's economy from one based on agriculture to a concentration on manufacturing and service industries. Muñoz Marín was also largely responsible for 'Operation Bootstrap', an economic development programme that began in 1948 and encouraged industrialization. It did so in part by granting tax holidays to corporations, most of them from the United States, that set up factories in the island.

After the Second World War, the United States was under pressure from the United Nations to change its colonial relationship with Puerto Rico. In response, the United States granted Puerto Rico its own constitution, which led to the creation in 1952 of the Estado Libre Asociado de Puerto Rico (the Free Associated State or Commonwealth). Since then, the status of Puerto Rico has been a constant issue: there is a small independence movement, but the island is split between supporters of the current Commonwealth status and those in favour of Puerto Rico becoming a state of the United States. In a referendum on this issue held in November 2012, a majority voted in favour of Puerto Rico becoming the 51st state of the United States. Another referendum in June 2017 even more emphatically supported statehood for Puerto Rico, with over 97 per cent of voters choosing this option. Moreover, the current governor, Ricardo Rosselló, was elected in 2017 on a platform that advocated statehood for Puerto Rico.

**FIGURE 16.1** *Luis Muñoz Marín.*
*Source:* © Bettmann/CORBIS.

Whatever the views of the Puerto Rican population, however, it is the US Congress that would have to agree to statehood for Puerto Rico. This is unlikely with a Republican-dominated Congress. At the same time that the issue of statehood is being debated, Puerto Rico is facing a huge debt crisis: in June 2017, it was $72 billion in debt with more than $49 billion in pension obligations. The outlook is therefore one of increasing austerity and hardship for many Puerto Ricans.[1] Interestingly, although Puerto Rico has become increasingly intertwined economically with the United States, it has retained the Spanish language and its own particular island identity. Three former Danish colonies, St. Thomas, St. John and St. Croix, are also part of the United States: the United States bought these islands from Denmark in 1917 for $25 million, largely for strategic reasons. Like Puerto Ricans, the people of these islands are citizens of the United States, but they cannot vote in US Presidential or Congressional elections.

By contrast, most of the Anglophone Caribbean has become independent, but only since the 1960s. In 1962, Jamaica and Trinidad were granted their independence from Britain, followed by Barbados and Guyana (formerly British Guiana) in 1966. In the 1970s and 1980s, many of the former British colonies in the eastern Caribbean also became independent, including Dominica, Grenada, St. Lucia, St. Kitts-Nevis, St. Vincent and Antigua. The Bahamas was given its independence in 1973 and Belize, formerly British Honduras, followed suit in 1981. This has left several islands in the Caribbean as effective colonies of Britain, because they are regarded as too small or too vulnerable to be independent. Now called British Overseas Territories, they consist of Anguilla, the British Virgin Islands, the Turks and Caicos Islands, the Cayman Islands and Montserrat.[2]

France and the Netherlands have followed very different paths than Britain in dealing with their former colonies in the Caribbean. In 1946, the French made French Guiana, Martinique and Guadeloupe overseas departments of France, effectively incorporating them as part of the metropolis. This has meant that these departments are represented in the French National Assembly. The French also have two other islands in the northeastern Caribbean that are known as French overseas collectivities. The first, St. Martin, is shared with the Dutch St. Maarten, and is the smallest island in the world to have been partitioned between two different countries for over 300 years. The other French island in this category, St. Barthélemy, was settled by the French in the seventeenth century, given to the Swedish in 1774 and returned to the French in 1877.

In the case of the Netherlands Antilles, which consist of Aruba, Bonaire, Curaçao, Saba, St. Eustatius and St. Maarten, the Dutch government granted them constitutional equality with the Netherlands and Suriname in 1954. This grouping formed the Kingdom of the Netherlands, although Suriname became independent in 1975. In 2010, the Netherlands Antilles was dissolved as a constitutional unit, with Curaçao and St. Maarten joining Aruba as separate countries within the Kingdom of the Netherlands, each having its own national government. The remaining Dutch islands, Bonaire, Saba and St. Eustatius, became special municipalities within the Netherlands.[3]

In light of the fragmented nature of the Caribbean, it is not surprising that there have been attempts at regional political and economic integration. The West Indies Federation was one of these: it was established by the British government to facilitate independence in many of its Caribbean colonies. The British view was that independence could only be viable on a regional basis. However, Britain did not take into account the lack of a regional identity among many of the Anglophone Caribbean countries and also the strong identification of Caribbean people with their individual colony or island. Established in 1958, the Federation foundered when the Jamaicans voted to withdraw after a referendum in 1961. Among other concerns, the Jamaicans feared that they would be subsidizing the small islands of the Federation; once Jamaica had made its decision, Trinidad followed soon after. The Federation was dissolved in 1962.

The Anglophone Caribbean has also been involved in a more lasting attempt at regional economic integration: the Caribbean Community (CARICOM) established in 1973. Its aim is to provide free trade and tariff protection among its members for goods made in the region; in addition, CARICOM seeks to promote regional integration and development. With its secretariat based in Guyana, CARICOM has expanded to include Suriname and Haiti. The smaller English-speaking states of the eastern Caribbean have also formed their own grouping, the Organization of Eastern Caribbean States, which shares a common currency and a common bank.

Despite these regional groupings and the political independence of large parts of the region, the Caribbean has had to deal with the political and economic impact of the United States. This has taken a variety of forms. In the first several decades of the twentieth century, the United States frequently occupied the independent countries of the region: Cuba, the Dominican Republic and Haiti. In different ways, this pattern has continued in the last half of the century as well.

The Cold War has played a significant part in these developments. In the case of the Dominican Republic, it has led the United States to support the dictatorship of Rafael Trujillo. Trujillo was chief of the national army and seized power in 1930 in the wake of the American withdrawal from the Dominican Republic. At that point, the Dominican Republic was suffering severely from the Great Depression, and Trujillo introduced an aggressive agrarian reform programme. He supported the peasantry by expropriating

**FIGURE 16.2** *Rafael Leonidas Trujillo.*
*Source:* © Bettmann/CORBIS.

and redistributing idle land and built canals and roads to aid the peasants' access to markets. As a result, the production of foodstuffs increased significantly and the Dominican Republic was saved from economic collapse.

However, under his rule, the Dominican Republic became a police state characterized by terror and repression. One of the worst atrocities of his regime – the so-called Parsley Massacre – was the 1937 killing of more than 20,000 Haitians living in the Dominican Republic. Trujillo personally ordered his army to slaughter the Haitians, many of whom worked in the Dominican Republic's sugar industry. This reflected the anti-Haitianism of the Trujillo regime, despite an outward show of support for the Haitian government. In the end, the Haitian government accepted a token indemnity for this atrocity of $750,000.[4]

In 1959, Trujillo faced an unsuccessful invasion supported by Cuba. Trujillo's response was to step up the terror and torture which had characterized his regime. This alienated many of his former supporters, including the Catholic Church. In May 1961, a group of conspirators backed by the United States and supported by the CIA assassinated him.[5] In the wake of the assassination, strikes and demonstrations forced members of Trujillo's family and his puppet president, Joaquín Balaguer, into exile.

The democratic elections which followed a year later returned a long-time opponent of Trujillo, Juan Bosch, the head of the Dominican Revolutionary Party. Bosch was a writer who had been in exile in Cuba and Costa Rica during the Trujillo regime. Although Bosch was elected by 60 per cent of the voters, a military coup ousted him from power less than a year later, because of fears of his progressive policies and the possibility of another Cuban revolution in the Caribbean. When the supporters of Bosch sought to restore him to office in 1965, the United States intervened militarily: the Americans sent in 23,000 troops to help quell the pro-Bosch forces.

A year later, Joaquín Balaguer, who had been president under Trujillo and who was favoured by the Americans, was again elected president. Although very different from the Trujillo regime, Balaguer's government was also characterized by military repression and corruption. At the same time, Balaguer sought to modernize the Dominican Republic and encouraged foreign investment. He remained in office until 1978 and returned again as president from 1987 to 1996. However, his government faced serious economic problems, including devaluation and inflation, and he was replaced by Leonel Fernández in 1996, who was elected again in 2004 and 2008. Unlike Trujillo's policy of isolationism, Fernández has sought to create links with the rest of the Caribbean. He has also encouraged the shift towards manufacturing, tourism and the service sector as drivers of the country's economy. His successor, Danilo Medina, formerly served as Fernández's chief of staff and has proven to be highly popular: he was easily re-elected in 2016.

However, Medina's administration has been marred by the expulsion of thousands of Dominicans of Haitian descent who were affected by a ruling of the Constitutional Court of the Dominican Republic. It ruled in 2013 that children born in the Dominican Republic to undocumented foreign parents since 1929 had never been entitled to Dominican nationality. The judgement disproportionately affected Dominicans of Haitian descent and, as a result, thousands of people have either been deported to Haiti or left the Dominican Republic fearing deportation.[6] But emigration, especially to the United States, has continued to be significant, and the remittances from these migrants have been an important element in the Dominican economy.

The United States not only backed Trujillo during most of his presidency but also supported another dictator, François Duvalier, in neighbouring Haiti. Although elected as president in 1957, Duvalier, who was known as Papa Doc, declared himself president for life in 1964 and made use of the *Tonton Macoutes*, his private security force, to help terrorize any opposition. Yet as with Trujillo, the United States favoured regimes which did not threaten the status quo, especially in the context of the Cold War and the threat from Cuba. Duvalier's son, Jean Claude, also known as Baby Doc, took over the government in 1971, but his dictatorship collapsed, partly because of the loss of American support. He fled the country in 1986, leaving a country which has remained the poorest in the Americas.[7]

The 1990s witnessed the accession to the presidency of Jean-Bertrand Aristide, a radical Catholic priest who had opposed Duvalier. Aristide was elected president with a huge majority in 1990 but deposed less than a year later by a military coup. He was returned to office again for two years from 1994 after the Americans, under the authorization of the United Nations, had sent in troops to occupy Haiti and remove the military regime. But despite Aristide's stated interest in improving the lot of the poor in Haiti and a further aborted period in office as president from 2001 to 2004, the situation for the mass of Haitians has deteriorated even further. This was magnified in January 2010, when Haiti was struck by a huge earthquake. Centred around the capital, Port-au-Prince, and the southwest of the island, the earthquake killed over 200,000 people and left over 1,000,000 homeless. Over 90 per cent of all buildings in the capital were destroyed. Yet despite billions of dollars of international aid, more than 50,000 people were still living in makeshift camps seven years after the earthquake.[8]

While Haiti has been independent since 1804, much of the Caribbean has only relatively recently become independent. At the same time, there are still islands in the Caribbean that are effectively colonies. As we have seen, independence for the small-island nations of the Caribbean has often been circumscribed by the presence and the power of the United States. But it is not only the United States that impinges on the Caribbean: Britain's decision in 2016 to leave the European Union (Brexit) is likely to have a significant impact, especially in the Anglophone Caribbean. As Ronald Sanders, the Antiguan ambassador to the United States, has pointed out, Brexit means that the Caribbean will lose a sympathetic voice in its relations with the European Union. This could affect many areas, including development assistance, since the remaining members of the European Union have no historical ties to the Caribbean.[9]

Another country that has shown increasing interest in the Caribbean has been the People's Republic of China. In the past decade alone, China has invested billions of dollars in the region. This has included funding major tourist and infrastructure projects as well as providing aid to countries in the region. For example, China has funded a long overdue north–south highway in Jamaica at an estimated cost of $600 million. At the same time, it has given Dominica over $100 million for development projects.

There have been questions about China's motivation in providing this funding. One view is that it forms part of China's investment strategy. In return for funding the major highway in Jamaica, for example, China has been given over 1,000 acres of land along the highway to build several luxury hotels. But there is another view that suggests that China's motivation is diplomatic: China is concerned about the number of countries in the Caribbean that support Taiwan in the United Nations. In this view, China is intent on maximizing its strategic alliances in the region.[10]

While both of these explanations are plausible, they point to the Caribbean's continued need for external support, whether from China, the United States or Europe. In general, then, the route from decolonization to independence has not been an easy one for the people of the Caribbean and continues to pose challenges for the region.

# CHAPTER SEVENTEEN

# Contemporary themes in the Hispanic and the wider Caribbean

A number of significant issues have affected the Hispanic and the wider Caribbean historically and continue to be important in the twenty-first century. Some of these issues – such as the illegal drug trade – have developed as a result of the Caribbean's geographical position between Latin America and the United States. The Caribbean is a major transhipment centre for drugs emanating from Colombia and destined for the United States and Europe. It is ideally located for this purpose and offers the potential of landing facilities and hidden coves to facilitate drug trafficking. Given the enormous wealth of the Colombian drug barons, it is possible for them to offer huge bribes to government officials and politicians to assist the drug trade.

This is precisely what has happened. For example, in 1985, the head of the government of the Turks and Caicos, along with two of his ministers, was arrested in Miami and charged with aiding the transhipment of drugs to the United States. The year before, one of the Bahamian ministers of government was accused of corruptly accepting money from drug smugglers. As Jorge I. Domínguez has suggested, 'The problems range from the possibility that a country might be seized by force to facilitate future drug traffic, to normal corruption, to the "purchasing" of a government such as that of the Turks and Caicos.'[1]

The drug trade has inevitably affected the economies of the region. But there have been even more significant developments which have helped to transform Caribbean economies. One of these was the model proposed by the St. Lucian economist, Arthur Lewis, in the 1940s to foster economic development in the region. His proposal for industrialization-by-invitation was taken up by Puerto Rico: the result of the 'Puerto Rican model', as it was called, was rapid economic growth for Puerto Rico. But it came at a price. It was capital intensive and did not create the large number of jobs which were needed. Moreover, the model had the effect of ruining Puerto Rican agriculture and making the island even more dependent on the United States. Yet despite these problems, other governments in the region have adopted similar programmes designed to attract foreign investment and to stimulate their economies.

One of the major problems for the Caribbean economies has been their traditional reliance on agricultural exports. From the time of slavery to the recent past, sugar production was important in most of the economies of the region. With the decline of sugar came some agricultural diversification: Jamaica, for example, developed a very significant banana industry in the late nineteenth century. Its banana production soon exceeded that of sugar and, in the early twentieth century, it was the world's leading banana producer. In the twentieth century, much of the eastern Caribbean – including St. Lucia, St. Vincent, Grenada and Dominica – became largely dependent on banana exports. There has also been diversification to produce other crops in the region such as coffee, cocoa, tobacco and citrus.

Mineral exports have also been significant in the last century: bauxite production has been a major element in the economies of Jamaica, Guyana and Suriname. At the same time, oil and gas exports from Trinidad have transformed its economy. Oil refining, rather than oil production, has been crucial in Aruba and Curaçao. Located close to oil-rich Venezuela, these former Dutch colonies witnessed massive investment by Dutch-Shell in the 1920s, creating the largest oil refinery in the world in Aruba.

Yet all of these areas pose potential problems for the Caribbean. Consider the problem of bananas. Banana exports to Europe were protected under the Lomé convention, which has meant that bananas gained access to the European markets at preferential rates. However, these agreements have been successfully challenged by other banana producers, especially in Central America. The result has been a very significant reduction in the number of small banana producers in the Anglophone Caribbean. According to Dennis A. Pantin, the number of active farmers in St. Lucia in the period from 1992 to 1998 declined by 36 per cent while in Grenada the figure was 80 per cent. Most banana producers in the eastern Caribbean now sell their crop under the Fairtrade label. This guarantees them a minimum price for their bananas and funds for reinvestment in their producer cooperatives. But Pantin argues that the long-term consequences of the decline of the banana industry have been increased unemployment and a potential for serious social tension. It is also apparent that sugar, which is still a significant employer in the region, is likely to have similar problems.[2]

A reliance on mineral exports creates comparable problems. When the Manley government levied big increases in the taxes on bauxite extraction in the 1970s, the multinational companies involved in the business shifted large parts of their production elsewhere in the world. In Trinidad, oil and gas production accounts for about 80 per cent of the value of its exports. When the oil price is high, as it was after the huge price rises of the early 1970s, Trinidad profited enormously. However, when the price of oil fell dramatically a decade later, there were serious economic problems for the country.

Tourism poses similar difficulties. On the one hand, tourism is one of the most important earners of foreign currency in the Caribbean. Many islands in the region depend on tourists to support their economies. Yet as with agricultural and mineral exports, tourism is highly dependent on external circumstances. A recession in North America or Europe can have a devastating impact on the number of tourists travelling to the region. Global economic fluctuations, then, are a factor outside of the region's control but which can seriously damage the islands' economies. In some places, there is also a problem of tourist revenues leaving the region. When tourists stay in foreign-owned hotels, for example, much of the profit is returned to European or North American shareholders rather than remaining in the Caribbean.

Tourist numbers can also be affected by concerns about health. The mosquito-borne Zika virus is a case in point. In December 2015, the Center for Disease Control in the United States confirmed that cases of the virus had been confirmed in Puerto Rico. Zika then spread across the Caribbean. The problem for tourists and people living in the region was the potential connection between Zika and microcephaly, a birth defect in babies born with an abnormally small head. Pregnant women and couples planning to have children were therefore warned not to travel to the affected areas in the Caribbean. Although Puerto Rican tourism was particularly affected by fears of the Zika virus, the impact of the virus on tourist numbers in the region as a whole is unclear. But the widespread concern about Zika is another example of the vulnerability of tourism in the region.

Tourism can also affect another important problem in the Caribbean: the environment. Short-term visitors to the region are not always aware of their ecological impact. Visiting relatively arid islands such as Antigua and the Bahamas, tourists from Europe and North America used to unlimited water supplies are often ignorant of the damage they can cause to the islands' water table and to the wider environment more generally. Yet tourists are only one of the threats to the Caribbean environment.

Another major problem for the region is climate change. Climate change has the potential to impact the Caribbean in a variety of ways. For example, a report from the UN Food and Agriculture Organization in 2016 predicted an increase in the frequency of droughts as a result of climate change. Since there are many Caribbean islands that are already affected by water shortages, more droughts could seriously damage their agricultural output as well as affecting tourism. Climate change has also been blamed for the rise in sea levels in the region. The Caribbean mirrors the global trend in rising sea levels but is particularly vulnerable to this problem because of its many low-lying shores and beaches. If sea levels continue to rise, this would have serious economic and social implications for many Caribbean countries.[3]

The skewed economic development of the region has also led to serious environmental degradation. The deforestation of large parts of the Caribbean has led to damaging soil erosion, most visibly in Haiti but also elsewhere. Many smaller plots of land have been subdivided so frequently and farmed so intensively that the land is no longer productive. Where minerals such as bauxite have been extracted, companies have sometimes left visible reminders of the damage they have caused: enormous lakes filled with the poisonous residues of their work.

The fragile ecologies of the region have also been affected by natural disasters. The area is prone to hurricanes, which have caused enormous damage. In 1995, which was one of the most active recent years for tropical storms and hurricanes, the cost to the region was several billion dollars. Hurricane Ivan in 2004 nearly destroyed Grenada, and 2005 witnessed a series of devastating hurricanes across the Caribbean. More recently, Hurricane Erika caused severe damage in Dominica in 2015, so much so that it was estimated that the reconstruction bill would total up to half of the country's annual GDP. Even worse was the effect of Hurricane Matthew in southern Haiti in 2016: at least 500 people were killed and 200,000 homes destroyed.

But two of the most destructive hurricanes ever to hit the region were Irma and Maria, both category-five hurricanes that struck the Caribbean in September 2017. Irma, which killed at least forty-three people, caused more than $10 billion in damage and made parts of the region – especially Barbuda – barely habitable. The British Virgin Islands, the Dutch and French parts of St Maarten/ St Martin, Tortola and Cuba also suffered extensive damage to homes and to infrastructure.[4] Irma was one of the most powerful hurricanes in the history of the Caribbean with wind speeds of between 130 and 185 mph and was followed soon in its wake by hurricane Maria. Maria also had a severe impact across the region but was particularly destructive in Dominica and Puerto Rico. The prime minister of Dominica reported that the storm killed at least twenty-seven people on the island and affected 80 per cent of the island's population. Agriculture was almost totally ruined as was much of the island's infrastructure. In Puerto Rico, Maria destroyed the electrical grid across the island and a month after the hurricane, 80 per cent of the island's population was still without power. Officially, sixty-four people died in Puerto Rico as a result of Maria; however, some estimates suggest that the figure is considerably higher because of the continuing lack of power and the effects on the health of Puerto Ricans.[5]

Volcanic activity in the region has also had very dramatic effects. The 1902 volcano eruption of Mt. Pelée in Martinique devastated its economic and cultural capital, Saint-Pierre, and killed 30,000 people. More recently, the Soufrière volcano in Montserrat erupted in 1997, rendering two-thirds of the island uninhabitable, including

**FIGURE 17.1** *The impact of Hurricane Maria in Dominica.*
*Source:* Public domain.

the capital, Plymouth. Roughly three-fourths of Montserrat's population of 12,000 people fled the island.

The fleeing islanders of Montserrat are among the most recent emigrants from the Caribbean, but they are part of a long history of migration within the region and outside of it as well. Indeed, the Caribbean itself is a region populated by immigrants. Having decimated the Amerindian population, Europeans, themselves immigrants, imported millions of Africans to work the plantations. After emancipation, large numbers of Asians were brought to the region: apart from the Indians who worked as indentured labourers primarily in Trinidad and British Guiana, there were roughly 100,000 Chinese who came to Cuba in the nineteenth century. Additionally, Suriname imported roughly 35,000 Indians and 24,000 Javanese labourers, while the French West Indies brought in nearly 100,000 Indians as well. Europeans also continued to come to the Caribbean in the nineteenth century, especially to Cuba, the Dominican Republic and Puerto Rico.

Moreover, many immigrants did not remain in the Caribbean; some, like the early Barbadian planters, helped to populate South

Carolina. Money and people flowed in and out of the region. As Dennis Conway has suggested:

> The triangular trade of sugar, manufactured goods, foodstuffs, timber, cotton, and tobacco ... cemented transnational and transatlantic mercantilist linkages, served planters' interests, and furthered interconnections, thereby deepening and entrenching the dependent relations of the Caribbean with external forces and influences. The wealth that was created in the region was always circulating out of it, and the region's people were to respond likewise as conditions worsened.[6]

When conditions in the Caribbean worsened for many people after emancipation, they left their homes in search of work and better pay. Large numbers of Barbadians migrated to Trinidad and to British Guiana and thousands of people from the small islands of the eastern Caribbean sought work in Trinidad. Later in the century, faced with the depression of the 1880s and the decline of the sugar industry, roughly 50,000 Jamaicans went to Panama to work on the French attempt to build the Panama Canal. When the Americans took over the project, 60,000 Barbadians, 80,000 Jamaicans and several thousand labourers from Guadeloupe and Martinique helped to construct the canal between 1900 and 1914. As Lara Putnam suggests, many of the Barbadians who went to work on the canal travelled to Panama under contract. But she estimates that around 25,000 Barbadians went on their steam, half of whom were probably women.[7] With the expansion of the sugar industry in Cuba and the Dominican Republic in the early twentieth century, over 100,000 Jamaicans went to work in Cuba, while thousands of West Indians from the Leeward Islands laboured in the Dominican Republic. Similarly, with the development of the oil refineries in Aruba and Curaçao in the 1920s, many West Indians migrated to work in the oil industry.

In the period after the Second World War, migration patterns changed: large numbers of Caribbean men and women migrated to the metropole. In labour-starved post-war Britain, for example, hospitals and transport services organized massive recruitment schemes to bring in workers from the Anglophone Caribbean. The first West Indian immigrants arrived from Jamaica on board the *Empire Windrush* in 1948, and one estimate put the total of migrants to Britain in the decade after 1951 at roughly 250,000. Concerned about the effects of this immigration, however, Britain passed the Commonwealth Immigration Act in 1962, severely restricting the flow of future migrants.[8] Elsewhere in Europe, France received about 200,000 migrants from Guadeloupe, Martinique and French Guiana, and the Netherlands in 1980 had roughly the same number of immigrants from its former colonies in the Caribbean. The Netherlands has had a particularly large number of migrants from Suriname. When Suriname became independent in 1975, roughly 40,000 Surinamese, mostly of Indian and Javanese descent, fled the country, fearing discrimination under the new regime.[9]

While hundreds of thousands of Caribbean people have migrated to Europe, the number going to the United States has been more than four million (see Table 17.1). This has partly been because of the easing

**TABLE 17.1** Distribution of Caribbean immigrants to the United States by country of birth, 2014.

| Region and Country | Number of Immigrants | Per cent (%) |
| --- | --- | --- |
| Cuba | 1,173,000 | 29.3 |
| Dominican Republic | 993,000 | 24.9 |
| Jamaica | 706,000 | 17.6 |
| Haiti | 628,000 | 15.7 |
| Trinidad and Tobago | 220,000 | 5.5 |
| Barbados | 51,000 | 1.3 |
| Grenada | 34,000 | 0.9 |
| Bahamas | 32,000 | 0.8 |
| Dominica | 28,000 | 0.7 |
| West Indies | 26,000 | 0.6 |
| St. Vincent and the Grenadines | 23,000 | 0.6 |
| Other Caribbean | 81,000 | 2.0 |
| Total: Caribbean | 4,000,000 | 100.0 |

Source: Migration Policy Institute tabulation of data from U.S. Census Bureau 2014 American Community Survey – http://www.migrationpolicy.org/article/caribbean-immigrants-united-states (accessed 28 April 2017).

of US immigration restrictions after 1965, but it is also a function of geography, economics and politics. The massive and continuing Cuban exodus following the Castro revolution has dramatically altered Miami, where there is a section known as 'Little Havana'. Between 1955 and 1970, one-third of the Puerto Rican population left the island for the United States, primarily to New York City. Similarly, nearly one million people from the Dominican Republic have migrated to the United States, while many impoverished Haitians have fled in makeshift boats, seeking access to Florida and the wider United States. In addition, Jamaica and Trinidad and Tobago have sent large numbers of migrants to the United States. Canada has also proved to be an increasingly important destination, especially for people from the Anglophone Caribbean.

Gender was an important factor in Caribbean migration to the United States. As Tyesha Maddox points out, there were more female immigrants than male immigrants to the United States in the early twentieth century. For example, in the period between 1920 and 1924, 29 per cent of immigrants arriving in the United States were Caribbean women while men made up just over 23 per cent of this figure. Maddox suggests that women were especially important in establishing immigrant social networks and in helping to found mutual aid societies and benevolent associations. Moreover, women also were primarily responsible for creating chains of migration that brought other women as well as men to the United States.[10]

Migration has inevitably had significant effects in the Caribbean itself. It has created problems in that it has deprived the Caribbean of some of its most productive people. Since a large proportion of emigrants are relatively young, it has meant that the demography of some parts of the region have been badly skewed, leaving behind an unbalanced population of generally older people. At the same time, the remittances of Caribbean migrants have been a very significant element in many Caribbean economies. As an example of the impact of remittance money, Bonham Richardson reported that Carriacou, a small island in the Grenadines with a population of around 6,000 people, received over $500,000 in remittances in one year in the 1970s.[11] Remittances, then, are a major contributor to the GNP of most Caribbean countries. Moreover, without emigration, much of the Caribbean would now be overpopulated, creating unsustainable social and economic tensions in those societies (see Table 17.2).

**TABLE 17.2** Caribbean populations and per capita income, 2003.

| Country | Population | Population Growth (%) | Per Capita Income (US$) |
|---|---|---|---|
| Antigua and Barbuda | 79,000 | 1.6 | 9,330 |
| Barbados | 271,000 | 0.4 | 9,270 |
| Belize | 274,000 | 2.9 | 3,740 |
| Cuba | 11,326,000 | 0.5 | N/A |
| Dominica | 71,000 | −0.1 | 3,380 |
| Dominican Republic | 8,739,000 | 1.6 | 2,130 |
| Grenada | 105,000 | 0.9 | 3,690 |
| Guyana | 769,000 | 0.4 | 890 |
| Haiti | 8,440,000 | 2.0 | 400 |
| Jamaica | 2,643,000 | 0.8 | 2,780 |
| St. Kitts and Nevis | 47,000 | 0.8 | 6,860 |
| St. Lucia | 161,000 | 1.4 | 4,040 |
| St. Vincent and the Grenadines | 109,000 | 0.2 | 3,250 |
| Trinidad and Tobago | 1,313,000 | 0.6 | 7,790 |

Source: World Bank – http://www.worldbank.org/data.

Caribbean migration, especially to the United States, has also thrown up significant differences between the metropole and the Caribbean. One of these is the varying pattern of race relations in the United States and the Caribbean. As Gordon Lewis pointed out, the pattern of discrimination in the United States was rooted in a black–white dichotomy; in this context, people were perceived as either black or white. In the Caribbean, however, the classificatory system has been more subtle, based among other things, on shades of colour. Moreover, in the Caribbean, class considerations have been significant: prejudice there can be softened by education and social status. For Lewis, this is the factor of 'social colour. In U.S. society, money talks; in Caribbean society, money whitens'.[12]

In parts of the Caribbean, the pattern of race relations has also been complicated by the arrival of immigrants from India, China and Indonesia after emancipation. Many of the Indian indentured labourers who worked on the sugar plantations remained in villages in the countryside; a significant number of blacks, on the other hand, migrated to the towns and worked in more urban occupations. This generalized spatial separation has also led to different patterns of voting, often resulting in ethnic groups supporting their own political parties. Cheddi Jagan, for example, remained the head of the largely Indian People's Political Party in Guyana and was supported overwhelmingly by voters of Indian descent. As we have seen, this becomes important, when one ethnic group forms the majority of the population and can therefore determine the outcome of elections.

Ethnic divisions have also been significant in blunting the Black Power Movement in the Caribbean, at least in the case of Trinidad. In 1970, Black Power demonstrations – initially led by students and academics from the University of the West Indies – rocked the government of Eric Williams. The 'February Revolution', as it was called, was taken up by the urban unemployed, but the severity of the protests had more to do with the socio-economic conditions in Trinidad than the banner of Black Power. Moreover, when the organizers sought to spread the message to the Indian heartland of Trinidad, they were met with relative indifference.

A different kind of division emerged in Trinidad in July 1990, when a group of over 100 black Muslims, the Jammat al-Muslimeen led by Abu Bakr, staged an attempted coup against the government. With other leading figures in his organization, Abu Bakr held Prime Minister A.N.R. Robinson and his cabinet hostage for seven days at the Red House, Trinidad's Parliament. The coup led to widespread rioting and looting, at a cost of millions of dollars and twenty-four dead. Although most Trinidadians did not support the coup, many agreed with the group's criticism of government corruption and social and economic inequality in Trinidad. The coup ended when Abu Bakr surrendered on condition that he and the other rebels would not be prosecuted.

The complex pattern of race relations and ethnic divisions in the Caribbean, along with concerns about the environment, drugs and migration, have all been highly significant contemporary themes in the region. A more recent issue – related to the region's history of slavery – is the campaign for reparations. The campaign was sparked by the publication of a book by the historian Hilary Beckles entitled *Britain's Black Debt: Reparations for Caribbean Slavery and Native Genocide*. Published in 2012, the book argued that Britain should pay reparations for the country's involvement in the slave trade and slavery in the Caribbean. In 2013, CARICOM agreed to take up the claim for reparations from Britain and other former colonial European countries and established a regional commission to organize the campaign. The commission, which is headed by Hilary Beckles, is not seeking payments to individuals; instead, it has developed a ten-point plan for 'reparative justice'. These points include an apology, funds for improved health programmes and a cancellation of debts. The British government's response thus far has been to condemn slavery but to deny any claims for reparations.[13]

A different issue that has emerged in the Caribbean is the debate over homosexuality. Across the region, there is widespread homophobia. This varies from the extreme case of Jamaica, where there is a significant history of physical abuse and attacks on gay men, to the more tacit acceptance of homosexuals in Puerto Rico. It may be, as Linden Lewis has suggested, that the explanation lies in the strength of sects such as Pentecostalism and Revivalism. Since these sects are strongly opposed to homosexuality, their concentration in various parts of the Caribbean may help to explain the regional differences in such attitudes.[14] Whatever the explanation, the issue of homophobia, like the other contemporary themes discussed in this chapter, is likely to remain important throughout the twenty-first century. But the Caribbean's contribution to world culture is far more likely to be remembered than its politics, economics and sexual attitudes.

# CHAPTER EIGHTEEN

# The cultures of
# the Caribbean

Despite its small size, the Caribbean has been a powerful exporter of culture in a variety of different fields. Caribbean music is probably the best-known export, but Caribbean literature and art have also had a significant impact on world culture. Moreover, there are similarities in the cultural output across the Caribbean. The cultural critic, Antonio Benítez-Rojo, maintains that there is a common Caribbean culture which is expressed through music, dance and rhythm and which is not affected by the political and linguistic differences which have characterized the region.[1]

Part of the creativity of the Caribbean lies in its creole culture and in the process of creolization. This has meant a blending of African and European traditions, with aspects of those cultures dominating at different times and in varying ways. The result has been largely unpredictable and constantly evolving. For Benítez-Rojo, the resulting creole culture is the product of the plantation, the institution which brought together Europeans and Africans to produce a range of commodities across the Caribbean. But the plantation did much more than produce sugar and rum: Benítez-Rojo suggests that it helped to create Caribbean culture. Using a highly instructive metaphor, he argues that the plantation was the big bang of the Caribbean universe

whose slow explosion throughout modern history threw out billions and billions of cultural fragments in all directions –

fragments of diverse kinds that, in their endless voyage, come together in an instant to form a dance step, a linguistic trope, the line of a poem, and afterward repel each other to re-form and pull apart once more.[2]

This was especially the case for Caribbean music, as African and European elements came together to produce new forms of music. The African past of the enslaved population has been crucial in that process. Moreover, Africa, like Europe, consists of a wide variety of cultures. The syncretic cultures which have emerged therefore often reflect a merging of different African cultures as well as different European cultures. The anthropologist, Ken Bilby, describes this process as 'inter-African syncretism'.[3]

For the enslaved, music was very important. Slaves held dances on the plantations and also had work songs, which were often characterized by a call and response style. Some of the songs of the enslaved were satirical, poking fun at their masters, while others made telling political points. An observer in Jamaica at the end of the eighteenth century, R. Renny, reported slaves in Kingston singing the following ditty:

One, two, tree,
All de same;
Black, white, brown,
All de same;
All de same,
One, two, tree ... .[4]

On a different level, the religious music of the enslaved was also significant. This music was played at slave funerals and was associated with Afro-Caribbean religions across the region, including Cuban *Santería*, Haitian *Vodou* and Jamaican *Kromanti*. In all of these Afro-Caribbean religions, there was 'song text in West African languages and the use of drums that closely resemble African drums with the same names'.[5] At the same time, these were also highly syncretic religions; *Santería*, for example, was a Yoruba-derived religion in which West African deities remained but were identified with Catholic saints. As a result, the Virgin de la Caridad, the patron saint of Cuba, is for many Cuban blacks also one of the most significant figures in *Santería*.

Caribbean folk music also owes a great deal to the syncretic music developed during slavery. African drumming patterns have been particularly important in this context. For example, the ritual of spirit possession linked to many Afro-Caribbean religions is created in part by a series of drums and other African instruments. But other forms of folk music reflect a more European origin. The *merengue* in the Dominican Republic began in Europe, but then added Afro-Caribbean elements such as its rhythms and call and response patterns. Like other folk music in the region, *merengue* texts often contain biting commentaries. One nationalist *merengue*, called 'La Protesta', was directed against the American occupation of the Dominican Republic from 1916 to 1924:

The Americans came in 1916,
trampling Dominican soil with their boots ... .
the Yankee intruders, we'll drive them out with machetes.'[6]

Like the *merengue*, the folk music elsewhere in the Caribbean – such as the Jamaican *mento*, the Puerto Rican *plena*, the Cuban *son* and *danzón* and the Martiniquan *biguine* – reflects a similar pattern of creolization.

Carnivals in the region also owe their origin to a European tradition. In Trinidad, which has the most famous carnival in the Caribbean, these began as celebrations by the French landed elite which lasted from Christmas to Ash Wednesday and which were characterized by masked balls. But these were taken over by ex-slaves after 1834 who changed carnival 'into a noisy, wild and disorderly amusement viewed with increasing disdain by the well-to-do and with suspicion by the authorities'.[7] The stick bands who participated in carnivals each had their own champion and their special *kalinda* songs, which became the basis for the calypso.

It is likely that calypso had its origins in the African custom of using songs and stories to criticize leaders. Merged with various elements of creole society, calypso developed at the turn of the twentieth century. By the 1920s regular calypso performances were held in special 'tents' ahead of carnival. Calypsonians commented on political events, often attacking local politicians but they also sang about relations between the sexes. This was especially the case during Second World War, when American servicemen were based in Trinidad and helped to stimulate the market for calypsos.

The most famous calypso of the period, Lord Invader's *Rum and Coca Cola*, was about the effect of the Americans on the women of Trinidad and sold over five million records in various versions.[8]

However, the leading calypsonian in the past fifty years has been the Mighty Sparrow (Francisco Slinger). Since the mid-1950s, Sparrow 'has superbly expressed the new surge of black nationalism and pride'. He was also a strong supporter of the future prime minister, Eric Williams, as is reflected in this calypso:

> Leave the damn doctor
> And don't get me mad
> Leave the damn doctor
> Or is murder in Trinidad

In another calypso, Sparrow sang about the development of black pride in the period after 1956:

> Well the way how things shaping up
> All this nigger business go stop
> I tell you soon in the West Indies
> It's please, Mister Nigger, please.

As Bridget Brereton has suggested, 'In the hands of Sparrow and his colleagues and rivals, calypso was taken to new levels of sophistication and wit, becoming an important cultural form as well as a major channel for political and social comment and protest.'[9]

There was another development in Trinidad which became a significant part of the national culture: the steel band. This music was produced by playing on tuned oil drums, which had been discarded from the island's oil industry. Growing out of the working-class ghettoes of Port of Spain in the late 1930s, steel band music was initially associated with hooliganism. However, like carnival, it was eventually embraced by all classes in Trinidad and became an integral part of Trinidad's musical culture.

Trinidad and the calypso have had an impact elsewhere in the Caribbean. In Barbados, one of the leading calypsonians, Gabby (Anthony Carter), has followed in the tradition of some of the more politically oriented Trinidad calypso singers. Gabby has produced a series of political calypsos which have met with government criticism but widespread public approval. For example, his calypso,

*Jack* (1982), called for Barbadians to have a right of access to all the island's beaches. The calypso included the words

> My navel string buried right here
> But a touris' one could be anywhere ... .[10]

In Jamaica, *mento*, the indigenous folk music of the island, has also been influenced by Trinidad calypso music. Under the influence of American rhythm-and-blues music, it developed into ska and then rocksteady and ultimately reggae. Asked to define reggae, Toots Hibbert, lead singer of the Maytals and the first performer to use the word in the title of a song in 1967, responded:

> Reggae means comin' from the people, y'know? Like a everyday thing. Like from the ghetto. From *majority*. Everyday thing that people use like food, we just put music to it and make a dance out of it. Reggae means *regular* people who are suffering, and don't have what they want.[11]

In addition, the Rastafarian influence on reggae has been enormous, and its most famous exponent has been Bob Marley. With his

**FIGURE 18.1** *Bob Marley, 1980.*
*Source:* © CORBIS.

emphasis on Africa and on radical social change in the 1970s, Marley created a worldwide audience for the message of the Rastafarians. One example of this was his song 'Revolution' from the *Natty Dread* album, in which Marley sings the words:

> Revelation, reveals the truth
> Revelation
> It take a revolution to make a solution.

Similarly, in the title track from the *Exodus* album, Marley paints a picture central to the Rastafarians of the exodus of 'Jah people' from Babylon (Jamaica) to Ethiopia:

> Open your eyes and look within.
> Are you satisfied with the life you're living?
> We know where we're going
> We know where we're from.
>
> We're leaving Babylon
> We're going to our father's land.
> Exodus!
> Movement of Jah people.[12]

In the 1980s, dancehall emerged, partly as a derivative of reggae but with a different focus. Dancehall was dominated by the lyrics of the disc jockeys who began to improvise raps over pre-recorded rhythm tracks. Eventually, this became known as 'toasting', and many of the lyrics of the major performers of dancehall proved to be highly controversial. Some were homophobic, often reflecting a fundamentalist reading of the Bible. Yet according to the dub poet, Linton Kwesi Johnson, some of the underlying rhythms of the more famous dancehall artists such as Shabba Ranks or Buju Banton are based on Afro-Caribbean religious cults. As a result, these rhythms are closer to the music of rural Jamaica than other popular music which preceded it.[13]

In Cuba, the music of Buena Vista Social Club evoked pre-revolutionary sounds and images. The group, made up of veteran Cuban musicians who had played in the clubs and casinos of Havana before the revolution, sold over two million records and won a number of Grammy awards. Buena Vista Social Club staged enormously popular concerts all over the world until the death of several of their leading members and was also the basis of a major film by Wim Wenders.

Caribbean migration has also had an influence on the music of the region. New York has become one of the centres of Caribbean music and is the home of *salsa*, the name given to Afro-Latin dance music which developed in the late 1960s and has been significant ever since. Its roots lie in Cuban folk and popular music, and many of its leading performers have been Cuban. But there are also elements in *salsa* from other parts of the Hispanic Caribbean and Latin America as well.[14]

Just as the music of the Caribbean has been closely identified with its folk traditions, writers in the region have increasingly reflected similar themes. In many cases, this has meant a recognition of the importance of the African past. In Cuba, Nicolás Guillén led a movement known as *Poesia negra* ('Black Poetry') from the late 1920s. In his *Son número 6*, Guillén described himself first as a Yoruba but also as an African more generally:

Yoruba soy,
cantando voy,
llorando estoy,
y cuando no soy yoruba,
soy congo, mandinga, carabalí.

[I am Yoruba
singing along,
weeping,
and when I am not Yoruba,
I am Kongo, Mandinka, Calabar.][15]

For Guillén, it was clear that the culture of Cuba as well as of the wider Caribbean was based on Africa. His own poetry therefore drew on Cuban folk music rhythms, language and folklore. Guillén was an important pan-Caribbean figure long before he became involved in the Cuban Revolution.[16]

Writers in Haiti and the Francophone Caribbean shared this interest in African culture. In Haiti, Jean Price-Mars and Jacques Roumain both sought inspiration from the creole-speaking population, from *Vodou* and from the African-based rhythms of their music. In the Francophone Caribbean, Aimé Césaire from Martinique and Léon Damas from French Guiana helped to develop the concept of *Négritude*, specifically valuing the African past and a black identity. Césaire's famous poem, *Cahier d'un Retour au Pays Natal (Notebook of a Return to my Native Land* (1939)) contains these memorable lines:

Eia for the royal Kailcedrate! [a giant African tree transplanted
to Martinique]

Eia for those who have never invented anything
For those who have never explored anything
for those who have never subdued anything
those who open themselves up, enraptured, to the essence
of things … .

Although the poem is written in both Martinican creole and
metropolitan French, Derek Walcott, himself a Nobel Prize-winning
poet and playwright from St. Lucia, noted that 'it sounds, at least
to a listener familiar with French patois, like a poem written totally
in Creole'.[17] Patrick Chamoiseau, a more recent Martinican writer,
also interweaves creole and French in his award-winning novel,
*Texaco* (1992).

In the Anglophone Caribbean, writers have emphasized similar
themes. The folk and the peasantry have been important in the
works of the Barbadians, George Lamming and Kamau Brathwaite.
Brathwaite, in particular, has emphasized the importance of creole
society in his work as an historian and a poet. Language has been
crucial for Brathwaite, and he coined the term 'Nation Language'
to describe creole speech, much of which was influenced by Africa.
In Jamaica, Louise Bennett, more widely known as 'Miss Lou', has
used creole in her verse to reflect the lives of the folk. In her poem,
'Colonization in Reverse', she pokes fun at the emigrants leaving
Jamaica for England in the 1950s:

Wat a joyful news, Miss Mattie
I feel like me heart gwine burs
Jamaica people colonizin
Englan in reverse ….
What a islan! What a people!
Man an woman, old an young
Just a-pack demand bag an baggage
An tun history unside dung![18]

Place has also remained crucial in the work of Anglophone Caribbean
writers. Most of the islands and colonies have been fought over by
Europeans and yet, for Derek Walcott, there is 'an absence of ruins'.
Building on this image, Louis James has suggested that

the real West Indian history was written not in its stones, but in African palm trees or Indian banana groves, in the living seeds brought from other worlds in the holds of privateers, in the cabinets of amateur botanists, and in the guts of slaves.[19]

But place could give way to voyaging, as in Walcott's *Omeros* (1990), which made use of Homer's *Odyssey* but where the voyage connected the worlds of the Caribbean and of Africa.

In more recent Caribbean literature, there is a different kind of place: a recognition of the importance of the diaspora. This is represented by three writers from the Hispanic and Francophone Caribbean: Christina Garcia from Cuba, Edwidge Danticat from Haiti and Junot Diaz from the Dominican Republic. Garcia, Danticat and Diaz all live in the United States and, according to Kezia Page, their novels reflect an acceptance of their new homes in the metropole as well as their origins in the Caribbean. For Page, this is evident in these writers' 'psychological closeness between "homes", one that facilitates a two-placed gaze and a double tongue'.[20] In examining three of their novels – Garcia's, *The Agüero Sisters* (1997), Danticat's *The Dew Breaker* (2004) and Diaz's *The Brief Wondrous Life of Oscar Wao* (2007) – Page points out they each focus on the contemporary politics in the region. More specifically, these novelists describe Caribbean people leaving the region to escape 'brutal' regimes: Castro's Cuba, the Duvaliers' Haiti and Trujillo's Dominican Republic. The authors are therefore describing a different type of migration: one intent on creating new communities in the diaspora but also revealing the violence associated with Caribbean dictatorships.

Much of the best writing of the Anglophone Caribbean has also been done abroad. Just as Césaire developed the concept of *négritude* while living in Paris, writers such as Lamming and the Trinidadians, Sam Selvon and V.S. Naipaul, have done most of their work in England. They have used the experience of the Caribbean diaspora to treat themes of displacement and exile. But in the process, they have retained the rhythms of popular speech and popular music. For example, Linton Kwesi Johnson, a leading dub poet who came to England from Jamaica at the age of eleven, has said that

I don't know how or why it happened, but from the moment I began to write in the Jamaican language music entered the poetry. There was always the beat, or a bass line, going on at the back of my head with the words.[21]

Some of the most significant films in the Caribbean have also reflected popular culture. For example, *The Harder They Come*, a film produced in Jamaica in 1972, was shot in Jamaican creole and was sympathetic to the plight of the urban poor of Kingston. For the film critic Keith Warner, *The Harder They Come* showed that 'the Caribbean people's time had come … '.[22] Twelve years later, *Rue Cases-Nègres* was a portrait of life for the poor of the French-speaking Caribbean which was based on the novel by Joseph Zobel. As with *The Harder They Come*, creole was used very effectively to reach a French-West Indian audience.

In Cuba, the highly developed film industry has dwarfed its Caribbean counterparts. Between 1959 and 1987, Cuba made 164 feature-length films, 1,026 shorts and 1,370 newsreels. Moreover, the Cuban Revolution has raised important questions about the role of cinema and the function of the intellectual in the revolution. One of the leading directors in Cuba, Tomás Gutiérrez Alea, made arguably the most important Cuban film of the 1960s, *Memorias del subdesarrollo* (*Memories of Underdevelopment*, 1968). As John King has suggested, the film 'deals with the consolidation of the Revolution in the face of US imperialist aggression, portraying a Revolution in process, a people constantly alert, and the need for commitment in all sectors of society'.[23] Other films explore subjects largely ignored before the revolution, such as slavery and slave resistance. The black film-maker, Sergio Giral, made a trilogy of films dealing with these themes in the 1970s: *El otro Francisco* (*The Other Francisco*, 1973), *Rancheador* (*Slave Hunter*, 1975) and *Maluala* (1979). Alea's brilliant *La última cena* (*The Last Supper*, 1976) goes even further in exploring the issue of slavery and also of Afro-Cuban religion. An even more important theme in Cuban films has been that of gender, and Pastor Vega's *Retrato de Teresa* (*Portrait of Teresa*, 1978) is an important example of a Cuban film coming to terms with the changing role of women as a result of the revolution.[24]

Like the literature and films of the Caribbean, art has also increasingly depicted aspects of popular culture. One of the most important of these has been Afro-Caribbean culture. This has been a significant theme in the work of Wilfredo Lam, a Cuban and the first Caribbean artist to be regarded as part of modern art history.

Lam was himself mixed race and the offspring of a Chinese father and a mother of African and European descent. According to the art historian and critic, Veerle Poupeye, Lam 'used Afro-Caribbean culture as a vehicle for socio-political commentary and once described his art as "an act of decolonization"'.[25]

Since Afro-Caribbean religions have been so significant in the region, artists have sought to depict elements of *Vodou*, *Santería* and Rastafarianism. Some of the 'primitive' (or not formally trained) painters of Haiti, such as Hector Hyppolite, have used images from *Vodou* in their work. Similarly, in Jamaica, the painter Mallica 'Kapo' Reynolds, who was a Revivalist bishop, has produced paintings and carvings linked to the Rastafarians.

Art has also been associated with other aspects of Caribbean popular culture. Artists have depicted carnivals in the Caribbean and also those established by Caribbean migrants in Brooklyn, Toronto and London. The Caribbean Artists' Movement in London (1966–72) included artists as well as writers and scholars from the region. One of the painters involved in this movement, Aubrey Williams from Guyana, had a leading role in fostering the Amerindian revival in Guyanese art.[26]

Popular culture in the Caribbean is not only reflected in its music, literature and art; there is also an important tradition of sport in the region. For the Anglophone Caribbean, this has meant cricket. Cricket has had a long history in the region: cricket clubs in Barbados were established early in the nineteenth century. By 1865, there was inter-colonial competition among the most important colonies in the region. But the significance of cricket does not lie simply in the game; cricket has been seen as an import from Britain but one which the West Indies have transformed. As Woodville Marshall has suggested:

> Cricket has transformed the region by presenting it with a major form of social expression and public art, and by giving West Indians, wherever they might be, a living tradition of achievement and thereby a sense of national identity ... .[27]

In dominating cricket and especially in defeating Britain, the West Indies have beaten the former colonial power at its own game. In some ways, this has also been the case for baseball, which has been so significant in the Hispanic Caribbean. But as with cricket, Cubans beat the United States in baseball in the 1992 and 1996 Olympics. Moreover, many of the better players in the American major leagues have come from the Dominican Republic and Puerto Rico.

Baseball is only one area in which the United States has had a cultural impact on the Caribbean. Basketball has become the major sport for many young people and has overtaken cricket in parts of the Anglophone Caribbean. American radio and television stations are available in the region and have made American popular culture widely known and often emulated. Christian religious stations emanating from the United States, and particularly those with an interest in evangelical religion, have attracted a huge following.

The most popular figure in Caribbean sports from 2008 onwards – and one of the most widely admired people in sports generally – is the Jamaican sprinter Usain Bolt. Bolt won nine Olympic gold medals in successive Olympics, beginning with Beijing in 2008, continuing in London in 2012 and concluding with Rio de Janeiro in 2016, although one of the gold medals was taken away because of a teammate's disqualification for a doping offence. He is the only sprinter to have won the Olympic 100-metre and 200-metre titles in three consecutive Olympics. In 2017, the year he retired from international competition, Bolt still held the world record for the 100-metre and the 200-metre dashes that he won in 2009.

Whether it is a question of sport, literature, art or music, there is an aspect of Caribbean culture which is common to the region as a whole. Benítez-Rojo suggests that it is Caribbean rhythms which are distinctive and very different from European rhythmic patterns. Discussing the depiction of Carnival in Cuba, for example, Benítez-Rojo points to particular paintings which

> work to capture the rhythms of the drums, of the dances, of the songs, of the fantastic dress and colors that this annual holiday, where the slaves were freed for one day, set out upon Havana's streets in an enormous carnivalesque spectacle.

More significantly, for Benítez-Rojo, 'it is precisely this rhythmic complexity ... that gives pan-Caribbean cultures a way of being, a style that is repeated through time and space in all its differences and variants'.[28]

# NOTES

## Chapter 1

1 Jalil Sued-Badillo, 'The Indigenous Societies at the Time of Conquest', in Jalil Sued-Badillo, ed., *General History of the Caribbean*, vol.1: *Autochthonous Societies* (London: Macmillan, 2003), p. 260. The discussion on the Amerindian chiefs that follows is based on Sued-Badillo's research.
2 Sued-Badillo, 'The Indigenous Societies at the Time of Conquest', p. 270.
3 For the best account of the Tainos, see Irving Rouse, *The Tainos: Rise and Decline of the People who Greeted Columbus* (New Haven: Yale University Press, 1992). Much of the discussion of the Tainos in this chapter is based on Rouse's treatment of them.
4 Rouse, *The Tainos*, p. 23. See also Peter Hulme, *Colonial Encounters: Europe and the Native Caribbean, 1492-1797* (London: Routledge, 1986).
5 Kenneth R. Andrews, *The Spanish Caribbean: Trade and Plunder, 1530-1630* (New Haven: Yale University Press, 1978), pp. 8–9.
6 Jerald T. Milanich and Susan Milbrath, eds, *First Encounters: Spanish Explorations in the Caribbean and the United States, 1492-1570* (Gainesville: University Press of Florida, 1989), pp. 67–8.
7 David Watts, *The West Indies: Patterns of Development, Culture and Environmental Change since 1492* (Cambridge: Cambridge University Press, 1987), p. 126.
8 Richard Dunn, *Sugar and Slaves: The Rise of the Planter Class in the English West Indies, 1624-1713* (Chapel Hill: The University of North Carolina Press, 1972), pp. 9, 10.
9 Hilary McD. Beckles, *White Servitude and Black Slavery in Barbados, 1627-1715* (Knoxville: University of Tennessee Press, 1989).

## Chapter 2

1 Stuart B. Schwartz, *Sugar Plantations in the Formation of Brazilian Society: Bahia, 1550-1834* (Cambridge: Cambridge University Press, 1985), ch. 1.

2  John J. McCusker and Russell R. Menard, 'The Sugar Industry in the Seventeenth Century: A New Perspective on the Barbadian "Sugar Revolution"', in Stuart B. Schwartz, ed., *Tropical Babylons: Sugar and the Making of the Atlantic World, 1450-1680* (Chapel Hill: University of North Carolina Press, 2004), pp. 295–6, 303.

3  Hilary McD. Beckles, 'The "Hub of Empire": the Caribbean and Britain in the Seventeenth Century', in Nicholas Canny, ed., *The Origins of Empire: British Overseas Enterprise to the Close of the Seventeenth Century*, vol 1: *The Oxford History of the British Empire* (Oxford: Oxford University Press, 1998), p. 232.

4  David Eltis, 'The Volume and Structure of the Transatlantic Slave Trade: A Reassessment', *William and Mary Quarterly*, 3rd series, 58, 1 (January 2001), p. 29. For an invaluable compilation of more than 35,000 voyages between 1514 and 1886, see *Voyages: The Transatlantic Slave Trade Database*, David Eltis, Martin Halbert et al., http://www.slavevoyages.org/.

5  Dunn, *Sugar and Slaves*, ch. 7.

6  Colin Palmer, 'The Slave Trade, African Slavers, and the Demography of the Caribbean to 1750', in Franklin Knight, ed., *The Slave Societies of the Caribbean*, vol 3: *General History of the Caribbean* (London, 1997), p. 28; Herbert S. Klein, *The Atlantic Slave Trade* (Cambridge: Cambridge University Press, 1999), p. 136.

7  Herbert S. Klein, Stanley L. Engerman, Robin Haines and Ralph Shlomowitz, 'Transoceanic Mortality: The Slave Trade in Comparative Perspective', *William and Mary Quarterly*, 3rd series, 58, 1 (January 2001): 101–2.

8  For a very useful treatment of the slave trade to the Chesapeake, see Lorena S. Walsh, 'The Chesapeake Slave Trade: Regional Patters, African Origins, and Some Implications', *William and Mary Quarterly*, 3rd series, 58, 1 (January 2001): 139–65.

9  Klein, *Atlantic Slave Trade*, p. 163.

10  Beckles, 'The "Hub of Empire"', p. 225.

11  Dunn, *Sugar and Slaves*, p. 77.

12  'Extracts from Henry Whistler's Journal of the West India Expedition', cited in Dunn, *Sugar and Slaves*, p. 77.

# Chapter 3

1  After Britain passed legislation to abolish its slave trade in 1807 (which took effect on 1 January 1808), it put pressure on other countries to follow suit. By 1815, all the major continental powers had agreed to do so and, by 1830, Cuba and Brazil had agreed to

abandon the slave trade as well. Thereafter, the slave trade was officially illegal.

2 Stanley L. Engerman and B.W. Higman, 'The Demographic Structure of the Caribbean Slave Societies in the Eighteenth and Nineteenth Centuries', in Franklin Knight, ed., *The Slave Societies of the Caribbean*, vol III: *General History of the Caribbean* (London: UNESCO Publishing, 1997), pp. 79–80.

3 Philip D. Morgan, 'The Black Experience in the British Empire, 1680-1810', in P. J. Marshall, ed., *The Eighteenth Century*, vol 2: *The Oxford History of the British Empire* (Oxford: Oxford University Press, 1998), p. 477.

4 Franklin W. Knight, *Slave Society in Cuba during the Nineteenth Century* (Madison: University of Wisconsin Press, 1970), p. 61. Slaves often formed very close and enduring bonds with other enslaved people who were on the same ship crossing the Atlantic – hence the term 'shipmate'.

5 Engerman and Higman, 'The Demographic Structure of the Caribbean Slave Societies', p. 77.

6 O. Nigel Bolland, *The Formation of a Colonial Society: Belize, from Conquest to Crown Colony* (Baltimore: Johns Hopkins University Press, 1977), p. 56.

7 Mrs [A. C.] Carmichael, *Domestic Manners and Social Condition of the White, Coloured, and Negro Population of the West Indies*, 2 vols. (London: Whittaker, Treacher, and Co., 1833), vol. 1, pp. 282–3.

8 Dale Tomich, 'Une Petite Guinée: Provision Ground and Plantation in Martinique, 1830-1848', in Ira Berlin and Philip Morgan, eds, *The Slaves' Economy: Independent Production by Slaves in the Americas* (London: Frank Cass, 1991), p. 81.

9 Ira Berlin and Philip Morgan, 'Introduction', in Idem, eds, *The Slaves' Economy*, pp. 7–8.

10 Edward Long, *The History of Jamaica*, 3 vols. (London, 1774), vol. 2, pp. 410–1.

# Chapter 4

1 The term *free people of colour* is used here to denote men and women who were coloured or black and born free or manumitted; it is used interchangeably with the terms *free coloureds* and *freedpeople*.

2 Arnold A. Sio, 'Marginality and Free Coloured Identity in Caribbean Slave Society', *Slavery and Abolition: A Journal of Comparative Studies* 8 (September 1987): 166.

3　Michelle Reid-Vasquez, *The Year of the Lash: Free People of Color in Cuba and the Nineteenth-Century Atlantic World* (Athens, GA: University of Georgia Press, 2011), p. 22.

4　David W. Cohen and Jack P. Greene, eds, *Neither Slave Nor Free: The Freedmen of African Descent in the Slave Societies of the New World* (Baltimore: Johns Hopkins University Press, 1972), pp. 4, 14.

5　Gad J. Heuman, *Between Black and White: Race, Politics, and the Free Coloreds in Jamaica, 1792-1865* (Westport, CT: Greenwood Press, 1981), p. 6. See also Daniel Livesay, 'Privileging Kinship: Family and Race in Eighteenth-Century Jamaica', *Early American Studies: An Interdisciplinary Journal* 14, 4 (2016): 688–711.

6　Léo Elisabeth, 'The French Antilles', in Cohen and Greene, ed., *Neither Slave nor Free*, p. 145.

7　Jerome S. Handler, 'Joseph Rachell and Rachael Pringle-Polgreen: Petty Entrepreneurs', in David G. Sweet and Gary B. Nash, eds, *Struggle and Survival in Colonial America* (Berkeley: University of California Press, 1981), p. 387. For a more recent interpretation, see Marisa J. Fuentes, 'Power and Historical Figuring: Rachael Pringle-Polgreen's Troubled Archive', *Gender & History* 22, 3 (2010): 564–84.

8　N. A. T. Hall, 'Anna Heegaard – Enigma', *Caribbean Quarterly* 22 (June–September 1976): 69.

9　This pattern was significant in Suriname. See Rosemary Brana-Shute, 'Approaching Freedom: The Manumission of Slaves in Suriname, 1760-1828', *Slavery & Abolition* 10, 3(December 1989): 56–7.

# Chapter 5

1　B. W. Higman, *Plantation Jamaica, 1750-1850: Capital and Control in a Colonial Economy* (Kingston: University of the West Indies Press, 2005).

2　Trevor Burnard, 'Et in Arcadia Ego: West Indian Planters in Glory, 1674–1784', *Atlantic Studies* 9, 1 (2012): 27.

3　Dunn, *Sugar and Slaves*, pp. 268–9.

4　[Charles Walker], 'Charles Walker's Letter from Puerto Rico, 1835-1837', annotated with an introduction by Kenneth Scott, *Caribbean Studies* 5 (April 1965): 43, cited in Francisco A. Scarano, *Sugar and Slavery in Puerto Rico: The Plantation Economy of Ponce, 1800-1850* (Madison: University of Wisconsin Press, 1984), p. 55.

5　Dunn, *Sugar and Slaves*, p. 113.

6　Thistlewood left an extensive diary, and Douglas Hall has quoted extensively from it in his *In Miserable Slavery: Thomas Thistlewood in Jamaica, 1750-86* (London: Macmillan Caribbean, 1989). See also the most important study of Thistlewood: Trevor Burnard, *Mastery, Tyranny, and Desire: Thomas Thistlewood and His Slaves in the Anglo-Jamaican World* (Chapel Hill: University of North Carolina Press, 2004).

7  Kathleen Mary Butler, *The Economics of Emancipation: Jamaica & Barbados, 1823-1843* (Chapel Hill: University of North Carolina Press, 1995), pp. 101–2; Verene A. Shepherd, comp. and ed., *Women in Caribbean History* (Kingston, 1999), pp. 31–2.

8  Long, *The History of Jamaica*, p. 279.

9  Moira Ferguson, ed., *The History of Mary Prince, A West Indian Slave: Related by Herself* (London: Pandora Press, 1987), p. 56.

10  Bryan Edwards, *The History, Civil and Commercial, of the British Colonies in the West Indies*, 2 vols. (London, 1793), bk. 4, chap. 1, p. 7.

11  Elsa V. Goveia, *Slave Society in the British Leeward Islands at the End of the Eighteenth Century* (New Haven: Yale University Press, 1965), p. 207.

12  For more information on the Haitian Revolution, see Chapter 7.

13  Scarano, *Sugar and Slavery in Puerto Rico*, chap. 4.

14  Knight, *Slave Society in Cuba During the Nineteenth Century*, pp. 86–90.

# Chapter 6

1  William Bosman, *A New and Accurate Description of the Coast of Guinea Divided into the Gold, the Slave, and the Ivory Coasts* (London, 1705), p. 365, cited in Richard Rathbone, 'Some Thoughts on Resistance to Enslavement in West Africa', in Gad Heuman, ed., *Out of the House of Bondage: Runaways, Resistance and Marronage in Africa and the New World* (London: Frank Cass, 1986), p. 18.

2  David Richardson, 'Shipboard Revolts, African Authority, and the Atlantic Slave Trade', *William and Mary Quarterly*, 3rd series, 58, 1 (January, 2001): 74–5.

3  Waldemar Westergaard, *The Danish West Indies under Company Rule, 1671-1754* (New York: Macmillan, 1917), p. 246.

4  Long, *The History of Jamaica*, pp. 447–8. See also the interactive map of the rebellion curated by Vincent Brown, *Slave Revolt in Jamaica, 1760-1761: A Cartographic Narrative* (Axis Maps, 2013): http://revolt.axismaps.com.

5  Michael Craton, *Testing the Chains: Resistance to Slavery in the British West Indies* (Ithaca, 1982), chap. 11.

6  David Barry Gaspar, *Bondmen & Rebels: A Study of Master-Slave Relations in Antigua* (Baltimore: Johns Hopkins University Press, 1985).

7  Barbara Bush, 'Hard Labor: Women, Childbirth, and Resistance in British Caribbean Slave Societies', in David Barry Gaspar and Darlene Clark Hine, eds, *More than Chattel: Black Women and Slavery in the Americas* (Bloomington: Indiana University Press, 1996): 193–217. See also Katherine Paugh, 'The Politics of Childbearing in the British Caribbean and Atlantic World during Age of Abolition', *Past & Present* 221, 1 (2013): 119–60.

8  For a discussion of the development of obeah in Barbados, see Jerome S. Handler, 'Slave Medicine and Obeah in Barbados, circa 1650 to 1834', *New West Indian Guide* 74, 1 and 2 (2000): 57–90. Brian L. Moore and Michele A. Johnson treat obeah after emancipation in Jamaica; see their *Neither Led nor Driven: Contesting British Cultural Imperialism in Jamaica, 1865-1920* (Kingston: University of the West Indies Press, 2004). For the most recent treatments of obeah, see Randy M. Browne, 'The "Bad Business" of Obeah: Power, Authority, and the Politics of Slave Culture in the British Caribbean', *William and Mary Quarterly*, 3d series, 68, 3 (2011): 451–80 and Diana Paton, *The Cultural Politics of Obeah: Religion, Colonialism and Modernity in the Caribbean World* (Cambridge: Cambridge University Press, 2015).

9  P. A. Bishop, 'Runaway Slaves in Jamaica, 1740-1807: A Study Based on Newspaper Advertisements Published During that Period for Runaways' (unpublished MA thesis, University of the West Indies, 1970), p. 11.

10  Gad Heuman, 'Runaway Slaves in Nineteenth-Century Barbados', in idem, ed., *Out of the House of Bondage*, p. 110.

11  On this point and on *petit marronage* more generally, see Simon P. Newman, 'Rethinking Runaways in the British Atlantic World: Britain, the Caribbean, West Africa and North America', *Slavery and Abolition* 38, 1 (2017): 49–75.

12  Richard Price, 'Introduction: Maroons and their Communities', in idem, ed., *Maroon Societies: Rebel Slave Communities in the Americas* (Garden City, NY: Anchor Press, 1973): 1–30. Much of the discussion which follows is based on Price's excellent treatment of the Maroons. For the most recent treatment of the Maroons, see Jean Besson, *Transformation of Freedom in the Land of the Maroons: Creolization in the Cockpits, Jamaica* (Kingston: Ian Randle Publishers, 2016).

# Chapter 7

1 David Geggus, 'The Haitian Revolution', in Hilary Beckles and Verene Shepherd, eds, *Caribbean Slave Society and Economy: A Student Reader* (Kingston: Ian Randle, 1991), p. 405.
2 Geggus, 'The Haitian Revolution'.
3 Carolyn E. Fick, 'The Saint Domingue Slave Insurrection of 1791: A Socio-Political and Cultural Analysis', *The Journal of Caribbean History* 25, 1 and 2 (1991): 6.
4 David Geggus, 'The Bois-Caïman Ceremony', *The Journal of Caribbean History* 25, 1 and 2 (1991): 51.
5 Geggus, 'Haitian Revolution', p. 411.
6 John K. Thornton, 'African Soldiers in the Haitian Revolution', *The Journal of Caribbean History* 25, 1 and 2 (1991): 58–80.
7 Laurent Dubois, *Avengers of the New World: The Story of the Haitian Revolution* (Cambridge, MA: Harvard University Press, 2004), pp. 173–4.
8 Dubois, *Avengers of the New World*, p. 278.
9 David Barry Gaspar, 'La Guerre des Bois: Revolution, War, and Slavery in Saint Lucia, 1793-1838', in idem and David Patrick Geggus, eds, *A Turbulent Time: The French Revolution and the Greater Caribbean* (Bloomington: Indiana University Press, 1997), p. 105.
10 Gaspar, 'La Guerre des Bois', p. 106. See also Laurent Dubois, *A Colony of Citizens: Revolution & Slave Emancipation in the French Caribbean, 1787-1804* (Chapel Hill: University of North Carolina Press, 2004), pp. 232–6.
11 Geggus, 'Haitian Revolution', p. 417.

# Chapter 8

1 Eric Williams, *Capitalism & Slavery* (1944; reprint, New York: Capricorn Books, 1966), p. 210.
2 Roger Anstey, 'Capitalism and Slavery: A Critique', *Economic History Review*, 2nd series, XXI (1968): 307–20; Roger Anstey, *The Atlantic Slave Trade and British Abolition, 1760-1810* (London: Prometheus Books, 1975).
3 Seymour Drescher, *Econocide: British Slavery in the Era of Abolition* (Pittsburgh: University of Pittsburgh Press, 1977).

4  Claudius Fergus, 'Dread of Insurrection: Abolitionism, Security, and Labor in Britain's West Indian Colonies, 1760-1823', *William and Mary Quarterly*, 3rd series, 66, 4 (2009): 772.

5  Howard Temperley, *British Antislavery, 1833-1870* (London: Longman, 1972), p. 12; Hilary McD. Beckles, *A History of Barbados: From Amerindian Settlement to Nation-State* (Cambridge: Cambridge University Press, 1990), p. 86.

6  Craton, *Testing the Chains*, p. 261.

7  William A. Green, *British Slave Emancipation: The Sugar Colonies and the Great Experiment, 1830-1865* (Oxford: Oxford University Press, 1976), chap. 5.

8  Michael Craton, 'Forms of Resistance to Slavery', in Franklin Knight, ed., *Slave Societies of the Caribbean*, vol 3, *General History of the Caribbean* (London: UNESCO Publishing, 1997), pp. 252–4.

9  Rebecca J. Scott, *Slave Emancipation in Cuba: The Transition to Free Labor, 1860-1899* (Princeton: Princeton University Press, 1985).

# Chapter 9

1  Reid-Vasquez, *The Year of the Lash*, p. 22.

2  For the most recent study of *La Escalera*, see Aisha K. Finch, *Rethinking Slave Rebellion in Cuba: La Escalera and the Insurgencies of 1841-1844* (Chapel Hill: University of North Carolina Press, 2015).

3  Knight, *Slave Society in Cuba during the Nineteenth Century*, p. 284.

4  Heuman, *Between Black and White*, pp. 23–4.

5  Ibid., p. 28.

6  Rev. George W. Bridges, *The Annals of Jamaica*, 2 vols. (London, 1828), vol. 2, p. 371; *The Jamaica Journal*, 22 November 1823.

7  Jerome S. Handler, *The Unappropriated People: Freedmen in the Slave Society of Barbados* (Baltimore: Johns Hopkins University Press, 1974), p. 197; James A. Thome and Horace J. Kimball, *Emancipation in the West Indies* (New York, 1838), p. 79.

8  Verena Martinez-Alier, *Marriage, Class and Colour in Nineteenth-century Cuba: A Study of Racial Attitudes and Sexual Values in a Slave Society* (Cambridge: Cambridge University Press, 1974), p. 96.

9  Bolland, *The Formation of a Colonial Society*, p. 94.

10 Anthony Trollope, *The West Indies and the Spanish Main*, 2nd ed., (London, 1860), pp. 81–2.

11 M. G. Lewis, *Journal of a West India Proprietor, 1815-17*, edited with an introduction by Mona Wilson (London, 1929), p. 143.

# Chapter 10

1 Richard Frucht, 'From Slavery to Unfreedom in the Plantation Society of St. Kitts, W.I.', in Vera Rubin and Arthur Tuden, eds, *Comparative Perspectives on Slavery in New World Plantation Societies* (New York: New York Academy of Sciences, 1977), p. 384.

2 *Supplement to The Royal Gazette*, 13–20 September 1834.

3 For a recent treatment of the resistance in Trinidad, see Claudius Fergus, *Revolutionary Emancipation: Slavery and Abolitionism in the British West Indies* (Baton Rouge: Louisiana State University Press, 2013), pp. 187–8.

4 Colonial Office records, National Archives, London [hereafter CO] 137/194, Sligo to Spring Rice, 9 December 1834, no. 91.

5 Thomas C. Holt, *The Problem of Freedom: Race, Labor, and Politics in Jamaica and Britain, 1832-1938* (Baltimore: Johns Hopkins University Press, 1992), p. 64.

6 Mimi Sheller, 'Quasheba, Mother, Queen: Black Women's Public Leadership and Political Protest in Post-Emancipation Jamaica, 1834-65', *Slavery & Abolition* 19 (December 1998): 93, 94.

7 Scott, *Slave Emancipation in Cuba*, p. 129.

8 Holt, *The Problem of Freedom*, pp. 144, 154; Michel-Rolph Trouillot, *Peasants and Capital: Dominica in the World Economy* (Baltimore: Johns Hopkins University Press, 1988), p. 78.

9 CO 137/242, Smith to Glenelg, 23 March 1839, no. 65, encl: Report of Tho. Abbott, Westmoreland, 28 February.

10 *British Parliamentary Papers* (hereafter *PP*), 1839, (107-V), XXXVII, Colebrooke to Glenelg, 15 October 1838, p. 390, encl no. 2: Phillips to the President, 1 October, p. 393; CO 71/87, Colebrooke to Glenelg, 15 October 1838, no. 232, encl: report of Howard Lloyd, stipendiary magistrate, 25 September.

11 Swithin Wilmot, '"Females of Abandoned Character?": Women and Protest in Jamaica, 1838-65' in Verene Shepherd, Bridget Brereton and Barbara Bailey, eds, *Engendering History: Caribbean Women in Historical Perspective* (Kingston: Ian Randle Publishers, 1995), p. 280.

12 Bridget Brereton, 'Family Strategies, Gender, and the Shift to Wage Labour in the British Caribbean', in Bridget Brereton and Kevin A. Yelvington, eds, *The Colonial Caribbean in Transition: Essays on Postemancipation Social and Cultural History* (Kingston: University of the West Indies Press, 1999), pp. 98–9, 105.

13 Michael Louis, '"An Equal Right to the Soil": The Rise of a Peasantry in St. Lucia, 1838-1900' (PhD thesis, Johns Hopkins University, 1981), p. 25; *PP*, 1839, (107-IV), XXXVI, MacGregor to Glenelg,

18 September 1838, no. 249, p. 503, encl. A: Richard & Munn to Captain Clarke, 24 August.

14  For an important study of the effects of the Baptist missionaries on Jamaica, see Catherine Hall, *Civilising Subjects: Metropole and Colony in the English Imagination, 1830-1867* (Oxford: Blackwell, 2002).

15  Bridget Brereton, *Race Relations in Colonial Trinidad, 1870-1900* (Cambridge: Cambridge University Press, 1979), p. 178.

16  Gaiutra Bahadur, *Coolie Woman: The Odyssey of Indenture* (London: C Hurst & Co, 2013), p. 128.

# Chapter 11

1   Russell E. Chace, Jr., 'Protest in Post-Emancipation Dominica: The "Guerre Negre" of 1844', *Journal of Caribbean History* 23 (1989): 130.

2   Woodville K. Marshall, '"Vox Populi": The St. Vincent Riots and Disturbances of 1862', in B. W. Higman, ed., *Trade, Government and Society in Caribbean History, 1700-1920* (Kingston: Heinemann, 1983), pp. 94–7. Emphasis added by Marshall.

3   Bridget Brereton, 'Post-Emancipation Protest in the Caribbean: The "Belmanna Riots" in Tobago, 1876', *Caribbean Quarterly* 30, 3 and 4 (1984): 110–23.

4   Isaac Dookhan, *A History of the Virgin Islands of the United States* (Epping, Essex: Caribbean University Press, 1974), pp. 227–31.

5   Natasha Lightfoot, '"Their Coats were Tied Up like Men": Women Rebels in Antigua's 1858 Uprising', *Slavery & Abolition: A Journal of Slave and Post-Slave Studies* 31, 4 (December 2010): 528.

6   Lightfoot, 'Their Coats were Tied Up like Men', pp. 530, 536.

7   Gad Heuman, *The Killing Time: The Morant Bay Rebellion in Jamaica* (London: Macmillan Caribbean, 1994), p. 8.

8   Gad Heuman, 'Post-Emancipation Resistance in the Caribbean: An Overview', in Karen Fog Olwig, ed., *Small Islands, Large Questions: Society, Culture and Resistance in the Post-Emancipation Caribbean* (London: Frank Cass, 1995), p. 129.

9   Heuman, *The Killing Time*, p. 23.

10  Rosamunde A. Renard, 'Labour Relations in Post-Slavery Martinique and Guadeloupe, 1848-1870', in Hilary Beckles and Verene Shepherd, eds, *Caribbean Freedom: Economy and Society from Emancipation to the Present* (Kingston: Ian Randle Publishers, 1993), pp. 80–92.

11  Christine Chivallon and David Howard, 'Colonial Violence and Civilising Utopias in the French and British Empires: The Morant Bay

Rebellion (1865) and the Insurrection of the South (1870)', *Slavery & Abolition* 38, 3 (September 2017): 542.

12  Takkara Keosha Brunson, 'Constructing Afro-Cuban Womanhood: Race, Gender, and Citizenship in Republican-Era Cuba, 1902-1958' (PhD Dissertation, University of Texas at Austin, 2011), p. 91.

13  Aline Helg, *Our Rightful Share: The Afro-Cuban Struggle for Equality, 1886-1912* (Chapel Hill: University of North Carolina Press, 1995), p. 5.

# Chapter 12

1  For a comprehensive study of J. J. Thomas, see Faith Smith, *Creole Recitations: John Jacob Thomas and Colonial Formation in the Late Nineteenth-Century Caribbean* (Charlottesville, VA: University Press of Virginia, 2002).

2  Bridget Brereton, 'The Development of an Identity: The Black Middle Class of Trinidad in the Later Nineteenth Century', in Hilary Beckles and Verene Shepherd, eds, *Caribbean Freedom: Society and Economy to the Present* (Kingston, 1993), pp. 281–2; Patrick Bryan, *The Jamaican People, 1880-1902* (London: Macmillan Caribbean, 1991), pp. 258–9.

3  Joy Lumsden, 'A Forgotten Generation: Black Politicians in Jamaica, 1884-1914', in Brian Moore and Swithin Wilmot, eds, *Before and After 1865: Education, Politics and Regionalism in the Caribbean* (Kingston: Ian Randle, 1998), pp. 117–20.

4  Rupert Lewis, *Marcus Garvey: Anti-Colonial Champion* (London: Karia Press, 1987), p. 26.

5  Amy Jacques Garvey, *Garvey and Garveyism* (London: Frank Cass, 1963), p. xii.

6  Dalea Bean, *Jamaican Women & the World Wars: On the Front Lines of Change* (London: Palgrave Macmillan, 2018), p. 116.

7  Robert A. Hill, ed., *The Marcus Garvey and Universal Negro Improvement Association Papers*, vol. 7, *November 1927–August 1940* (Berkeley: University of California Press, 1990), p. L.

8  Barry Chevannes, *Rastafari: Roots and Ideology* (Syracuse, NY: Syracuse University Press, 1994).

9  Richard D. E. Burton, *Afro-Creole: Power, Opposition and Play in the Caribbean* (Ithaca: Cornell University Press, 1997), p. 130.

10  M. G. Smith, Roy Augier and Rex Nettleford, *The Rastafari Movement in Kingston, Jamaica* (Mona, Jamaica: Institute of Social and Economic Research, 1960).

11 Burton, *Afro-Creole*, p. 131.
12 Alistair Hennessy, *Intellectuals in the Twentieth-Century Caribbean*, vol. 2, *Unity in Variety: The Hispanic and Francophone Caribbean* (London: Macmillan Caribbean, 1992), p. 21.

# Chapter 13

1 Lester D. Langley, *The United States and the Caribbean in the Twentieth Century* (Athens, Georgia: University of Georgia Press, 1982), p. 18. See also Louis A. Pérez Jr., *The War of 1898: The United States and Cuba in History and Historiography* (Chapel Hill: University of North Carolina Press, 1998).
2 Luis E. Aguilar, 'Cuba, c. 1860-c. 1930', in Leslie Bethell, ed., *Cuba: A Short History* (Cambridge: Cambridge University Press, 1993), p. 43.
3 Langley, *The United States and the Caribbean in the Twentieth Century*, pp. 138–46.
4 Anthony P. Maingot, *The United States and the Caribbean* (London: Macmillan Caribbean, 1994), p. 35.
5 Grace Louise Sanders, 'La Voix des Femmes: Haitian Women's Rights, National Politics and Black Activism in Port-au-Prince and Montreal, 1934-1986' (PhD dissertation, University of Michigan, 2013), p. 78.
6 Sanders, La Voix des Femmes.
7 Bruce J. Calder, *The Impact of Intervention: The Dominican Republic during the U.S. Occupation of 1916-1924* (Austin: University of Texas Press, 1984), p. 246.
8 Calder, *The Impact of Intervention*, p. 249.

# Chapter 14

1 Bonham C. Richardson, 'Prelude to Nationalism? Riots and Land Use Changes in the Lesser Antilles in the 1890s', in Wim Hoogbergen, ed., *Born Out of Resistance: On Caribbean Cultural Creativity* (Utrecht: ISOR-Publications, 1995), pp. 208–9.
2 Bryan, *The Jamaican People, 1880-1900*, pp. 271–4; Walter Rodney, *A History of the Guyanese Working People, 1881-1905* (Kingston: Heinemann, 1981), chap. 8.
3 Richard Hart, 'Origin and Development of the Working Class in the English-Speaking Caribbean Area, 1897-1937', in Malcolm Cross and Gad Heuman, eds, *Labour in the Caribbean: From Emancipation to Independence* (London: Macmillan Caribbean, 1988), pp. 43–50.

4 O. Nigel Bolland, *On the March: Labour Rebellions in the British Caribbean, 1934-39* (Kingston: University of the West Indies Press, 1995), p. 46.

5 Bolland, *On the March*, p. 59.

6 For the most recent treatment of the riots in St. Vincent, see Adrian Fraser, *The 1935 Riots in St. Vincent: From Riots to Adult Suffrage* (Kingston: University of the West Indies Press, 2016).

7 Bolland, *On the March,* chap. 8.

8 Ibid., pp. 119–20.

9 For more on Bustamante, Manley and the riots in Jamaica, see Colin A. Palmer, *Freedom's Children: The 1938 Labor Rebellion and the Birth of Modern Jamaica* (Chapel Hill: University of North Carolina Press, 2014).

10 Bolland, *On the March*, p. 154.

11 Franklin W. Knight, 'The Caribbean in the 1930s', in Bridget Brereton, ed., *The Caribbean in the Twentieth Century*, vol 5: *General History of the Caribbean* (London: Macmillan, 2004), p. 72.

# Chapter 15

1 Hugh Thomas, *The Cuban Revolution* (New York: Eyre & Spottiswoode, 1971), p. 65.

2 Louis A. Pérez, Jr., 'Cuba, *c.* 1930-1959', in Leslie Bethell, ed., *Cuba: A Short History* (Cambridge: Cambridge University Press, 1993), pp. 88–9.

3 Pérez, Jr., 'Cuba, *c.* 1930-1959', p. 102.

4 Marifeli Pérez-Stable, 'The Cuban Revolution and its Impact on the Caribbean', in Bridget Brereton, ed., *The Caribbean in the Twentieth Century*, vol 5: *General History of the Caribbean* (London: Macmillan, 2004), p. 297.

5 Antoni Kapcia, *Cuba, Island of Dreams* (Oxford: Berg, 2000), p. 207.

6 Pérez-Stable, 'The Cuban Revolution and its Impact on the Caribbean', p. 310.

7 Ada Ferrer, 'Listening to Obama in Cuba', http://nacla.org/news/2016/03/28/listening-obama-cuba (accessed 22 March 2017).

8 Anthony J. Payne, *Politics in Jamaica* (Kingston: Frances Pinter, 1994), p. 30.

9 Tony Thorndike, *Grenada: Politics, Economics and Society* (London: C Hurst & Co, 1985).

10 Brian Meeks, *Caribbean Revolutions and Revolutionary Theory: An Assessment of Cuba, Nicaragua and Grenada* (London: Macmillan Caribbean, 1993), p. 65.

11 For an important recent assessment of Jagan, see Colin A. Palmer, *Cheddi Jagan and the Politics of Power: British Guiana's Struggle for Independence* (Chapel Hill: University of North Carolina Press, 2014).

12 Stephen J. Randall and Graeme S. Mount, *The Caribbean Basin: An International History* (London: Routledge, 1998), pp. 104–7; 134–7.

# Chapter 16

1 Mary Williams Walsh, 'How Puerto Rico is Grappling with a Debt Crisis', *The New York Times*, /www.nytimes.com/interactive/2017/business/dealbook/puerto-rico-debt-bankruptcy.html (accessed 22 June 2017).

2 Peter Clegg and David Killingray, eds, *The Non-Independent Territories of the Caribbean and Pacific: Continuity or Change?* (London: Institute of Commonwealth Studies, 2012).

3 Gert Oostindie, *Paradise Overseas – The Dutch Caribbean: Colonialism and its Transatlantic Legacies* (Oxford: Macmillan Caribbean, 2005).

4 Richard Lee Turits, 'A World Destroyed, A Nation Imposed: The 1937 Haitian Massacre in the Dominican Republic', *Hispanic American Historical Review* 82, 3 (August 2002): 589–636.

5 Alex von Tunzelmann, *Red Heat: Conspiracy, Murder and the Cold War in the Caribbean* (London: Simon & Shuster, 2011), pp. 262–5.

6 Michele Wucker, 'The Dominican Republic's Shameful Deportation Legacy', FP, http://foreignpolicy.com/2015/10/08/dominican-republic-haiti-trujillo-immigration-deportation/ (accessed 21 June 2017).

7 Wucker, 'The Dominican Republic's Shameful Deportation Legacy', p. 424.

8 Jesselyn Cook, '7 Years After Haiti's Earthquake, Millions Still Need Aid', *The World Post*, 12 January 2017, http://www.huffingtonpost.com/entry/haiti-earthquake-anniversary_us_5875108de4b02b5f858b3f9c (accessed 16 March 2017).

9 Sir Ronald Sanders, 'The Implications of Brexit for the Caribbean's Future Relationship with Britain and the EU', *The Round Table* 105, 5 (2016): 519–29.

10 Sandra Laville, 'Beijing Highway: $600m Road just the Start of China's Investments in the Caribbean', *The Guardian*, /www.theguardian.com/world/2015/dec/24/beijing-highway-600m-road-just-the-start-of-chinas-investments-in-caribbean (accessed 10 April 2017); Ezra Fieser, 'Why is China Spending Billions in the Caribbean?' /www.pri.org/stories/2011-04-22/why-china-spending-billions-caribbean (accessed 10 April 2017).

# Chapter 17

1 Jorge I. Domínguez, 'The Caribbean Question: Why Has Liberal Democracy (Surprisingly) Flourished?', in Jorge I. Domínguez, Robert A. Pastor and R. DeLisle Worrell, eds, *Democracy in the Caribbean: Political, Economic, and Social Perspectives* (Baltimore: Johns Hopkins Press, 1993), p. 21.

2 Dennis A. Pantin, 'The Economies of the Caribbean', in Richard S. Hillman and Thomas J. D'Agostino, eds, *Understanding the Contemporary Caribbean* (Boulder, 2003), p. 141. See also the article by Oliver Balch, 'Banana Production Battered by Market Pressures – and the Caribbean Weather', *The Guardian*, 24 October 2013: https://www.theguardian.com/sustainable-business/future-banana-production-windward-islands (accessed 4 April 2017).

3 For the report from the U.N. Food and Agriculture Organization, see Tasnim Abdi, 'Caribbean Region to see Increased Drought, UN says', in *The Christian Science Monitor*, 18 September 2016 (http://www.csmonitor.com/Business/The-Bite/2016/0918/Caribbean-region-to-see-increased-drought-UN-says (accessed 6 April 2017).

4 'Hurricane Irma: Caribbean Counts the Cost of Deadly Storm', www.bbc.co.uk/news/business-41192158 (accessed 13 September 2017).

5 'Dominica Devastated by Hurricane Maria', *Caribbean Insight*, vol. 39, issue 52, 29 September–13 October 2017, p. 1 (accessed 19 October 2017); 'Puerto Ricans Struggle to Survive in Storm's Aftermath', *Caribbean Insight*, vol. 39, issue 53, 13 October–29 October 2017, p. 10 (accessed 19 October 2017); 'Official Toll in Puerto Rico:64. Actual Deaths May be 1,052', https://www.nytimes.com/interactive/2017/12/08/us/puerto-rico-hurricane-maria-death-toll.html (accessed 31 January 2018).

6 Dennis Conway, 'The Caribbean Diaspora', in Hillman and D'Agostino, *Understanding the Contemporary Caribbean*, p. 338.

7 Lara Putnam, *Radical Moves: Caribbean Migrants and the Politics of Race in the Jazz Age* (Chapel Hill, NC: University of North Carolina Press, 2013), p. 26.

8 For an important study of migration from Barbados to Britain using oral life-stories, see Mary Chamberlain, *Narratives of Exile and Return* (London: Macmillan Caribbean, 1997).

9 Bonham C. Richardson, 'Caribbean Migrations, 1838-1985', in Franklin W. Knight and Colin A. Palmer, eds, *The Modern Caribbean* (Chapel Hill: University of North Carolina Press, 1989), chap. 10.

10 Tyesha Maddox, 'More than Auxiliary: West Indian Social Organizations, Citizenship, Political Activism, and the Construction

of Caribbean American Identity', unpublished paper, Association of
Caribbean Historians Conference, Tobago, 2017, pp. 13–5.

11  Maddox, 'More than Auxiliary', p. 224.

12  Gordon K. Lewis, 'The Contemporary Caribbean: A General
Overview', in Sidney W. Mintz and Sally Price, eds, *Caribbean
Contours* (Baltimore: Johns Hopkins University Press, 1985), p. 237.

13  Hilary McD. Beckles, *Britain's Black Debt: Reparations for Caribbean
Slavery and Native Genocide* (Kingston: University of West Indies
Press, 2012). For the Caribbean Reparation Commission's ten-point
plan, see its website: http://caricomreparations.org/

14  Linden Lewis, ed., *The Culture of Gender and Sexuality in the
Caribbean* (Gainesville, FL: University Press of Florida, 2003), p. 110.

# Chapter 18

1  Antonio Benítez-Rojo, *The Repeating Island: The Caribbean and the
Postmodern Perspective* (Durham: Duke University Press, 1996), p. 35.

2  Antonio Benítez-Rojo, 'Three Words Toward Creolization', in O.
Nigel Bolland, ed., *The Birth of Caribbean Civilisation: A Century of
Ideas about Culture and Identity, Nation and Society* (Kingston: Ian
Randle, 2004), p. 162.

3  Kenneth M. Bilby, 'The Caribbean as a Musical Region', in Sidney
W. Mintz and Sally Price, eds, *Caribbean Contours* (Baltimore: Johns
Hopkins University Press, 1985), p. 183.

4  Edward Brathwaite, *The Development of Creole Society in Jamaica,
1770-1820* (Oxford: Oxford University Press, 1971), p. 208.

5  Peter Manuel, *Caribbean Currents: Caribbean Music from Rumba to
Reggae* (Philadelphia: Temple University Press, 1995), p. 6.

6  Manuel, *Caribbean Currents*, p. 101.

7  Peter van Koninsbruggen, *Trinidad Carnival: A Quest for National
Identity* (London: Macmillan Education, 1997), pp. 15–6.

8  The most popular version was sung by the Andrews Sisters in the
United States, which replaced the lyrics of the original with one more
suited to the American market.

9  Bridget Brereton, *A History of Modern Trinidad, 1783-1962*
(Kingston: Heinemann, 1981), p. 225.

10  Curwen Best, *Roots to Popular Culture: Barbadian Aesthetics: Kamau
Brathwaite to Hardcore Styles* (London: Macmillan Caribbean,
2001), p. 158.

11  Carolyn Cooper, 'Hip-Hopping Across Cultures: Crossing Over
from Reggae to Rap and Back', in Verene A. Shepherd and Glen

L. Richards, eds, *Questioning Creole: Creolisation Discourses in Caribbean Culture* (Kingston: Ian Randle, 2002), p. 268.

12 Carolyn Cooper, *Noises in the Blood: Orality, Gender and the 'Vulgar' Body of Jamaican Popular Culture* (London: Macmillan Caribbean, 1994), pp. 121–2.

13 Manuel, *Caribbean Currents*, p. 177.

14 Bilby, 'The Caribbean as a Musical Region', p. 208.

15 Lorna V. Williams, 'The African Presence in the Poetry of Nicolás Guillén', in Margaret E. Crahan and Franklin W. Knight, eds, *Africa and the Caribbean: The Legacies of a Link* (Baltimore: Johns Hopkins University Press, 1979), pp. 124–5.

16 Louis James, *Caribbean Literature in English* (Harlow: Longman, 1999), p. 106.

17 James, *Caribbean Literature in English*, pp. 107–8.

18 James Ferguson, *Traveller's Literary Companion to the Caribbean* (London: In Print Publishing, 1997), p. 65.

19 James, *Caribbean Literature in English*, p. 101.

20 Kezia Page, 'From Diasporic Sensibility to Close Transnationalism: *The Agüero Sisters, The Dew Breaker* and *The Brief Wondrous Life of Oscar Wao*', in Michael A. Bucknor and Alison Donnell, eds, *The Routledge Companion to Anglophone Caribbean Literature* (London: Routledge, 2011), p. 227.

21 Page, 'From Diasporic Sensibility to Close Transnationalism', p. 127.

22 Keith Q. Warner, *On Location: Cinema and Film in the Anglophone Caribbean* (London: Macmillan Caribbean, 2000), p. 80.

23 John King, *Magical Reels: A History of Cinema in Latin America* (London: Verso, 1990), p. 156.

24 King, *Magical Reels*, pp. 158–61.

25 Veerle Poupeye, *Caribbean Art* (London: Thames and Hudson, 1998), p. 9.

26 Poupeye, *Caribbean Art*, pp. 81, 90, 140, 152.

27 Woodville Marshall, 'The Worrell-Sobers Revolution', in Hilary Beckles, ed., *An Area of Conquest: Popular Democracy and West Indies Cricket Supremacy* (Kingston: Ian Randle, 1994), p. 31.

28 Benítez-Rojo, *The Repeating Island*, pp. 79–80.

# SUGGESTIONS FOR FURTHER READING

## Chapter 1

Kenneth R. Andrews, *The Spanish Caribbean: Trade and Plunder, 1530–1630* (New Haven, 1978).

Hilary McD. Beckles, *White Servitude and Black Slavery in Barbados, 1627–1715* (Knoxville, 1989).

Kristen Block, *Ordinary Lives in the Early Caribbean: Religion, Colonial Competition, and the Politics of Profit* (Athens, GA, 2012).

Kristen Block and Jenny Shaw, 'Subjects Without an Empire: The Irish in the Early Modern Caribbean', *Past & Present* 210, no. 1 (2011): 33–60.

Carl Bridenbaugh and Roberta Bridenbaugh, *No Peace Beyond the Line: The English in the Caribbean, 1624–1690* (New York, 1972).

Alfred W. Crosby, *The Columbian Exchange: Biological and Cultural Consequences of 1492* (Westport, CT, 1972).

Richard Dunn, *Sugar and Slaves: The Rise of the Planter Class in the English West Indies, 1624–1713* (Chapel Hill, 1972).

Peter Hulme, *Colonial Encounters: Europe and the Native Caribbean, 1492–1797* (London, 1986).

Peter Hulme and Neil L. Whitehead, eds., *Wild Majesty: Encounters with Caribs from Columbus to the Present Day* (Oxford, 1992).

J. R. McNeill, *Mosquito Empires: Ecology and War in the Greater Caribbean, 1620–1914* (Cambridge, 2010).

Jerald T. Milanich and Susan Milbrath, eds., *First Encounters: Spanish Explorations in the Caribbean and the United States, 1492–1570* (Gainesville, 1989).

Irving Rouse, *The Tainos: Rise and Decline of the People Who Greeted Columbia* (New Haven, 1992).

Linda M. Rupert, *Creolization and Contraband: Curaçao in the Early Modern Atlantic World* (Athens, GA, 2012).

Carl Ortwin Sauer, *The Early Spanish Main* (Berkeley, 1966).

Jenny Shaw, *Everyday Life in the Early English Caribbean: Irish, Africans, and the Construction of Difference* (Athens, GA, 2013).

Jalil Sued-Badillo, 'The Indigenous Societies at the Time of Conquest', in Jalil Sued-Badillo, ed., *General History of the Caribbean, volume 1: Autochthonous Societies* (London, 2003).

David Watts, *The West Indies: Patterns of Development, Culture and Environmental Change since 1492* (Cambridge, 1987).

Samuel M. Wilson, *Hispaniola: Caribbean Chiefdoms in the Age of Columbus* (Tuscaloosa, 1990).

Natalie A. Zacek, *Settler Society in the English Leeward Islands, 1670–1776* (New York, 2010).

# Chapter 2

Hilary McD. Beckles, 'The "Hub of Empire": the Caribbean and Britain in the Seventeenth Century', in Nicholas Canny, ed., *The Origins of Empire: British Overseas Enterprise to the Close of the Seventeenth Century, volume 1: The Oxford History of the British Empire* (Oxford, 1998).

Hilary McD. Beckles, *White Servitude and Black Slavery in Barbados, 1627–1715* (Knoxville, 1989).

Carl Bridenbaugh and Roberta Bridenbaugh, *No Peace Beyond the Line: The English in the Caribbean, 1624–1690* (New York, 1972).

Trevor Burnard, 'The Atlantic Slave and African Ethnicities in Seventeenth-Century Jamaica', in David Richardson, Suzanne Schwarz and Anthony Tibbles, eds., *Liverpool and Transatlantic Slavery* (Liverpool, 2007).

Trevor Burnard, 'The Planter Class', in Gad Heuman and Trevor Burnard, eds., *The Routledge History of Slavery* (New York, 2011), pp. 187–203.

Richard S. Dunn, *Sugar and Slaves: The Rise of the Planter Class in the English West Indies, 1624–1713* (Chapel Hill, 1972).

David Eltis, 'The Slave Economies of the Caribbean: Structure, Performance, Evolution and Significance', in Franklin W. Knight, ed., *The Slave Societies of the Caribbean, volume 3: General History of the Caribbean* (London, 1997).

David Eltis, 'The Volume and Structure of the Transatlantic Slave Trade: A Reassessment', *William and Mary Quarterly, 3rd series* 58, no. 1 (January 2001): 17–46.

David Eltis and David Richardson, *Atlas of the Transatlantic Slave Trade* (New Haven, 2010).

David Eltis and David Richardson, eds., *Routes to Slavery: Direction, Ethnicity and Mortality in the Atlantic Slave Trade* (London, 1997).

Larry Gragg, *Englishmen Transplanted: The English Colonization of Barbados, 1627–1660* (Oxford, 2003).

Jerome S. Handler, 'Slave Medicine and Obeah in Barbados, circa 1650 to 1834', *New West Indian Guide* 74, no. 1 and 2 (2000): 57–90.

Jerome S. Handler, 'The Middle Passage and the Material Culture of Captive Africans', *Slavery & Abolition: A Journal of Slave and Post-Slave Studies* 30, no. 1 (2009): 1–26.

Jerome S. Handler and M. L. Tuite, The Atlantic Slave Trade and Slave Life in the Americas: A Visual Record, http://www.slaveryimages.org.

Herbert S. Klein, *The Atlantic Slave Trade* (Cambridge, 1999).

Herbert S. Klein, Stanley L. Engerman, Robin Haines and Ralph Shlomowitz, 'Transoceanic Mortality: The Slave Trade in Comparative Perspective', *William and Mary Quarterly, 3rd series* 58, no. 1 (January, 2001): 93–117.

John J. McCusker and Russell R. Menard, 'The Sugar Industry in the Seventeenth Century: A New Perspective on the Barbadian "Sugar Revolution"', in Stuart B. Schwartz, ed., *Tropical Babylons: Sugar and the Making of the Atlantic World, 1450–1680* (Chapel Hill, 2004).

Sidney W. Mintz, *Sweetness and Power: The Place of Sugar in Modern History* (New York, 1985).

Colin Palmer, 'The Slave Trade, African Slavers, and the Demography of the Caribbean to 1750', in Franklin Knight, ed., *The Slave Societies of the Caribbean, volume 3: General History of the Caribbean* (London, 1997).

Marcus Rediker, *The Slave Ship: A Human History* (New York, 2007).

Stuart B. Schwartz, *Sugar Plantations in the Formation of Brazilian Society: Bahia, 1550–1834* (Cambridge, 1985).

*Voyages: The Transatlantic Slave Trade Database*, David Eltis, Martin Halbert et al., http://www.slavevoyages.org/

James Walvin, *Black Ivory: A History of British Slavery* (London, 1992).

# Chapter 3

## *Primary sources*

A. C. Carmichael, *Domestic Manners and Social Condition of the White, Coloured, and Negro Population of the West Indies*, 2 volumes (London, 1833).

Edward Long, *The History of Jamaica*, 3 volumes (London, 1774).

# *Secondary sources*

Ira Berlin and Philip Morgan, eds., *The Slaves' Economy: Independent Production by Slaves in the Americas* (London, 1991).

J. Harry Bennett Jr., *Bondsmen and Bishops: Slavery and Apprenticeship on the Codrington Plantations of Barbados, 1710–1838* (Berkeley, 1958).

O. Nigel Bolland, *The Formation of a Colonial Society: Belize, from Conquest to Crown Colony* (Baltimore, 1977).

Edward Brathwaite, *The Development of Creole Society in Jamaica, 1770–1820* (Oxford, 1971).

Vincent Brown, *The Reaper's Garden: Death and Power in the World of Atlantic Slavery* (Cambridge, MA, 2008).

Randy M. Browne, *Surviving Slavery in the British Caribbean* (Philadelphia, 2017).

Trevor Burnard, *Planters, Merchants, and Slaves: Plantation Socieites in British America, 1650–1820* (Chicago, 2015).

James Dator, 'Frank Travels: Space, Power and Slave Mobility in the British Leeward Islands, c. 1700–1730', *Slavery & Abolition: A Journal of Slave and Post-Slave Studies* 36, no. 2 (2015): 335–59.

Gabriel Debien, *Les Esclaves aux Antilles Françaises* (Basse-Terre, 1974).

Audra A. Diptee, *From Africa to Jamaica: The Making of an Atlantic Slave Society, 1775–1807* (Gainesville, 2010).

D. A. Dunkley, *Agency of the Enslaved: Jamaica and the Culture of Freedom in the Atlantic World* (Lanham, MD, 2013).

Richard Dunn, *A Tale of Two Plantations: Slave Life and Labor in Jamaica and Virginia* (Cambridge, MA, 2014).

Stanley L. Engerman and B. W. Higman, 'The Demographic Structure of the Caribbean Slave Societies in the Eighteenth and Nineteenth Centuries', in Franklin Knight, ed., *The Slave Societies of the Caribbean, volume 3: General History of the Caribbean* (London, 1997).

Elsa V. Goveia, *Slave Society in the British Leeward Islands at the End of the Eighteenth Century* (New Haven, 1965).

Jerome S. Handler and Frederick W. Lange, *Plantation Slavery in Barbados: An Archaeological and Historical Investigation* (Cambridge, MA, 1978).

Herbert S. Klein, *Slavery in the Americas: A Comparative Study of Virginia and Cuba* (Chicago, 1967).

Franklin W. Knight, *Slave Society in Cuba during the Nineteenth Century* (Madison, 1970).

Paul E. Lovejoy and David V. Trotman, 'Enslaved Africans and their Expectations of Slave Life in the Americas: Towards a Reconsideration of Models of "Creolisation"', in Verene A. Shepherd and Glen L.

Richards, eds., *Questioning Creole: Creolisation Discourses in Caribbean Culture* (Kingston, 2002).

Roderick A. McDonald, *The Economy and Material Culture of Slaves: Goods and Chattels on the Sugar Plantations of Jamaica and Louisiana* (Baton Rouge, 1993).

Sidney W. Mintz, *Caribbean Transformations* (Chicago, 1974).

Philip D. Morgan, 'The Black Experience in the British Empire, 1680–1810', in P. J. Marshall, ed., *The Eighteenth Century, volume 2: The Oxford History of the British Empire* (Oxford, 1998).

Philip D. Morgan, 'The Cultural Implications of the Atlantic Slave Trade: African Regional Origins, American Destinations and New World Developments', *Slavery & Abolition: A Journal of Slave and Post-Slave Studies* 18 (April 1997): 122–45.

Orlando Patterson, *The Sociology of Slavery: An Analysis of the Origins, Development and Structure of Negro Slave Society in Jamaica* (London, 1967).

Justin Roberts, 'Uncertain Business: A Case Study of Barbadian Plantation Management, 1770–93', *Slavery & Abolition: A Journal of Slave and Post-Slave Studies* 32 (June 2011): 247–68.

Francisco A. Scarano, *Sugar and Slavery in Puerto Rico: The Plantation Economy of Ponce, 1800–1850* (Madison, 1984).

Verene A. Shepherd, *Livestock, Sugar and Slavery: Contested Terrain in Colonial Jamaica* (Kingston, 2009).

Richard B. Sheridan, 'The Formation of Caribbean Plantation Society, 1689–1748', in P. J. Marshall, ed., *The Eighteenth Century, volume 2: The Oxford History of the British Empire* (Oxford, 1998).

Dale Tomich, 'Une Petite Guinée: Provision Ground and Plantation in Martinique, 1830–1848', in Ira Berlin and Philip Morgan, eds., *The Slaves' Economy: Independent Production by Slaves in the Americas* (London, 1991).

James Walvin, *Black Ivory: A History of British Slavery* (London, 1992).

# Chapter 4

Rosemary Brana-Shute, 'Approaching Freedom: The Manumission of Slaves in Suriname, 1760–1828', *Slavery & Abolition: A Journal of Slave and Post-Slave Studies* 10, no. 3 (December 1989): 40–63.

Carl C. Campbell, *Cedulants and Capitulants: The Politics of Coloured Opposition in the Slave Society of Trinidad, 1783–1838* (Port of Spain, 1992).

David W. Cohen and Jack P. Greene, eds., *Neither Slave Nor Free: The Freedmen of African Descent in the Slave Societies of the New World* (Baltimore, 1972).

Edward L. Cox, *Free Coloreds in the Slave Societies of St. Kitts and Grenada, 1763–1833* (Knoxville, 1984).

Gabriel Debien, *Les Esclaves aux Antilles Françaises* (Basse-Terre, 1974).

Léo Elisabeth, 'The French Antilles', in David W. Cohen and Jack P. Greene, eds., *Neither Slave Nor Free: The Freedmen of African Descent in the Slave Societies of the New World* (Baltimore, 1972).

Marisa J. Fuentes, *Dispossessed Lives: Enslaved Women, Violence, and the Archive* (Philadelphia, 2016).

Marisa J. Fuentes, 'Power and Historical Figuring: Rachael Pringle Polgreen's Troubled Archive', *Gender & History* 22, no. 3 (2010): 564–84.

David Barry Gaspar and Darlene Clark Hine, eds., *Beyond Bondage: Free Women of Color in the Americas* (Urbana, 2004).

David Patrick Geggus, *Slavery, War, and Revolution: The British Occupation of St. Domingue, 1793–1798* (Oxford, 1982).

Gwendolyn Midlo Hall, 'Saint Domingue', in David W. Cohen and Jack P. Greene, eds., *Neither Slave Nor Free: The Freedmen of African Descent in the Slave Societies of the New World* (Baltimore, 1972).

N. A. T. Hall, 'Anna Heegaard – Enigma', *Caribbean Quarterly* 22 (June-September 1976): 62–73.

N. A. T. Hall, 'The 1816 freedman petition in the Danish West Indies: Its background and consequences', *Boletin de estudios Latinoamericanos y del Caribe* 29 (1980): 55–73.

Jerome S. Handler, 'Joseph Rachell and Rachael Pringle-Polgreen: Petty Entrepreneurs', in David G. Sweet and Gary B. Nash, eds., *Struggle and Survival in Colonial America* (Berkeley, 1981).

Jerome S. Handler, *The Unappropriated People: Freedmen in the Slave Society of Barbados* (Baltimore, 1974).

Gad J. Heuman, *Between Black and White: Race, Politics, and the Free Coloreds in Jamaica, 1792–1865* (Westport, CT, 1981).

H. Hoetink, 'Surinam and Curaçao', in David W. Cohen and Jack P. Greene, eds., *Neither Slave Nor Free: The Freedmen of African Descent in the Slave Societies of the New World* (Baltimore, 1972).

Franklin W. Knight, 'Cuba', in David W. Cohen and Jack P. Greene, eds., *Neither Slave Nor Free: The Freedmen of African Descent in the Slave Societies of the New World* (Baltimore, 1972).

Jane Landers, ed., *Against the Odds: Free Blacks in the Slave Societies of the Americas* (London, 1996).

Daniel Livesay, 'Privileging Kinship: Family and Race in Eighteenth-Century Jamaica', *Early American Studies: An Interdisciplinary Journal* 14, no. 4 (2016): 688–711.

Daniel Livesay, 'The decline of Jamaica's interracial households and the fall of the planter class, 1733–1823', *Atlantic Studies* 9, no. 1 (2012): 107–23.

Melanie J. Newton, *The Children of Africa in the Colonies: Free People of Color in Barbados in the Age of Emancipation* (Baton Rouge, 2008).

Michele Reid-Vazquez, *The Year of the Lash: Free People of Color in Cuba and the Nineteenth-Century Atlantic World* (Athens, GA, 2011).

Arnold A. Sio, 'Marginality and Free Coloured Identity in Caribbean Slave Society', *Slavery & Abolition: A Journal of Slave and Post-Slave Studies* 8 (September 1987): 166–82.

R. A. J. Van Lier, *Frontier Society: A Social Analysis of the History of Surinam* (The Hague, 1971).

Pedro L. V. Welch, with Richard A. Goodridge, *'Red' & Black Over White: Free Coloured Women in Pre-Emancipation Barbados* (Bridgetown, 2000).

# Chapter 5

## *Primary sources*

Bryan Edwards, *The History, Civil and Commercial, of the British Colonies in the West Indies*, 2 volumes (London, 1793).

Moira Ferguson, ed., *The History of Mary Prince, A West Indian Slave: Related by Herself* (London, 1987).

Edward Long, *The History of Jamaica*, 3 volumes (London, 1774).

## *Secondary sources*

Hilary McD. Beckles, *Centering Women: Gender Discourses in Caribbean History* (Kingston, 1999).

Edward Brathwaite, *The Development of Creole Society in Jamaica, 1770–1820* (Oxford, 1971).

Trevor Burnard, 'Et in Arcadia ego: West Indian planters in glory, 1674–1784', *Atlantic Studies* 9, no. 1 (2012): 19–40.

Trevor Burnard, *Mastery, Tyranny, and Desire: Thomas Thistlewood and His Slaves in the Anglo-Jamaican World* (Chapel Hill, 2004).

Trevor Burnard, *Planters, Merchants, and Slaves: Plantation Societies in British North America* (Chicago, 2015).

Barbara Bush, *Slave Women in Caribbean Society, 1650–1838* (London, 1990).

Kathleen Mary Butler, *The Economics of Emancipation: Jamaica & Barbados, 1823–1843* (Chapel Hill, 1995).

Michael Craton and James Walvin, *A Jamaica Plantation: The History of Worthy Park, 1670–1970* (Toronto, 1970).

Gabriel Debien, *Les Esclaves aux Antilles Françaises* (Basse-Terre, 1974).

Richard S. Dunn, *Sugar and Slaves: The Rise of the Planter Class in the English West Indies, 1624–1713* (Chapel Hill, 1972).

David Patrick Geggus, *Slavery, War, and Revolution: The British Occupation of St. Domingue, 1793–1798* (Oxford, 1982).

Elsa V. Goveia, *Slave Society in the British Leeward Islands at the End of the Eighteenth Century* (New Haven, 1965).

Douglas Hall, *In Miserable Slavery: Thomas Thistlewood in Jamaica, 1750–86* (London: Macmillan Caribbean, 1989).

B. W. Higman, *Plantation Jamaica, 1750–1850: Capital and Control in a Colonial Economy* (Kingston, 2005).

Howard Johnson and Karl Watson, eds., *The White Minority in the Caribbean* (Kingston, 1998).

Cecily Jones, 'Contesting the Boundaries of Gender, Race and Sexuality in Barbadian Plantation Society', *Women's History Review* 12, no. 2 (2003): 195–231.

Franklin W. Knight, *Slave Society in Cuba during the Nineteenth Century* (Madison, 1970).

Franklin Knight, ed., *The Slave Societies of the Caribbean, volume 3: General History of the Caribbean* (London, 1997).

David Lambert, *White Creole Culture, Politics and Identity during the Age of Abolition* (Cambridge, 2005).

Christer Petley, 'Rethinking the fall of the planter class', *Atlantic Studies* 9, no. 1 (2012): 1–17.

Christer Petley, *Slaveholders in Jamaica: Colonial Society and Culture during the Era of Abolition* (London, 2009).

Christer Petley, *White Fury: A Jamaican Slaveholder and the Age of Revolution* (Oxford, 2018).

Robert L. Paquette, *Sugar Is Made with Blood: The Conspiracy of La Escalera and the Conflict between Empires over Slavery in Cuba* (Middletown, CT, 1988).

Francisco A. Scarano, *Sugar and Slavery in Puerto Rico: The Plantation Economy of Ponce, 1800–1850* (Madison, 1984).

Verene A. Shepherd, comp. and ed., *Women in Caribbean History* (Kingston, 1999).

S. D. Smith, *Slavery, Family and Gentry Capitalism in the British Atlantic: The World of the Lascelles, 1648–1834* (Cambridge, 2006).

James Walvin, *Black Ivory: A History of British Slavery* (London, 1992).

# Chapter 6

## Primary source

Edward Long, *The History of Jamaica*, 3 volumes (London, 1774).

## Secondary sources

Manuel Barcia, *Seeds of Insurrection: Domination and Resistance on Western Cuban Plantations, 1808–1845* (Baton Rouge, 2008).

Jean Besson, *Transformation of Freedom in the Land of the Maroons: Creolization in the Cockpits, Jamaica* (Kingston, 2016).

Kenneth Bilby, *True-Born Maroons* (Gainesville, 2005).

Vincent Brown, 'Slave Revolt in Jamaica, 1760–1761: A Cartographic Narrative', *Axis Maps*, 2013, http://revolt.axismaps.com.

Randy M. Browne, 'The "Bad Business" of Obeah: Power, Authority, and the Politics of Slave Culture in the British Caribbean', *William and Mary Quarterly*, 3rd series 68, no. 3 (2011): 451–80.

Barbara Bush, *Slave Women in Caribbean Society, 1650–1838* (London, 1990).

Mavis C. Campbell, *The Maroons of Jamaica, 1655–1796: A History of Resistance, Collaboration & Betrayal* (Trenton, NJ, 1990).

Matt D. Childs, *The 1812 Aponte Rebellion in Cuba and the Struggle against Atlantic Slavery* (Chapel Hill, 2006).

Michael Craton, 'Forms of Resistance to Slavery', in Franklin Knight, ed., *Slave Societies of the Caribbean, volume 3: General History of the Caribbean* (London, 1997).

Michael Craton, *Testing the Chains: Resistance to Slavery in the British West Indies* (Ithaca, 1982).

David Barry Gaspar, *Bondmen & Rebels: A Study of Master-Slave Relations in Antigua* (Baltimore, 1985).

David Barry Gaspar and Darlene Clark Hine, eds., *More than Chattel: Black Women and Slavery in the Americas* (Bloomington, 1996).

Jerome S. Handler, 'Slave Medicine and Obeah in Barbados, circa 1650 to 1834', *New West Indian Guide* 74, no. 1 and 2 (2000): 57–90.

Gad Heuman, ed., *Out of the House of Bondage: Runaways, Resistance and Marronage in Africa and the New World* (London, 1986).

Brian L. Moore and Michele A. Johnson, *Neither Led nor Driven: Contesting British Cultural Imperialism in Jamaica, 1865–1920* (Kingston, 2004).

Marietta Morrissey, *Slave Women in the New World: Gender Stratification in the Caribbean* (Lawrence, KS, 1989).

Michael Mullin, *Africa in America: Slave Acculturation and Resistance in the American South and the British Caribbean, 1736–1831* (Urbana, 1992).

Simon P. Newman, 'Rethinking runaways in the British Atlantic world: Britain, the Caribbean, West Africa and North America', *Slavery & Abolition: A Journal of Slave and Post-Slave Studies* 38, no. 1(2017): 49–75.

Diana Paton, *The Cultural Politics of Obeah: Religion, Colonialism and Modernity in the Caribbean World* (Cambridge, 2015).

Diana Paton and Maarit Forde, eds., *The Politics of Caribbean Religion and Healing* (Durham, 2012).

Katherine Paugh, 'The Politics of Childbearing in the British Caribbean and Atlantic World during Age of Abolition', *Past & Present* 221, no. 1 (2013): 119–60.

Katherine Paugh, *The Politics of Reproduction: Race, Medicine, and Fertility in the Age of Abolition* (Oxford, 2017).

Richard Price, *Alabi's World* (Baltimore, 1990).

Richard Price, *Maroon Societies: Rebel Slave Communities in the Americas* (Garden City, NY, 1973).

Richard Rathbone, 'Some Thoughts on Resistance to Enslavement in West Africa', in Gad Heuman, ed., *Out of the House of Bondage: Runaways, Resistance and Marronage in Africa and the New World* (London, 1986).

Rhoda Reddock, 'Women and Slavery in the Caribbean: A Feminist Perspective', *Latin American Perspectives* 12, no. 1 (1985): 63–80.

David Richardson, 'Shipboard Revolts, African Authority, and the Atlantic Slave Trade', *William and Mary Quarterly, 3rd series* 58, no. 1 (January 2001): 69–92.

Verene Shepherd, Bridget Brereton and Barbara Bailey, eds., *Engendering History: Caribbean Women in Historical Perspective* (Kingston, 1995).

Alvin O. Thompson, *Flight to Freedom: African Runaways and Maroons in the Americas* (Kingston, 2006).

Sasha Turner, *Contested Bodies: Pregnancy, Childbearing, and Slavery in Jamaica* (Philadelphia, 2017).

Emily West, Camillia Cowling, Diana Paton and Maria Helena Machado, eds., 'Special Issue: Mothering Slaves: Motherhood, Childlessness and the Care of Children in Atlantic Slave Societies', *Slavery & Abolition: A Journal of Slave and Post-Slave Studies* 38, no. 2 (June 2017): 223–440.

Waldemar Westergaard, *The Danish West Indies under Company Rule, 1671–1754* (New York, 1917).

# Chapter 7

## *Primary source*

Marcus Rainsford, *An Historical Account of the Black Empire of Hayti*,
Paul Younquist and Gregory Pierrot, eds. (Durham, NC, 2013 [orig.
pub. 1805]).

## *Secondary sources*

Robin Blackburn, *The Overthrow of Colonial Slavery, 1776–1848*
(London, 1988).
Trevor Burnard and John Garrigus, *The Plantation Machine: Atlantic
Capitalism in French Saint-Domingue and British Jamaica*
(Philadelphia, 2016).
Paul Cheney, *Cul de Sac: Patrimony, Capitalism, and Slavery in French
Saint Domingue* (Chicago, 2017).
Edward L. Cox, *Free Coloreds in the Slave Societies of St. Kitts and
Grenada, 1763–1833* (Knoxville, 1984).
Michael Craton, 'Forms of Resistance to Slavery', in Franklin Knight, ed.,
*Slave Societies of the Caribbean, volume 3: General History of the
Caribbean* (London, 1997).
Laurent Dubois, *A Colony of Citizens: Revolution & Slave Emancipation
in the French Caribbean, 1787–1804* (Chapel Hill, 2004).
Laurent Dubois, *Avengers of the New World: The Story of the Haitian
Revolution* (Cambridge, 2004).
Carolyn E. Fick, *The Making of Haiti: The Saint Domingue Revolution
from Below* (Knoxville, 1990).
Carolyn E. Fick, 'The Saint Domingue Slave Insurrection of 1791: A
Socio-Political and Cultural Analysis', *The Journal of Caribbean
History* 25, no. 1 and 2 (1991): 1–40.
Julia Gaffield, *Haitian Connections in the Atlantic World: Recognition
after Revolution* (Chapel Hill, NC, 2015).
Julia Gaffield, ed., *The Haitian Declaration of Independence: Creation,
Context, and Legacy* (Charlottesville, 2016).
John D. Garrigus, *Before Haiti: Race and Citizenship in French Saint-
Domingue* (New York, 2006).
David Barry Gaspar and David Patrick Geggus, eds., *A Turbulent Time:
The French Revolution and the Greater Caribbean* (Bloomington,
1997).

David Geggus, 'The Bois-Caïman Ceremony', *The Journal of Caribbean History* 25, no. 1 and 2 (1991): 41–57.

David Geggus, 'The Haitian Revolution', in Hilary Beckles and Verene Shepherd, eds., *Caribbean Slave Society and Economy: A Student Reader* (Kingston, 1991).

David Patrick Geggus, *Haitian Revolutionary Studies* (Bloomington, 2002).

David Patrick Geggus, *Slavery, War, and Revolution: The British Occupation of St. Domingue, 1793–1798* (Oxford, 1982).

David Patrick Geggus and Norman Fiering, eds., *The World of the Haitian Revolution* (Bloomington, 2009).

Malick W. Ghachem, *The Old Regime and the Haitian Revolution* (Cambridge, 2012).

Phillipe Girard, *Toussaint Louverture: A Revolutionary Life* (New York, 2016).

C. L. R. James, *The Black Jacobins: Toussaint L'Ouverture and the San Domingo Revolution* (1938; reprint, New York, 1963).

Jane G. Landers, *Atlantic Creoles in the Age of Revolutions* (Cambridge, MA, 2010).

Thomas O. Ott, *The Haitian Revolution, 1789–1804* (Knoxville, 1973).

Jeremy D. Popkin, *You Are All Free: The Haitian Revolution and the Abolition of Slavery* (Cambridge, 2010).

Alyssa Goldstein Sepinwall, *Haitian History: New Perspectives* (London, 2012).

Rebecca J. Scott and Jean M. Hébrard, *Freedom Papers: An Atlantic Odyssey in the Age of Emancipation* (Cambridge, MA, 2012).

John K. Thornton, 'African Soldiers in the Haitian Revolution', *The Journal of Caribbean History* 25, no. 1 and 2 (1991): 58–80.

# Chapter 8

Roger Anstey, *The Atlantic Slave Trade and British Abolition, 1760–1810* (London, 1975).

Roger Anstey, 'Capitalism and Slavery: A Critique', *Economic History Review, 2nd series* XXI (1968): 307–20.

Hilary McD. Beckles, *A History of Barbados: From Amerindian Settlement to Nation-State* (Cambridge, 1990).

Robin Blackburn, *The American Crucible: Slavery, Emancipation and Human Rights* (London, 2011).

Robin Blackburn, *The Overthrow of Colonial Slavery, 1776–1848* (London, 1988).

Christopher Leslie Brown, 'Abolition of the Atlantic Slave Trade', in Gad Heuman and Trevor Burnard, eds., *The Routledge History of Slavery* (New York, 2011): 281–97.

Christopher Leslie Brown, *Moral Capital: Foundations of British Abolitionism* (Chapel Hill, 2006).

Emilia Viotti da Costa, *Crowns of Glory, Tears of Blood: The Demerara Slave Rebellion of 1823* (New York, 1994).

Michael Craton, *Testing the Chains: Resistance to Slavery in the British West Indies* (Ithaca, 1982).

Michael Craton, 'Forms of Resistance to Slavery', in Franklin Knight, ed., *Slave Societies of the Caribbean, volume 3: General History of the Caribbean* (London, 1997).

Seymour Drescher, *Abolition: A History of Slavery and Antislavery* (Cambridge, 2009).

Seymour Drescher, *Econocide: British Slavery in the Era of Abolition* (Pittsburgh, 1977).

Claudius Fergus, '"Dread of insurrection": Abolitionism, Security, and Labor in Britain's West Indian Colonies, 1760–1823', *William and Mary Quarterly, 3rd series* 66, no. 4 (2009): 757–80.

William A. Green, *British Slave Emancipation: The Sugar Colonies and the Great Experiment, 1830–1865* (Oxford, 1976).

Gad Heuman, 'A Tale of Two Jamaican Rebellions', In Wim Hoogbergen, ed., *Born Out of Resistance: On Caribbean Cultural Creativity* (Utrecht, 1995).

Thomas C. Holt, *The Problem of Freedom: Race, Labor, and Politics in Jamaica and Britain, 1832–1938* (Baltimore, 1992).

Jane G. Landers, *Atlantic Creoles in the Age of Revolutions* (Cambridge, MA, 2010).

Gelien Matthews, *Caribbean Slave Revolts and the British Abolitionist Movement* (Baton Rouge, 2006).

Robert L. Paquette, *Sugar Is Made with Blood: The Conspiracy of La Escalera and the Conflict between Empires over Slavery in Cuba* (Middletown, CT, 1988).

David Beck Ryden, *West Indian Slavery and British Abolitionism, 1783–1807* (Cambridge, 2010).

Christopher Schmidt-Nowara, *Empire and Antislavery: Spain, Cuba and Puerto Rico, 1833–1874* (Pittsburgh, 1999).

Rebecca J. Scott, *Slave Emancipation in Cuba: The Transition to Free Labor, 1860–1899* (Princeton, 1985).

Barbara L. Solow and Stanley L. Engerman, *British Capitalism & Caribbean Slavery: The Legacy of Eric Williams* (Cambridge, 1987).

Howard Temperley, *British Antislavery, 1833–1870* (London, 1972).

Mary Turner, *Slaves and Missionaries: The Disintegration of Jamaican Slave Society, 1787–1834* (Urbana, 1982).

James Walvin, *The Zong: A Massacre, The Law and The End of Slavery* (New Haven, 2011).

Eric Williams, *Capitalism & Slavery* (1944; reprint, New York, 1966).

# Chapter 9

## *Primary sources*

Rev. George W. Bridges, *The Annals of Jamaica*, 2 volumes (London, 1828).

M. G. Lewis, *Journal of a West India Proprietor, 1815–17*, ed. with an introduction by Mona Wilson (London, 1929).

James A. Thome and Horace J. Kimball, *Emancipation in the West Indies* (New York, 1838).

Anthony Trollope, *The West Indies and the Spanish Main*, 2nd ed. (London, 1860).

## *Secondary sources*

O. Nigel Bolland, *The Formation of a Colonial Society: Belize, from Conquest to Crown Colony* (Baltimore, 1977).

Carl C. Campbell, *Cedulants and Capitulants: The Politics of Coloured Opposition in the Slave Society of Trinidad, 1783–1838* (Port of Spain, 1992).

David W. Cohen and Jack P. Greene, *Neither Slave Nor Free: The Freedmen of African Descent in the Slave Societies of the New World* (Baltimore, 1972).

Edward L. Cox, *Free Coloreds in the Slave Societies of St. Kitts and Grenada, 1763–1833* (Knoxville, 1984).

Léo Elisabeth, 'The French Antilles', in David W. Cohen and Jack P. Greene, eds., *Neither Slave Nor Free: The Freedmen of African Descent in the Slave Societies of the New World* (Baltimore, 1972).

Aisha K. Finch, *Rethinking Slave Rebellion in Cuba: La Escalera and the Insurgencies of 1841–1844* (Chapel Hill, 2015).

John Garrigus, 'Free coloureds', in Gad Heuman and Trevor Burnard, eds., *The Routledge History of Slavery* (New York, 2011): 234–47.

Jerome S. Handler, *The Unappropriated People: Freedmen in the Slave Society of Barbados* (Baltimore, 1974).

Gad J. Heuman, *Between Black and White: Race, Politics and the Free Coloreds in Jamaica, 1792–1865* (Westport, CT, 1981).

Franklin W. Knight, *Slave Society in Cuba during the Nineteenth Century* (Madison, 1970).

Daniel Livesay, *Children of Uncertain Fortune: Mixed-Race Jamaicans in Britain and the Atlantic Family, 1733–1833* (Chapel Hill, 2018).

Verena Martinez-Alier, *Marriage, Class and Colour in Nineteenth-Century Cuba: A Study of Racial Attitudes and Sexual Values in a Slave Society* (Cambridge, 1974).

Melanie J. Newton, *The Children of Africa in the Colonies: Free People of Color in Barbados in the Age of Emancipation* (Baton Rouge, 2008).

Michele Reid-Vazquez, *The Year of the Lash: Free People of Color in Cuba and the Nineteenth-Century Atlantic World* (Athens, GA, 2011).

# Chapter 10

## *Primary source*

Diana Paton, ed., *A Narrative of Events, since the First of August, 1834, by James Williams, an Apprenticed Labourer in Jamaica* (Durham, NC, 2001).

## *Secondary sources*

Gaiutra Bahadur, *Coolie Woman: The Odyssey of Indenture* (London, 2013).

Jean Besson, *Martha Brae's Two Histories: European Expansion and Caribbean Culture-Building* (Chapel Hill, 2002).

Robin Blackburn, *The American Crucible: Slavery, Emancipation and Human Rights* (London, 2011).

O. Nigel Bolland, '*Systems of Domination after Slavery: The Control of Land and Labour in the British West Indies after 1838*', in Hilary Beckles and Verene Shepherd, eds., *Caribbean Freedom: Economy and Society from Emancipation to the Present* (Kingston, 1993).

Bridget Brereton, 'Family Strategies, Gender, and the Shift to Wage Labour in the British Caribbean', in Bridget Brereton and Kevin A. Yelvington, eds., *The Colonial Caribbean in Transition: Essays on Postemancipation Social and Cultural History* (Kingston, 1999).

Bridget Brereton, *Race Relations in Colonial Trinidad, 1870–1900* (Cambridge, 1979).

Victor Bulmer-Thomas, *The Economic History of the Caribbean since the Napoleonic Wars* (Cambridge, 2012).

Russell E. Chace, Jr., 'Protest in Post-Emancipation Dominica: The "Guerre Negre" of 1844', *Journal of Caribbean History* 23 (1989): 118–41.

Philip D. Curtin, *Two Jamaicas: The Role of Ideas in a Tropical Colony, 1830–1865* (Cambridge, 1955).

Nicholas Draper, *The Price of Emancipation: Slave-ownership, Compensation and British Society at the End of Slavery* (Cambridge, 2010).

Claudius Fergus, *Revolutionary Emancipation: Slavery and Abolitionism in the British West Indies* (Baton Rouge, 2013).

Richard Frucht, 'From Slavery to Unfreedom in the Plantation Society of St. Kitts, W.I.', in Vera Rubin and Arthur Tuden, eds., *Comparative Perspectives on Slavery in New World Plantation Societies* (New York, 1977).

William A. Green, *British Slave Emancipation: The Sugar Colonies and the Great Experiment, 1830–1865* (Oxford, 1976).

Catherine Hall, *Civilising Subjects: Metropole and Colony in the English Imagination, 1830–1867* (Oxford, 2002).

Douglas Hall, *Five of the Leewards, 1834–70: The Major Problems of the Post-Emancipation Period in Antigua, Barbuda, Montserrat, Nevis and St. Kitts* (London, 1971).

Aline Helg, *Our Rightful Share: The Afro-Cuban Struggle for Equality, 1886–1912* (Chapel Hill, 1995).

Gad J. Heuman, *Between Black and White: Race, Politics and the Free Coloreds in Jamaica, 1792–1865* (Westport, CT., 1981).

Thomas C. Holt, *The Problem of Freedom: Race, Labor, and Politics in Jamaica and Britain, 1832–1938* (Baltimore, 1992).

Madhavi Kale, *Fragments of Empire: Capital, Slavery, and Indian Indentured Labor Migration in the British Caribbean* (Philadelphia, 1998).

Keith Lawrence, *A Question of Labour: Indentured Immigration into Trinidad and British Guiana, 1875–1917* (Kingston, 1994).

Roderick A. McDonald, *Between Slavery and Freedom: Special Magistrate John Anderson's Journal of St. Vincent during the Apprenticeship* (Philadelphia, 2001).

Woodville Marshall, '"We be wise to many more tings": Blacks' Hopes and Expectations of Emancipation', in Hilary Beckles and Verene Shepherd, eds., *Caribbean Freedom: Economy and Society from Emancipation to the Present* (Kingston, 1993).

Brian L. Moore, *Race, Power and Social Segmentation in Colonial Society: Guyana After Slavery, 1838–1891* (New York, 1987).

Diana Paton, 'Decency, Dependence and the Lash: Gender and the British Debate over Slave Emancipation, 1830–34', *Slavery & Abolition: A Journal of Slave and Post-Slave Studies* 17 (December 1996): 163–184.

Diana Paton, *No Bond but the Law: Punishment, Race, and Gender in Jamaican State Formation, 1780–1870* (Durham, 2004).

Rosamunde A. Renard, 'Labour Relations in Post-Slavery Martinique and Guadeloupe, 1848–1870', in Hilary Beckles and Verene Shepherd, eds., *Caribbean Freedom: Economy and Society from Emancipation to the Present* (Kingston, 1993).

Rebecca J. Scott, *Degrees of Freedom: Louisiana and Cuba after Slavery* (Cambridge, MA, 2005).

Rebecca J. Scott, *Slave Emancipation in Cuba: The Transition to Free Labor, 1860–1899* (Princeton, 1985).

Clem Seecharan, *'Tiger in the Stars': The Anatomy of Indian Achievement in British Guiana, 1919–29* (London, 1997).

Mimi Sheller, *Democracy After Slavery: Black Publics and Peasant Radicalism in Haiti and Jamaica* (London, 2000).

Mimi Sheller, 'Quasheba, Mother, Queen: Black Women's Public Leadership and Political Protest in Post-Emancipation Jamaica, 1834–65', *Slavery & Abolition: A Journal of Slave and Post-Slave Studies* 19 (December 1998): 90–117.

Robert S. Shelton, 'A Modified Crime: The Apprenticeship System in St. Kitts', *Slavery & Abolition: A Journal of Slave and Post-Slave Studies* 16 (December 1995): 331–45.

Matthew J. Smith, *Liberty, Fraternity, Exile: Haiti and Jamaica after Emancipation* (Chapel Hill, 2014).

David Vincent Trotman, *Crime in Trinidad: Conflict and Control in a Plantation Society, 1838–1900* (Knoxville, 1986).

Michel-Rolph Trouillot, *Peasants and Capital: Dominica in the World Economy* (Baltimore, 1988).

Maureen Warner-Lewis, *Archibald Monteath: Igbo, Jamaican, Moravian* (Kingston, 2007).

Swithin Wilmot, '"Females of Abandoned Character?": Women and Protest in Jamaica, 1838–65', in Verene Shepherd, Bridget Brereton and Barbara Bailey, eds., *Engendering History: Caribbean Women in Historical Perspective* (Kingston, 1995).

Donald Wood, *Trinidad in Transition: The Years after Slavery* (London, 1968).

# Chapter 11

O. Nigel Bolland, 'Systems of Domination after Slavery: The Control of Land and Labour in the British West Indies after 1838', *Comparative Studies in Society and History* 23, no. 4 (1981): 591–619.

Bridget Brereton, 'Post-Emancipation Protest in the Caribbean: The "Belmanna Riots" in Tobago, 1876', *Caribbean Quarterly* 30, no. 3 and 4 (1984): 110–23.

Bridget Brereton, *Race Relations in Colonial Trinidad, 1870–1900* (Cambridge, 1979).

Russell E. Chace, Jr., 'Protest in Post-Emancipation Dominica: The "Guerre Negre" of 1844', *Journal of Caribbean History* 23 (1989): 118–41.

Christine Chivallon and David Howard, 'Colonial violence and civilising utopias in the French and British empires: The Morant Bay Rebellion (1865) and the Insurrection of the South (1870)', *Slavery & Abolition: A Journal of Slave and Post-Slave Studies* 38, no. 3 (September, 2017): 534–58.

Michael Craton, 'Continuity Not Change: The Incidence of Unrest Among Ex-Slaves in the British West Indies, 1838–1876', *Slavery & Abolition: A Journal of Slave and Post-Slave Studies* 9, no. 2 (1988): 144–70.

Isaac Dookhan, *A History of the Virgin Islands of the United States* (Epping, Essex, 1974).

Ada Ferrer, *Insurgent Cuba: Race, Nation, and Revolution, 1868–1898* (Chapel Hill, 1999).

Douglas Hall, *Free Jamaica, 1838–1865: An Economic History* (New Haven, 1959).

Aline Helg, *Our Rightful Share: The Afro-Cuban Struggle for Equality, 1886–1912* (Chapel Hill, 1995).

Gad Heuman, 'Post-Emancipation Resistance in the Caribbean: An Overview', in Karen Fog Olwig, ed., *Small Islands, Large Questions: Society, Culture and Resistance in the Post-Emancipation Caribbean* (London, 1995).

Gad Heuman, *The Killing Time: The Morant Bay Rebellion in Jamaica* (London, 1994).

Gad Heuman and David V. Trotman, eds., *Contesting Freedom: Control and Resistance in the Post-Emancipation Caribbean* (London, 2005).

Clinton A. Hutton, *Colour for Colour, Skin for Skin: Marching with the Ancestral Spirits into War Oh at Morant Bay* (Kingston, 2015).

Claude Levy, *Emancipation, Sugar, and Federalism: Barbados and the West Indies, 1833–1876* (Gainesville, 1980).

Natasha Lightfoot, '"Their Coats were Tied Up like Men": Women Rebels in Antigua's 1858 Uprising', *Slavery & Abolition: A Journal of Slave and Post-Slave Studies* 31 (December 2010): 527–45.

Natasha Lightfoot, *Troubling Freedom: Antigua and the Aftermath of British Emancipation* (Durham, 2015).

Woodville K. Marshall, '"Vox Populi": The St. Vincent Riots and
Disturbances of 1862', in B. W. Higman, ed., *Trade, Government and
Society in Caribbean History, 1700–1920* (Kingston, 1983).
Rosamunde A. Renard, 'Labour Relations in Post-Slavery Martinique and
Guadeloupe, 1848–1870', in Hilary Beckles and Verene Shepherd, eds.,
*Caribbean Freedom: Economy and Society from Emancipation to the
Present* (Kingston, 1993).
Mimi Sheller, *Democracy After Slavery: Black Publics and Peasant
Radicalism in Haiti and Jamaica* (London, 2000).
Dale Tomich, 'Contested Terrains: Houses, Provision Grounds & the
Reconstitution of Labour in Post-Emancipation Martinique', in Mary
Turner, ed., *From Chattel Slaves to Wage Slaves: The Dynamics of
Labour Bargaining in the Americas* (Kingston, 1995).

# Chapter 12

## *Primary sources*

Robert A. Hill, ed., *The Marcus Garvey and Universal Negro
Improvement Association Papers, volume 7: November 1927 – August
1940* (Berkeley, 1990).
Robert A. Hill, ed., *The Marcus Garvey and Universal Negro
Improvement Association Papers, volume 11: The Caribbean Diaspora,
1910–1920* (Durham, NC, 2011).

## *Secondary sources*

Leonard E. Barrett, *The Rastafarians: The Dreadlocks of Jamaica*
(Kingston, 1977).
Bridget Brereton, 'The Development of an Identity: The Black Middle
Class of Trinidad in the Later Nineteenth Century', in Hilary Beckles
and Verene Shepherd, eds., *Caribbean Freedom: Society and Economy
to the Present* (Kingston, 1993).
Dalea Bean, *Jamaican Women & the World Wars: On the Front Lines of
Change* (London, 2018).
Patrick Bryan, *The Jamaican People, 1880–1902* (London, 1991).
Richard D. E. Burton, *Afro-Creole: Power, Opposition, and Play in the
Caribbean* (Ithaca, 1997).
Richard D. E. Burton and Fred Reno, *French and West Indian:
Martinique, Guadeloupe and French Guiana Today* (London, 1995).

Horace Campbell, *Rasta and Resistance: From Marcus Garvey to Walter Rodney* (London, 1985).

Barry Chevannes, *Rastafari: Roots and Ideology* (Syracuse, NY, 1994).

Barry Chevannes, ed., *Rastafari and Other African-Caribbean Worldviews* (London, 1997).

D. A. Dunkley, 'Suppression of L.P. Howell', *New West Indian Guide* 87, no. 1/2 (2013): 62–93.

D. A. Dunkley, with C. Hutton, M. Barnett and J. Niaah, eds., *Leonard Percival Howell and the Genesis of Rastafari* (Kingston, 2015).

Ennis B. Edmonds, *Rastafari: A Very Short Introduction* (Oxford, 2013).

Adam Ewing, *The Age of Garvey: How a Jamaican Activist Created a Mass Movement and Changed Global Black Politics* (Princeton, 2016).

Colin Grant, *Negro with a Hat: The Rise and Fall of Marcus Garvey* (London, 2009).

Alistair Hennessy, ed., *Intellectuals in the Twentieth-Century Caribbean, volume 2: Unity in Variety: The Hispanic and Francophone Caribbean* (London, 1992).

Conrad James and John Perivolaris, *The Cultures of the Hispanic Caribbean* (London, 2000).

Winston James, *Holding Aloft the Banner of Ethiopia: Caribbean Radicalism in Early Twentieth Century America* (London, 1998).

Rupert Lewis, *Marcus Garvey: Anti-Colonial Champion* (London, 1987).

Rupert Lewis and Patrick Bryan, *Garvey: His Work and Impact* (Kingston, 1988).

Joy Lumsden, 'A Forgotten Generation: Black Politicians in Jamaica, 1884–1914', in Brian Moore and Swithin Wilmot, eds., *Before and After 1865: Education, Politics and Regionalism in the Caribbean* (Kingston, 1998).

Brian L. Moore and Michele A. Johnson, *Neither Led nor Driven: Contesting British Cultural Imperialism in Jamaica, 1865–1920* (Kingston, 2004).

Brian L. Moore and Michele A. Johnson, *'They Do As They Please': The Jamaican Struggle for Cultural Freedom after Morant Bay* (Kingston, 2011).

Nathaniel Samuel Murrell, William David Spencer and Adrian Anthony McFarlane, eds., *Chanting Down Babylon The Rastafari Reader* (Kingston, 1998).

Pedro Peréz Sarduy and Jean Stubbs, eds., *AfroCuba: An Anthology of Cuban Writing on Race, Politics and Culture* (London, 1993).

Faith Smith, *Creole Recitations: John Jacob Thomas and Colonial Formation in the Late Nineteenth-Century Caribbean* (Charlottesville, 2002).

M. G. Smith, Roy Augier and Rex Nettleford, *The Rastafari Movement in Kingston, Jamaica* (Mona, Jamaica, 1960).

Judith Stein, *The World of Marcus Garvey: Race and Class in Modern Society* (Baton Rouge, 1986).

# Chapter 13

Luis E. Aguilar, 'Cuba, c. 1860-c. 1930', in Leslie Bethell, ed., *Cuba: A Short History* (Cambridge, 1993).

Charles Arthur and Michael Dash, eds., *A Haiti Anthology: Libète* (London, 1999).

Victor Bulmer-Thomas, *The Economic History of the Caribbean since the Napoleonic Wars* (Cambridge, 2012).

Bruce J. Calder, *The Impact of intervention: The Dominican Republic during the U.S. Occupation of 1916–1924* (Austin, 1983).

Peter Chapman, *Bananas: How the United Fruit Company Shaped the World* (Edinburgh, 2009).

J. Michael Dash, *Literature and Ideology in Haiti, 1915–1961* (London, 1981).

Ada Ferrer, *Insurgent Cuba: Race, Nation, and Revolution, 1868–1898* (Chapel Hill, 1999).

Lillian Guerra, *The Myth of José Martí: Conflicting Nationalisms in Early Twentieth-Century Cuba* (Chapel Hill, 2005).

Richard S. Hillman and Thomas J. D. Agostino, *Understanding the Contemporary Caribbean* (Boulder, 2003).

Lester D. Langley, *The United States and the Caribbean in the Twentieth Century* (Athens, GA, 1982).

Anthony P. Maingot, *The United States and the Caribbean* (London, 1994).

John Bartlow Martin, *U.S. Policy in the Caribbean* (Boulder, 1978).

Steven Palmer, *Launching Global Health: The Caribbean Odyssey of the Rockefeller Foundation* (Ann Arbor, MI, 2010).

Teresita Martínez-Vergne, *Nation and Citizen in the Dominican Republic, 1880–1916* (Chapel Hill, 2005).

David Nicholls, *From Dessalines to Duvalier: Race, Colour and National Independence in Haiti* (Cambridge, 1979).

Louis A. Pérez Jr., *The War of 1898: The United States and Cuba in History and Historiography* (Chapel Hill, 1998).

Whitney T. Perkins, *Constraint of Empire: The United States and Caribbean Interventions* (Westport, CT, 1981).

Stephen J. Randall and Graeme S. Mount, *The Caribbean Basin: An International History* (London, 1998).

Matthew J. Smith, Liberty, Fraternity, *Exile: Haiti and Jamaica after Emancipation* (Chapel Hill, 2014).
Matthew J. Smith, *Red and Black in Haiti: Radicalism, Conflict and Political Change, 1934–1957* (Chapel Hill, 2009).
John Lawrence Tone, *War and Genocide in Cuba, 1895–1898* (Chapel Hill, 2006).

# Chapter 14

## *Primary source*

*The West India Royal Commission, 1938–1939* (London, 1945).

## *Secondary sources*

O. Nigel Bolland, *On the March: Labour Rebellions in the British Caribbean, 1934–39* (Kingston, 1995).
O. Nigel Bolland, *The Politics of Labour in the British Caribbean* (Kingston, 2001).
Bridget Brereton, ed., *The Caribbean in the Twentieth Century, volume 5: General History of the Caribbean* (London, 2004).
Patrick Bryan, *The Jamaican People, 1880–1902* (London, 1991).
Peter Clegg, *The Caribbean Banana Trade: From Colonialism to Globalization* (Houndmills, Basingstoke, 2002).
Adrian Fraser, *The 1935 Riots in St. Vincent: From Riots to Adult Suffrage* (Kingston, 2016).
Richard Hart, 'Origin and Development of the Working Class in the English-Speaking Caribbean Area, 1897–1937', in Malcolm Cross and Gad Heuman, eds., *Labour in the Caribbean: From Emancipation to Independence* (London, 1988).
Glenford Howe, *Race, War and Nationalism: A Social History of West Indians in the First World War* (Kingston, 2002).
Franklin Knight, 'The Caribbean in the 1930s', in Bridget Brereton, ed., *The Caribbean in the Twentieth Century, volume 5: General History of the Caribbean* (London, 2004).
Gordon K. Lewis, *The Growth of the Modern West Indies* (London, 1968).
Colin A. Palmer, *Freedom's Children: The 1938 Labor Rebellion and the Birth of Modern Jamaica* (Chapel Hill, 2014).

Bonham C. Richardson, *The Caribbean in the Wider World, 1492–1992: A Regional Geography* (Cambridge, 1992).

Bonham C. Richardson, 'Prelude to Nationalism? Riots and Land Use Changes in the Lesser Antilles in the 1890s', in Wim Hoogbergen, ed., *Born Out of Resistance: On Caribbean Cultural Creativity* (Utrecht, 1995).

Walter Rodney, *A History of the Guyanese Working People, 1881–1905* (Kingston, 1981).

Richard Smith, *Jamaican Volunteers in the First World War: Race, Masculinity and the Development of National Consciousness* (Manchester, 2004).

Elisabeth Wallace, *The British Caribbean: From the Decline of Colonialism to the End of Federation* (Toronto, 1977).

# Chapter 15

## *Primary source*

Michael Manley, *The Politics of Change: A Jamaican Testament* (London, 1974).

## *Secondary sources*

Colin Barber and Henry B. Jeffrey, *Guyana: Politics, Economics and Society* (London, 1986).

Michelle Chase, *Revolution within the Revolution: Women and Gender Politics in Cuba, 1952–1962* (Chapel Hill, 2015).

Steve Cushion, *A Hidden History of the Cuban Revolution: How the Working Class Shaped the Guerrilla Victory* (New York, 2016).

Jorge Dominguez, 'Cuba since 1959', in Leslie Bethell, ed., *Cuba: A Short History* (Cambridge, 1993).

Ada Ferrer, 'Listening to Obama in Cuba', http://nacla.org/news/2016/03/28/listening-obama-cuba (accessed 22 March 2017).

Wendy C. Grenade, ed., *The Grenada Revolution: Reflections and Lessons* (Jackson, MS, 2015).

Lillian Guerra, *Visions of Power in Cuba: Revolution, Redemption and Resistance, 1959–1971* (Chapel Hill, 2012).

Jorge Heine, *A Revolution Aborted: The Lessons of Grenada* (Pittsburgh, 1990).

Gerald Horne, *Cold War in a Hot Zone: The United States Confronts Labor and Independence Struggles in the British West Indies* (Philadelphia, 2007).

Howard Jones, *The Bay of Pigs* (New York, 2008).

Antoni Kapcia, *Cuba in Revolution: A History Since the Fifties* (Chicago, 2008).

Antoni Kapcia, *Cuba, Island of Dreams* (Oxford, 2000).

Brian Meeks, *Caribbean Revolutions and Revolutionary Theory: An Assessment of Cuba, Nicaragua and Grenada* (London, 1993).

James Millette, 'Decolonization, populist movements and the formation of new nations, 1945–70', in Bridget Brereton, ed., *The Caribbean in the Twentieth Century, volume 5: General History of the Caribbean* (London, 2004).

Colin A. Palmer, *Cheddi Jagan and the Politics of Power: British Guiana's Struggle for Independence* (Chapel Hill, 2014).

Anthony J. Payne, *Politics in Jamaica* (Kingston, 1994).

Louis A. Pérez, Jr., 'Cuba, *c.* 1930–1959', in Leslie Bethell, ed., *Cuba: A Short History* (Cambridge, 1993).

Marifeli Pérez-Stable, ed., *Looking Forward: Comparative Perspectives on Cuba's Transition* (Notre Dame, IN, 2007).

Marifeli Pérez-Stable, 'The Cuban Revolution and its impact on the Caribbean', in Bridget Brereton, ed., *The Caribbean in the Twentieth Century, volume 5: General History of the Caribbean* (London, 2004).

Marifeli Pérez-Stable, *The Cuban Revolution: Origins, Course, and Legacy* (New York, 1993).

Stephen J. Randall and Graeme S. Mount, *The Caribbean Basin: An International History* (London, 1998).

Lars Schoultz, *That Infernal Little Cuban Republic: The United States and the Cuban Revolution* (Chapel Hill, 2009).

Evelyn Huber Stephens and John D. Stephens, *Democratic Socialism in Jamaica: The Political Movement and Social Transformation in Dependent Capitalism* (Princeton, 1986).

Hugh Thomas, *The Cuban Revolution* (New York, 1971).

Tony Thorndike, *Grenada: Politics, Economics and Society* (London, 1985).

Alex von Tunzelmann, *Red Heat: Conspiracy, Murder and the Cold War in the Caribbean* (London, 2011).

# Chapter 16

César J. Ayala and Rafael Bernabe, *Puerto Rico in the American Century: A History since 1898* (Chapel Hill, 2007).

Peter Clegg and David Killingray, eds., *The Non-Independent Territories of the Caribbean and Pacific: Continuity or Change?* (London, 2012).

Jesselyn Cook, '7 Years After Haiti's Earthquake, Millions Still Need Aid', *The World Post*, 12 January 2017, http://www.huffingtonpost.com/entry/haiti-earthquake-anniversary_us_5875108de4b02b5f858b3f9c (accessed 16 March 2017).

Ezra Fieser, 'Why is China spending billions in the Caribbean?' https://www.pri.org/stories/2011-04-22/why-china-spending-billions-caribbean (accessed 10 April 2017).

Juan Manuel García-Passalacqua, 'The Role of the Puerto Rican People in the Caribbean', in Jorge I. Domínguez, Robert A. Pastor and R. DeLisle Worrell, eds., *Democracy in the Caribbean: Political, Economic, and Social Perspectives* (Baltimore, 1993).

Jonathan Hartlyn, 'The Dominican Republic: Contemporary Problems and Challenges', in Jorge I. Domínguez, Robert A. Pastor and R. DeLisle Worrell, eds., *Democracy in the Caribbean: Political, Economic, and Social Perspectives* (Baltimore, 1993).

Richard S. Hillman and Thomas J. D'Agostino, eds., *Understanding the Contemporary Caribbean* (Boulder, 2003).

Rosemarijn Hoefte and Peter Meel, eds., *Twentieth-Century Suriname: Continuities and Discontinuities in a New World Society* (Kingston, 2001).

Franklin Knight, 'The Societies of the Caribbean since Independence', in Jorge I. Domínguez, Robert A. Pastor and R. DeLisle Worrell, eds., *Democracy in the Caribbean: Political, Economic, and Social Perspectives* (Baltimore, 1993).

Sandra Laville, 'Beijing highway: $600m road just the start of China's investments in the Caribbean', *The Guardian*, https://www.theguardian.com/world/2015/dec/24/beijing-highway-600m-road-just-the-start-of-chinas-investments-in-caribbean (accessed 10 April 2017).

Gert Oostindie, *Paradise Overseas – The Dutch Caribbean: Colonialism and its Transatlantic Legacies* (Oxford, 2005).

Sir Ronald Sanders, 'The Implications of Brexit for the Caribbean's Future Relationship with Britain and the EU', *The Round Table* 105, no. 5 (2016): 519–29.

Alex von Tunzelmann, *Red Heat: Conspiracy, Murder and the Cold War in the Caribbean* (London, 2011).

Richard Lee Turits, 'A World Destroyed, A Nation Imposed: The 1937 Haitian Massacre in the Dominican Republic', *Hispanic American Historical Review* 82, no. 3 (August 2002): 589–636.

Mary Williams Walsh, 'How Puerto Rico is Grappling with a Debt Crisis', *The New York Times*, https://www.nytimes.com/

interactive/2017/business/dealbook/puerto-rico-debt-bankruptcy.html (accessed 22 June 2017).

Michele Wucker, 'The Dominican Republic's Shameful Deportation Legacy', *FP*, http://foreignpolicy.com/2015/10/08/dominican-republic-haiti-trujillo-immigration-deportation/ (accessed 21 June 2017).

# Chapter 17

Tasnim Abdi, 'Caribbean region to see increased drought, UN says', *The Christian Science Monitor*, 18 September 2016, http://www.csmonitor.com/Business/The-Bite/2016/0918/Caribbean-region-to-see-increased-drought-UN-says (accessed 6 April 2017).

Oliver Balch, 'Banana production battered by market pressures – and the Caribbean weather', *The Guardian*, 24 October 2013, https://www.theguardian.com/sustainable-business/future-banana-production-windward-islands (accessed 4 April 2017).

Hilary McD. Beckles, *Britain's Black Debt: Reparations for Caribbean Slavery and Native Genocide* (Kingston, 2012).

Victor Bulmer-Thomas, *The Economic History of the Caribbean since the Napoleonic Wars* (Cambridge, 2012).

Mary Chamberlain, *Narratives of Exile and Return* (London, 1997).

Jorge I. Domínguez, 'The Caribbean Question: Why Has Liberal Democracy (Surprisingly) Flourished?' in Jorge I. Domínguez, Robert A. Pastor and R. DeLisle Worrell, eds., *Democracy in the Caribbean: Political, Economic, and Social Perspectives* (Baltimore, 1993).

'Dominica Devastated by Hurricane Maria', *Caribbean Insight* 39, no. 52 (29 September – 13 October 2017): 1 (accessed 19 October 2017).

Richard S. Hillman and Thomas J. D'Agostino, eds., *Understanding the Contemporary Caribbean* (Boulder, 2003).

'Hurricane Irma: Caribbean counts the cost of deadly storm', www.bbc.co.uk/news/business-41192158 (accessed 13 September 2017).

Franklin W. Knight and Colin A. Palmer, eds., *The Modern Caribbean* (Chapel Hill, 1989).

Linden Lewis, ed., *The Culture of Gender and Sexuality in the Caribbean* (Gainesville, FL, 2003).

Edgardo Meléndez, *Sponsored Migration: The State and Puerto Rican Postwar Migration to the United States* (Columbus, OH, 2017).

James Millette, 'Decolonization, Populist Movements and the Formation of New Nations, 1945–70', in Bridget Brereton, ed., *The Caribbean in the Twentieth Century, volume 5: General History of the Caribbean* (London, 2004).

Sidney W. Mintz and Sally Price, eds., *Caribbean Contours* (Baltimore, 1985).

Velma Newton, *The Silver Men: West Indian Labour Migration to Panama, 1850–1914* (Kingston, 1984).

Gert Oostindie, ed., *Dutch Colonialism, Migration and Cultural Heritage* (Leiden, 2008).

'Puerto Ricans struggle to survive in storm's aftermath', *Caribbean Insight* 39, no. 53 (13 October – 29 October 2017): 10 (accessed 19 October 2017).

Lara Putnam, *Radical Moves: Caribbean Migrants and the Politics of Race in the Jazz Age* (Chapel Hill, NC, 2013).

Bonham C. Richardson, *The Caribbean in the wider world, 1492–1992: A regional geography* (Cambridge, 1992).

Bonham C. Richardson, *Panama Money in Barbados, 1900–1920* (Knoxville, 1985).

Stuart B. Schwartz, *Sea of Storms: A History of Hurricanes in the Greater Caribbean from Columbus to Katrina* (Princeton, NJ, 2016).

Alyssa Goldstein Sepinwall, *Haitian History: New Perspectives* (London, 2012).

Deborah Thomas, *Exceptional Violence: Embodied Citizenship in Transnational Jamaica* (Durham, NC, 2011).

Elizabeth M. Thomas-Hope, *Explanation in Caribbean Migration, Perception and the Image: Jamaica, Barbados, St. Vincent* (London, 1992).

Jie Zong and Jeanne Balalova, 'Caribbean Immigrants in the United States', *Migration Policy Institute*, 14 September 2016, http://www.migrationpolicy.org/article/caribbean-immigrants-united-states (accessed 28 April 2017).

# Chapter 18

Hilary McD. Beckles, *The Development of West Indies Cricket*, 2 volumes (Kingston, 1998).

Antonio Benítez-Rojo, *The Repeating Island: The Caribbean and the Postmodern Perspective* (Durham, 1996).

Antonio Benítez-Rojo, 'Three Words Toward Creolization', in O. Nigel Bolland, ed., *The Birth of Caribbean Civilisation: A Century of Ideas about Culture and Identity, Nation and Society* (Kingston, 2004).

Curwen Best, *Roots to Popular Culture: Barbadian Aesthetics: Kamau Brathwaite to Hardcore Styles* (London, 2001).

Kenneth M. Bilby, 'The Caribbean as a Musical Region', in Sidney W. Mintz and Sally Price, eds., *Caribbean Contours* (Baltimore, 1985).

Edward Brathwaite, *The Development of Creole Society in Jamaica, 1770–1820* (Oxford, 1971).

Bridget Brereton, *A History of Modern Trinidad, 1783–1962* (Kingston, 1981).

Carolyn Cooper, 'Hip-Hopping Across Cultures: Crossing Over from Reggae to Rap and Back', in Verene A. Shepherd and Glen L. Richards, eds., *Questioning Creole: Creolisation Discourses in Caribbean Culture* (Kingston, 2002).

Carolyn Cooper, *Noises in the Blood: Orality, Gender and the 'Vulgar' Body of Jamaican Popular Culture* (London, 1994).

James Ferguson, *Traveller's Literary Companion to the Caribbean* (London, 1997).

C. L. R. James, *Beyond a Boundary* (London, 1963).

Louis James, *Caribbean Literature in English* (Harlow, 1999).

Winston James, A Fierce *Hatred of Injustice: Claude McKay's Jamaican Poetry of Rebellion* (London, 2001).

John King, *Magical Reels: A History of Cinema in Latin America* (London, 1990).

Franklin W. Knight and Teresita Martínez Vergne, eds., *Contemporary Caribbean Cultures and Societies in a Global Context* (Chapel Hill, 2005).

Peter van Koninsbruggen, *Trinidad Carnival: A Quest for National Identity* (London, 1997).

Peter Manuel, *Caribbean Currents: Caribbean Music from Rumba to Reggae* (Philadelphia, 1995).

Woodville Marshall, 'The Worrell-Sobers Revolution', in Hilary Beckles, ed., *An Area of Conquest: Popular Democracy and West Indies Cricket Supremacy* (Kingston, 1994).

Rex Nettleford, 'Ideology, identity, culture', in Bridget Brereton, ed., *The Caribbean in the Twentieth Century, volume 5: General History of the Caribbean* (London, 2004).

Sidney W. Mintz, *Caribbean Transformations* (Chicago, 1974).

Sidney W. Mintz, *Three Ancient Colonies: Caribbean Themes and Variations* (Cambridge, MA, 2010).

Kezia Page, 'From Diasporic Sensibility to Close Transnationalism: The Agüero Sisters, The Dew Breaker and The Brief Wondrous Life of Oscar Wao', in Michael A. Bucknor and Alison Donnell, eds, *The Routledge Companion to Anglophone Caribbean Literature* (London, 2011).

Veerle Poupeye, *Caribbean Art* (London, 1998).

Kenneth Ramchand, *The West Indian Novel and its Background* (Kingston, 2004).

Deborah Thomas, *Modern Blackness: Nationalism, Globalization, and the Politics of Culture in Jamaica* (Kingston, 2004).

Ann Walmsley and Stanley Greaves, *Art in the Caribbean: An Introduction* (London, 2010).

Keith Q. Warner, *On Location: Cinema and Film in the Anglophone Caribbean* (London, 2000).

Lorna V. Williams, 'The African Presence in the Poetry of Nicolás Guillén', in Margaret E. Crahan and Franklin W. Knight, *Africa and the Caribbean: The Legacies of a Link* (Baltimore, 1979).

# INDEX